D1587911

£2-50

16/31

THE AFRICAN AWAKENING

the same author

REI   ON SOUTHERN AFRICA
YBREAK IN CHINA
RMANY: WHAT NOW?
PARTISAN PICTURE

•

GOLDEN HORN
HIGHWAY FORTY

THE
AFRICAN
AWAKENING

by

BASIL DAVIDSON

JONATHAN CAPE
THIRTY BEDFORD SQUARE
LONDON

FIRST PUBLISHED 1955

PRINTED IN GREAT BRITAIN IN THE CITY OF OXFORD
AT THE ALDEN PRESS
BOUND BY A. W. BAIN & CO. LTD., LONDON

CONTENTS

BY WAY OF INTRODUCTION

ALL the way up and down Africa, from the hills of Cyrenaica as far as Table Mountain, from the Atlantic coast to the Indian Ocean and through green and tawny solitudes between, there is in our day an awakening among African peoples to the way they live, and the different way they wish to live. There is desire for many-sided change, for movement into the modern world, for an end to subjection and a beginning of equality.

Everywhere present although often hard to find, this African awakening seems likely to count in history among the fundamental movements of humanity in the twentieth century. Like all great movements toward the unity of the human race, it is full of stress and conflict, of hesitation, doubt, false starts and wrong directions; and yet always beneath this troubled surface, and true to its liberating nature, it is strong with hope and clear with hopeful purpose. Humanity rejoins itself, grows larger in this unifying process, grows stronger with new ideas and new potentialities.

What follows is an attempt, necessarily partial and tentative, to describe and explain this African awakening against a background of the great central region formed by the Belgian Congo, the French Congo and the Portuguese colony of Angola. I have chosen this background because these countries are the Darkest Africa of European tradition, because this region contains within itself many fruitful contrasts, and because the contemporary literature of the Congo Basin, at least in English, is extremely meagre.

But mostly I have chosen the Congo and Angola as a background to the African awakening because here we are close to its most intimate beginnings. What is elsewhere sure and obvious — in Nigeria, in the Gold Coast, in Uganda, the French Sudan, the Ivory Coast, not to mention the countries of Africa to the north of the Sahara, which lie outside the

9

purview of this book — is dubious and obscure in the Congo and Angola. Dubious in purpose and often difficult to find; and yet, perhaps for that very reason, all the more convincing and attractive to inquiry. What is elsewhere great is small here: small, and yet certainly present, demanding recognition, growing in many devious ways, not to be denied.

Although mainly about the Belgian Congo and Angola, this book is the fruit of some four years' study and travel in British, French, Belgian and Portuguese colonies in Africa, as well as in self-governing Southern Rhodesia, and in the Union of South Africa. For making possible this study and travel I have greatly to thank Dr. Stringfellow Barr and his colleagues of the Foundation for World Government, Charlottesville, Virginia, whose generous and unquestioning aid has been a pattern of what such aid should be. The Foundation is of course in no way responsible for what I have written.

THE AFRICAN AWAKENING

A traveller may proceed alone amongst them without the least fear of brigands, or robbers, or ravages.

IBN BATTUTAH in 1352

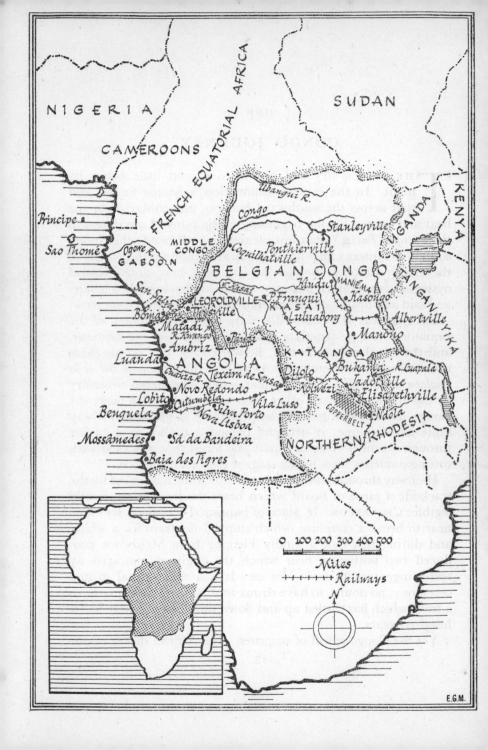

ONE

CONGO JOURNEY

THE air was dry and hot by day; and little better by
night. In the evening thunderless lightning forked and
spat across the southward horizon; one choked with the
heat and longed for the beginning of the rains. Late diners in
the *Pourquoi Pas*, a restaurant pleasantly built beside the Congo
so that its lanterns may float in thin reflection on the waters of
the river, consoled themselves with iced beer and Zeeland
oysters at two pounds a dozen: others lay back in their chairs
and said and drank and ate no more, exhausted until tomorrow.

But that was at Stanleyville, sixty miles to the north of the
Equator. Now we are sixty miles to the south of the Equator,
and the weather is different. Between these two points there
runs the eventful stretch of railway — of the *Chemin de Fer de la
Lualaba et des Grands Lacs Africains* — that is rendered necessary
by the Stanley Falls and other snags and rapids which make the
Congo unnavigable here. I suspect there is no other railway
quite like this one: it struggles behind a timber-fired engine
through a tunnel of dense equatorial forest that is walled with
rotting nameless trees which stagger past at slow speed.

Half way through this tunnel some romantic has nailed by the
trackside a piece of board which bears the inscription, faintly
legible: L'EQUATEUR. In place of baptismal ceremony we came
near to break a coupling, which stopped the train for a while;
and during this halt a kindly Fleming from Melsbroek produced two bottles of beer which the engineer managed by
secret ingenuity to freeze for us. It is a thing equal to any
ceremony, no doubt, to have drunk iced beer on the Equator in
a train which has rattled up and down this line for nearly half a
hundred years.

Yet the Congo is full of surprises. The African driver of our

13

train, evidently a man of iron nerve, brought us into Ponthierville only an hour late. At Ponthierville the wide Congo stream becomes navigable again, and is called the Lualaba. Here we embarked forthwith in the *Baron Delbeck*, which would sail at dawn. And here the rains began, the weather changed, the mornings turned cool with mist and pleasant sunlight. Early today it was so cool that Arkady Platonovich positively stamped his way up and down the deck in order to get warm.

Now it is days since our African deck-hands cheerfully took a fire hose to the odd score or so of would-be African passengers for whom no room could be found: since we cast off moorings at Ponthierville, and pushed away upstream against this broad impassive river.

It seems like weeks. Hour after hour the *Baron Delbeck*, venerable stern-wheeler, flaps his water-jewelled paddle into this dreaming sepia flood, while on either side and behind us and ahead of us the equatorial forest totters to the river bank in grey-green fungoid desolation, and makes our only skyline. We are thousands of miles from the Atlantic Ocean, as many thousands from the Indian. Take a pencil and prick it in the dark green middle of Africa. That is where we are.

Rarely do we pass bankside villages; but then the excitement is all the more because each is full of fifty people or so, and kids leap into the river and swim shouting into our wake. The two nuns who are going to Lokandu to help with an outbreak of meningitis watch them approvingly. Arkady Platonovich, who likes children, comes out of his cabin and cries encouragement, and even the railway engineer, a sad Ligurian from Sestri in the Gulf of Genoa, brightens a little.

Now and then the *Baron* lets forth four sharp hoots as we near a couple of European bungalows or a corrugated-iron warehouse. 'Come out in a canoe and collect your mail': the Sociologist has explained the meaning of this signal. Now and then we stop for timber fuel, because the *Baron* uses no other, although later this year he may be undergoing his own personal and private industrial revolution, and acquire an oil-fired engine. Now and then we stop for trading goods: casks labelled UNION MATCH — VIA MATADI, or, surprisingly, GUINNESS IS GOOD FOR YOU: or nameless boxes and bundles and cases which have shunted up and down the Congo for countless months until they arrive at a store among the trees, dignified with a name and signifying civilization to half a dozen Europeans and half a thousand Africans, and nothing at all to the rest of the world.

There are passengers too. A Pakistani trader came aboard this morning and has since disturbed the Settler by installing himself and his children and his wife — a frail girl as pale and wistful as Rossetti's Beatrice — on the European deck. 'And that's not the worst of it, either,' the Settler confides gloomily. 'Nowadays the Blacks have a right to come up here if they've got a *carte de mérite* or whatever it is. You'll see — in a few years there'll be no stopping them. Just to please the United Nations, eh?' He is really upset. 'Though, mind you,' he reflects, 'they still eat after us.'

Even the Sociologist cannot quite find it in himself to approve this headlong pace of social advancement, when non-Europeans are actually admitted in their ones and twos — yes, and even in their threes and fours — to European travelling quarters. I learnt this morning that he passed the night on deck rather than share his cabin with a mulatto; and that is why, no doubt, his temper is rather short today.

Yet it is impossible to be cross for long on a journey so calm and comfortable as this. At these rare stopping places along the river bank we lean over the rail and admire the lingering girls upon the shore. The Sociologist gossips about them; the Surveyor points out where he camped last season and suffered still another bout of malaria; and Arkady Platonovich, never downhearted, makes everyone feel a little better than he really is. There is also the sentiment that we all belong to Africa, to this shabby wilderness where poverty and desolation are not disgraceful, being the common state of things, and which never seem to overcome the energy and power of humanity — of this strange African humanity that is the same as any other and yet entirely different from any other. Against this shared experience the troubles over segregation dwindle and disappear. The Congo is a world to itself: more specially African, it seems to me, than any other part of Africa I know.

The girls are brilliant on the river bank. They are handsome with an Arab strain — for this stretch of the Congo was once a centre of the Arab slave trade, the heart of Tippoo Tib's country — and wear striped cotton gowns and curious turbans, pendant ear-rings and bangles of ivory or painted wood. Fashions are Victorian, just as the missionaries first brought them; mutton-chop sleeves and a bustle being the latest thing among the well-to-do. The well-to-do also lacquer their finger nails; and those who are no better than they should be do the same, but with more abandon, with an outrageous joy in life, and wear their dresses off the shoulder.

Beside these girls the men in tattered shirts and shorts are lustreless and sad, for here the pattern is always the same: there is a handful of Europeans in command, directing, watching, while the African men run and stumble, robbed of dignity. Here and there an African *évolué* — a clerk or supercargo — has dressed himself in European clothing and is sharply trying to acquire dignity, in the gaining of which he evidently finds it necessary to treat his fellow Africans as the Europeans treat them; or rather worse, perhaps, because his need for reassurance is even greater than the European need.

For all that, laughter and excitement prevail; and delightful is this river journey. Around eleven, when the sun begins to burn more fiercely, Arkady Platonovich arrives with a cheerful apology and wants to know whether it wouldn't be right to break a bottle. *Ecraser* is the verb he uses: in the literal sense, no doubt, of what an officer and gentleman should once have done in Petersburg, flinging it over his shoulder at the wall behind.

'Let's break a bottle,' he says; and that is when, idly in a row beneath the canvas awning, with our feet on the *Baron's* smart white rail (for he keeps himself up in spite of advanced years), we call for iced Congo beer and begin talking. We go on talking, Arkady Platonovich and the Italian and the Settler and the Sociologist and me, all day and all evening; and the end of this conversation is nowhere in sight. I do not think it has an end.

By this time we are beyond personalities, and are deep into philosophy. Africa is strong for philosophy. Yesterday the Italian from Sestri was telling us why. He is livid with malaria, and his blue eyes have the pallid stare, never quite focusing, of those who are raked with fever. He has malaria because everyone along the river has it, but more especially because his contract with the Congo Government takes him on long surveying trips into the forest. There he lives in the company of a dozen Africans whose language he cannot understand, catches malaria, and thinks deeply about the world. 'I think how I'm going to pull through. I think about the goal I've got ahead of me. You see, I've got something to live for.' He is putting every hard-won penny into the money-box of his dreams — a cottage near the beach at Nervi beside the gentle Mediterranean, and messing about in boats and strolling through summer evenings, and forgetting the equatorial nightmare. He is mad about boats: he believes they promote self-reliance as well as opening the gate to happiness. 'My grandfather sailed to America, you know, in a boat not twenty metres long . . .' He believes it is good for him to meditate on things which promote self-reliance; and perhaps it is. Africa is full of Europeans relying on a dream of somewhere else.

Arkady Platonovich is also strong for philosophy, but of a purer less personal kind. We met on the train from Ponthierville when his book, oddly enough, was Ilf and Petrov's *Little Golden America*. He is a sturdy old man with glinting eyes and a healthy happiness in adversity: one of the things he wanted to know about was the Red Army during the war. 'I'm a mortal enemy of the regime, you know,' he offered gently, 'but I'm a Russian. Rrr-rien à faire!' He had left Russia with Denikin in 1923, lingered for a little in Constantinople and in Brussels,

B   17

and arrived in the Congo a year or so later. 'Go back to Europe?' His stubby fingers spread quickly and relaxed, as though the thing were too obvious for protest. 'And live in an attic?'

I do not know exactly what Arkady Platonovich is dreaming about while the endless river swings by impassively. Just when you think you are getting to the point, he is up and away, elusive, lost. He is also sorrowing over his only daughter, whose mother is one of those physically incomparable Watutsi from Ruanda Urundi, because she would not come back with him to their bush home but insisted on remaining in town. 'A half-caste girl in town, you know, and one who's handsome, *bien faite*. . . .'

That is also part of our talk. Could you have an African mistress in South Africa: or Southern Rhodesia? But the English, as everyone knows, are either not quite human or not quite honest . . . here along the river it is common form. How otherwise could a man live in this place, with European women so few and far between? 'And there's something else, too,' puts in the Sociologist earnestly: 'Since I've lived in the bush, you know, White women do not appeal to me. While a Native woman . . .' He launches away into his dreams, and for the time being is lost to us. The Italian, a practical man, explains to me that African *ménagères* generally cost about 600 francs (say £4 10s.) a month along the river: in the old days, even officials lost nothing by keeping one, but now, it seems, the thing is frowned on, and only *esprits forts* like the sub-governor of —— Province can afford to be suspected.

Unique in not dreaming is the Settler, a Walloon who is longing to return to Kivu where the blue eastern lakes lie amid clean mountains. The Settler is political: that is to say, he would like to be political but the Congo Government will not let him. The Congo Government is paternalist, refusing all political rights and responsibilities to Europeans and Africans alike. The Settler is discontented with the Congo Government. 'They're going too fast with the Native out here,' he says and keeps on saying. 'They're ruining this colony.' This is the extent of his philosophy; we know it backwards.

We might have less of the Settler's philosophy if it were not for the Sociologist, who cannot resist baiting him. The Sociologist is also a lost soul, sunk in singular erotic meditations; but he clings to his duty. He knows so much, I think, about the tribal habits of the Eastern Baluba people that he no longer believes anything general to be knowable, or worth knowing: in moments of lucidity he is nonetheless a warm upholder of the Congo Government.

'As for you,' he says to me: 'Everyone writes books about Africa. Mostly very bad ones. And they never ask the interesting questions, let alone trying to answer them.'

'What are the interesting questions?'

'I'll tell you.' They emerge, surprisingly, as general questions.

'There's only two that matter. But after all,' he checks suspiciously: 'You've been to West Africa and South Africa and the Lord knows where, and you still ask me that? These two questions — they're not peculiar to the Congo. They're the questions which the whole of Black Africa has to answer. They're the common denominator — the substratum, the foundation, the basis of any intelligent opinion.'

Solitude has made the Sociologist a little pugnacious with his fellow men, whom he rarely sees. 'First of all, if it's any good telling you, why did the Congo peoples (since we're in the Congo) stay in the Stone Age — all right, a kind of Bronze Age here and there — while the rest of the world moved on?' He slaps down his hand on the top of the rail. 'Secondly, what is going to happen *now* — when they've understood where they are and where we are, when they're convinced they've got to catch up? Those are the interesting questions, but you won't answer them because you can't. You've never thought about them.'

I am saved by the Settler, who cannot resist this opening. '*C'est fou*,' he breaks in. 'They stayed in the Stone Age because they're children. Because they're a lazy useless branch of the human race that never grew up. Couldn't grow up! As for *catching* up' — he speaks acidly as though these Africans had sadly wronged him, and waves a glass so wildly that drops of beer scatter over Arkady Platonovich, fortunately thinking of something else, of something quite his own. 'It'll take them generations.'

'You say that because it's your interest as a settler,' returns the Sociologist rudely. 'Well, I've known settlers who've lived for twenty years in the Congo without ever having a serious conversation with a Native. And then they talk about the Natives as though they actually knew anything! Just look at Kenya.'

He sweeps aside the Settler's retort, for these are fighting words, and goes on: 'The point today, in this year and age, is that the African peoples of the Congo — everywhere else, I dare say — can't stay in their tribalism, their "Stone Age", because they are up against the machine age. Right up against it. Aren't we industrializing the Congo? Bringing in machines, building factories? Yes, and if there is anything surprising about our Congo peoples, it's their native power of adjusting themselves, adapting themselves. It's not intelligence they've lacked. It's opportunity.'

These are opinions which the Settler answers with a weary smile and a sideways wink of contempt. Poor old Sociologist: anyone can see that he's punch-drunk with the forest, with queer ideas, unreal, unworkable . . . The Settler knows better. He 'knows the African', and he knows him for a knave or a fool. '*Mon cher*,' he says with friendly condescension, 'it'll take them generations. They're children, that's all. Children who've never grown up. A firm hand, and you're all right. Once let go . . .' he flings out his hands as if throwing everything away.

To this the Sociologist replies scathingly: 'Have you ever been in Jadotville?'

It is a skilful thrust, and it takes the Settler between wind and water. He grumbles offendedly: 'Oh, the big companies, of course. . . .'

But the Sociologist has played a trump card. For the drama of the Congo, intense, fast moving, magnificently full, is no longer contained in the old ideas for which the Settler stands: it escapes them with a speed and diversity of change which must surely count among the great events of this century. The Congo is still the Congo of yesterday; but it is also, here and there, the Congo of tomorrow.

Listening to the Sociologist, who is now hard in pursuit of the Settler, I think of the great engineering workshops of Jadotville, where African craftsmen are using tools precise to a hundredth of a millimetre; of the newly-electrified railway line between Jadotville and Kolwézi where Africans are driving electric locomotives of the newest type; of the immense waterways of the Ubangui and Congo and Kasai where Africans command tugs and barges and even river-steamers . . . And I also think of these great Congo cities which pullulate with village Africans learning to live urban lives, of the bars of Léopoldville, of the fun and games and dancing, the astonishing absence of violent crime for all the somersault in ways of life and family loyalty, the order and upward striving for all the disorder and downward striving of those naughty girls associated in *La Joie Kinoise*, *La Rose*, *La Délicatesse*. . . .

In all this there is much that needs explaining. But the Settler only shakes his head, speaks of 'the decadence of Africa', of the degradation of the tribal African as soon as he gets to town, of drink, of prostitution, of the collapse of family life. There is truth in what he is saying. All the same, this is no longer the only truth or the essential truth about the Congo. If it were, how explain the underlying pulse of hope and eagerness which beats in these cities?

The Settler and the Sociologist now reach familiar deadlock. Rashly, I intrude. 'Still,' I say, 'you've put a stopper on all political development. Now we, for instance — I mean, look at the Gold Coast —'

The Sociologist and the Settler take a quick look at one another, and by mutual consent fall upon me in a heap. On one thing at least they are emphatically agreed: the Gold Coast is going *much too fast*.

I am hauled out from under by Arkady Platonovich, who takes me aside and gives me a drink. Arkady Platonovich gestures vaguely at the wilted forest. 'The Congo — there's nowhere like it. I've lived here for thirty years. I shall leave my bones here.' He chuckles and goes on: 'You know, I've never made a penny, but . . . tell me, did you ever read *Dead Souls*? Do you remember Chichikov, who made a fortune out of nothing, absolutely nothing?' His malarial eyes are staring into the dense green emptiness along the bank. 'Just think,' he says dreamily, enjoying his private joke, 'what Chichikov mightn't have done with the Congo.'

But the Africans, the eleven million people of the Congo — what do they think of it all?

In the middle of the night we moor at a bankside village to take on wood. Awakened by the clatter, I go out of my cabin and lean on the rail and watch the gnomelike figures, their shoulders hunched grotesquely with burdens of wood, who run and slither under the glare of white lights mounted in the trees.

They might be thinking of nothing at all. Or of almost anything.

TWO

SHAMBA BOLONGONGO

THESE Congo peoples have lived for years beyond knowledge in the solitude of the equatorial forest. History, it might seem, has passed them by. Outwardly, nothing of their past survives: their slipshod thatch-and-plaster hamlets stand in muddied clearings in the forest as though time here had neither past nor future, but only now, only this.

Such was the familiar European thought: here were peoples who did not belong to the world as others belonged, who were humanly inferior. To civilize these peoples would be to give them peace, order, security: advantages, it was generally believed, they had proved utterly unable to achieve of themselves. For Mrs. Jellyby and her zealous Victorian clan, the people of Borrioboola Gha were living in a state of horrible disgrace. They were in sore need of knowing what was good for them, and of having it done to them, willy-nilly, by those who did know. And Mrs. Jellyby has left a numerous and powerful progeny.

They are weaker than they were. Nowadays it is quite common in Africa to meet with administrators who have parted from Mrs. Jellyby's confident sense of mission; and who, on the contrary, point out that European invasion and conquest have brought ruin to a tribal society otherwise admirably balanced for the most part, and generally capable of placing the good of the many above the good of the few. 'It is worth noting', wrote a former Belgian administrator not long ago, 'that some of the great tribes of the Central Congo, having more or less escaped the horrors of the slave trade, offered at the time of our arrival a degree of civilization that was admirable from more than one point of view.'

Anthropologists have tried and are trying to piece together

23

the truth of African history through the veil of myth and misunderstanding which has clothed the European invasion. What they are finding almost obliterates the picture of a wilderness inhabited by cannibals and given over to endless tribal warfare, terror, starvation. It becomes probable and even certain that many and perhaps most of the great social evils which European invaders encountered towards the end of the nineteenth century were evils which earlier European contact, not native African decadence, had itself promoted and inflamed. If these peoples had no civilization in the sense of literate urban culture, they are nonetheless now seen to have possessed an intricate and durable social order well adapted to their material circumstances, to the climate and the forest, to the tools and techniques they knew and could evolve.

This intricate tribal order was reflected with all its complex pattern of checks and balances in their systems of religion. These were not 'simple', simply because the missionary and explorer could not understand them: on the contrary, Africans had 'elaborate theologies, but these were developed in social relations, rather than in intellectual speculations. Indeed, because of this settling of theology in social relationships, their religions have a complexity which makes Christianity, Judaism, Islam, and Buddhism seem simple'.(1) These religions were not evidence of moral and social chaos: they were evidence, on the contrary, of moral and social order.

Some reflection of all this the later explorers could still note for themselves. Penetrating in 1904 into the old Bashongo kingdom between the Kasai and Sankuru rivers, the German explorer Frobenius wrote later that he 'could still find villages whose approaches were bordered on either side, for several miles, by four rows of palms, and whose houses were decorated with charm and were works of art'. He speaks of their silks and skins, their tools, their spoons, as of an artistry 'comparable to the creations of the Roman style in Europe'; and of the grace and dignity of these peoples, whether rich or poor, slave or free. 'I do not know any people of the North who can compare for unity of civilization with these primitives. Alas, these last "Islands of the Blest" were also submerged beneath the tidal wave of European civilization.' A little idyllic, no doubt; yet Frobenius was a careful reporter who was perfectly convinced, as his writings show, that he belonged to a master race himself.

These stories of the past are incomplete. They grow mysteriously out of legend, wither again in the soil of our ignorance. Yet their influence is persistent, unmistakable. Even with the relatively little knowledge that we have, one may scarcely approach the shadow of Shamba Bolongongo, ninety-third king of the Bashongo — or of others like him — with the confidently condescending eye that Mrs. Jellyby's was. There is something here that is much bigger, more important, more complete, than anyone had said. So much seems certain: much of the rest is still conjecture, must perhaps remain conjecture.

Shamba Bolongongo himself may be interviewed on his wooden throne, most weeks of the year, in the archaeological gallery of the British Museum, although at times they lock him away in the cellar. He is small and black and ancient — for he reigned about 1600, when memories of the Spanish Armada were still warm in Europe — and there is little to be learned from him. All around King Shamba, crouched on his throne in the tropical solitudes of the British Museum, there stand or sit attendant priests, witches with masks, young wives, youthful hunters brandishing spears: busts, portraits, statues wonderfully wrought in hard black wood by artists whose names will never be known. Look at these things how one may, they remain mysterious: there is no explaining them. They are beautiful, they are technically superb: but they are also a little frightening. They make on first seeing much the same impression of cruelty and crude superstition as might be made, no doubt, upon an African who, untouched by Christianity, set anxious eyes upon a medieval likeness of the Crucifixion.

Yet on closer seeing they are not crude, and possibly they are not cruel — or not cruel in any obvious sense. They have dignity, pride, the consciousness of order and orderly succession. They match the oral legends which give Shamba Bolongongo ninety-two kingly predecessors and the name of an enlightened monarch who brought in social reforms and improved ways of weaving raffia. There is every likelihood that life in Shamba's country was a good deal less difficult and dangerous than life in the kingdoms of Europe during his time: it is even said that he caused his warriors to throw away their spears and arrows, and to rely only on their knives. If tradition may hold, he disarmed his army and made it into a police force, and reigned over wide and peaceful lands where people lived better than before, the arts flourished, and life was relatively painless. His dynasty has long since failed and disappeared, for chiefs in the Congo have suffered the same destruction of authority and dignity that European domination has wrought elsewhere. His last successor Kwete Peshanga Kena — 120th in the line of oral tradition — fought the Belgian invaders in 1904 and was put down; and thereafter the story fades.

Yet it is towards King Shamba and other heroes no less remembered that nascent African nationalism now casts a backward glance. With the Bakongo, the Baluba, and other strongly surviving Congo peoples there begins to emerge a sense of nationhood rooted in their tribal loyalties, and sometimes transcending them; and in all this King Shamba has his part.

Often concealed in strange and unaccustomed garb, nationalism is present in the Congo today as surely as it is elsewhere in Africa. Europeans who deny this are really doing no more than echo the arguments of the Earl of Warwick in *Saint Joan*: 'A Frenchman! Where did you pick up that expression? Are these Burgundians and Bretons and Picards and Gascons beginning to call themselves Frenchmen, just as our fellows are beginning to call themselves Englishmen? They actually talk of France and England as their own countries. Theirs, if you please! What is to become of me and you if that way of thinking comes into fashion?'(2)

Of all this, indeed, one sees at first little or nothing. There appears at first, as one travels through the Congo, neither past nor future. The equatorial forest looks petrified in its lush decay as though these vast central regions of the Congo basin must have always been, and must always be, this same shabby and hopeless slum.

These first impressions are wrong impressions. Much of the Congo is as woefully poor as the rest of the colonial continent, because most of the wealth produced in the Congo is carried away and spent elsewhere. But the reality of the Congo is no longer mere stagnation, starving, despairing: in these mid-century years it reaches with a new confidence back into the past towards half-legendary figures like Shamba Bolongongo, and forward into the future towards new ways and new ideas. There may still be despair; but there is also hope, and the hope is later and greater than the despair. It is as though a section of humanity had long been lost to the rest of us, and only now was come in sight again.

The Belgian Congo is a country which is as big as Europe, and consists of the wide flat basin of one of the longest rivers in the world, together with rising ground on the north, east and south of this basin.

What is most remarkable about the geography of the Congo river itself, perhaps, is that from Bukama right round its north-ward and westward-curving stream to Matadi on the Atlantic Ocean, a distance of nearly two thousand miles (and most of it navigable), the river falls less than two thousand feet. Always flowing fast because of the great volume of water delivered by its tributaries, the Congo seems to wander and dream through the endless forest where vines chain tree to tree, and one slow bend in the river serves only to reveal the next. Here are the tropical sunsets, the terrible storms of thunderless lightning, the lashing rain among the palm trees, the silent people slipping through the forest or paddling dug-out canoes within the shelter of the river bank . . . just as the explorers first described them.

But there is also something else here; and it is this something else which expels the illusion of unending sameness, unending decay. Watching this thing, one sees that the peoples of the Congo are not rooted in a timeless present, but are changing from one kind of life to other kinds of life — changing faster than anyone might reasonably have thought possible, only a dozen years ago.

One caught a first glimpse of this at the river port of Stanleyville, terminal for water traffic which comes up-country from the capital at Léopoldville, eight hundred miles downstream. Here one may see Africans operating heavy cranes, driving bull-dozers, laying roads, unloading, packing, supervising: and this with an ease and sense of purpose which betoken men who understand what they are doing.

Now in all the Congo which is as big as Europe, this contrast between the old and the new — between the primitive forest with its apparently primitive inhabitants, and Africans working at semi-skilled and skilled jobs in industry — does not cease to surprise and mystify. How is it possible? Haven't we thought of Africans as the Settler on the *Baron Delbeck* thought of them — as children not yet grown up, likeable but second-rate, irresponsible? Yet it is difficult to think in such terms of these African industrial workers in the Congo. Not only are they up against the machine age: at certain points they are right into it.

At Stanleyville there were the port installations, all manned by Africans. On the old slow train to Ponthierville, rambling through its tunnel of forest behind its antediluvian wood-fired boiler, there was the African driver. Pushing up-river in the *Baron* one had further reminders of change. Far beyond Kindu, where the river flows out of the southern plateau of the Katanga into the dense Maniéma, there was the little scene I witnessed one afternoon at Muyumba.

Muyumba is actually marked on the map as though it were a town; but really there is nothing here except the end of a dusty road from tin mines in the bush, a couple of warehouses and an office, two cranes worked by hand, a few barges idle beside the

28

wharf. Within shouting distance of the office, under the shadow of a clump of gums, a group of African port hands snooze through the midday hours. Scrub grows into forest, and the wide brown river flows through both.

A pile of naked metal ingots glitter on the wharfside. This is what Muyumba is for. The pile consists of fifty lumps of pure tin; they are going to the United States.

John Kilongi comes out of the office and shouts to the snoozing port hands. A tug is now in sight, upstream, with a trailing string of barges in its wake: its African skipper leans out of his wheelhouse and shouts orders in Kiswahili, *lingua franca* in these parts: he and John Kilongi exchange greetings in the same language, for John is from the Kasai and the skipper is not. Their vernaculars differ. In time the barges are got alongside, the ingots of tin disappear aboard them; there are the usual inexplicable delays, and finally the tug casts off and the barges are cast off, the whole convoy shifts away down-river, and the port hands go back to sleep again.

Kilongi goes into his office and phones the mine. He is in charge of ninety men and is visited twice a week by the European in charge of mining transport. A trusted port representative, Kilongi has had two years of secondary school, speaks and writes some French, and receives 2700 francs a month (about £20), which is comparatively high pay for the rural areas. He unloads mining stores and loads up pure tin; and all this remains an African operation.

In the past, so long as Africans did only unskilled work, the economic gain was all on the European side. Metals were dragged out of the Congo by the spade-and-muscle power of Africans who could in no way draw upon the stock of knowledge which has gone to build the modern world. Now, at last, people like Kilongi are working with their brains as well as with their muscles: they are learning many new things and learning them fast. The economic gain is still greatly on the European side, but it is no longer only on the European side. There is at last a sharing of knowledge, a real diffusion of ideas.

Grudgingly, sparingly, no doubt: but in matters of this kind the beginning may be half the battle.

Towards the end of my journey in the Congo I came to Léopoldville. This is the administrative and economic capital, and, with Elisabethville at the other end of this enormous colony, is the most imposing city of all central Africa. Here the old notions of tropical Africa as dark and dangerous receive their *coup de grâce*: Léopoldville is nothing in the least like a 'hell-ridden hole rank with fever'. It is a pleasant and well-constructed city whose spires and skyscrapers loom amazingly through the morning mist as one drops down river or crosses Stanley Pool in the ferry from Brazzaville. To my loss, I reached Léopoldville for the first time by air from Angola; but it is much better to approach across the silver mirrors of Stanley Pool, for then one has a full and proper impact of the multitudinous quays and cranes that equip this port.

From here the barges, tugs and steamers travel for thousands of miles up the Congo, Kasai and Ubangui rivers, for this is the ocean terminal of the waterways of the Belgian Congo. Below Léopoldville the river runs into piling rapids which chase one another for two hundred miles down to Matadi, where the ocean estuary begins. These Congo rapids, it is said, offer enough electric power to illuminate all tropical Africa, and the means whereby the Congo peoples may one day overleap the handicaps of history.

This port of Léopoldville is operated by Africans under sparse European supervision. There is nowhere else in Africa south of the Sahara — in 'Black Africa' as distinct from 'White Africa', from Arab Africa, to the north of the Sahara — where anything like this is thought to be remotely possible. For most Europeans in Black Africa the port of Léopoldville represents, without exaggeration, something that is strictly impossible. Where is the magic wand?

Captain Pirie of the S.S. *Kigoma* is part of the answer. The S.S. *Kigoma* is not much of a command: she lies in a little lagoon above the port, an old stern-wheeler withdrawn from years of paddling up and down the Congo and Kasai, wedged between the river bank and a spit of grey mud. But Captain Pirie is well enough pleased. There are, at the moment, just forty-seven reasons for this. He takes me up to the passengers' deck and shows me forty-seven Africans in mariner's rig, bent earnestly over their text-books in cabins widened into class-rooms, learning the mysteries of sextant and steam pressure. The S.S. *Kigoma* is a navigational school for Africans training to command and operate the tugs and passenger steamers of OTRACO, one of the big Congo transport companies; and she is practically a revolution in her own right.

Captain Pirie is training ship's captains and engineers: the wireless operators employed for short-wave signalling in the larger boats are trained elsewhere. Since 1948, when OTRACO opened this school, about 120 pupils have gone through training: most of the earlier ones failed to pass their tests, ran away to work elsewhere, or were discarded. Most of the present 'promotion', the forty-seven of today, are promising better. 'We have learnt from earlier mistakes,' Captain Pirie explains: 'We used to take them directly on their applications and their general savvy. Now we give them a period of practical employment in the boats before selecting them for advanced training.'

He put forth a hand towards an African with an eager watchful face. 'That man will be a captain later this year. He'll command one of our biggest boats — something we'd never thought possible a few years ago — a boat carrying up to eight hundred tons of cargo and forty passengers.'

I am not sure of his name: I think it may have been Henry Molongo. He comes of the powerful Bakongo people who inhabit both banks of the lower reaches of the river, and was born in a little lost village somewhere out in the blue.

Why had he left home?

He had two answers, and both made sense. In the first place he could scarcely have earned enough money, had he stayed at home, to pay his poll-tax to the government and buy himself a wife. Yet this was not the only, nor even the principal, reason. Once, when very young, Henry had accompanied an uncle on a journey to the banks of the river: there he had seen miracles. He had seen men whose skins were other than his own, which might signify little; but whose ways signified much. They flew in the sky and travelled in wheeled monsters; they went on the river in ships without paddles.

This vision of another world could have frightened many children. It failed to frighten small Henry Molongo. One understood that he turned these things over in his mind, and determined to get into this other world no matter how difficult the getting might prove. He evidently saw this journey into the modern world in no high-falutin' philosophical sense. He saw it as a journey in space and time: as a challenge to his manhood but also as a bread-and-butter question. First, get out of this village, and as soon as possible. Leave the forest behind. Go to the town and work for the men who own and master these new things. Understand them. Live their kind of life.

Henry Molongo's quest is the characteristic story of Africa's youth in this day and age. Little by little, while the story emerged, one could frame a picture of this small Henry Molongo coming to town, making ridiculous mistakes, stumbling over himself and everyone else, shouted at, clouted at: but learning, learning all the time, avidly, obstinately, heroically. Until at last he carved out for himself a job as steamer deck hand. Until he rose to be bos'n. Until he induced *them* — the authorities, the possessors of knowledge — to send him on a course to learn navigation aboard the S.S. *Kigoma*.

Henry Molongo is a valid contemporary of the middle years of this century. He is right on the rising tip of history's wave. He and others like him have discovered that they have a future: also, that they have a past.

But why now, why not before? Where is the link between King Shamba the Reformer, reigning sovereign in 1600, and Henry Molongo of today? Why all these years in quest of community with the rest of the world?

THREE

THE COMING OF DIOGO CÃO

THE quest begins in 1482. It is then that the people of
Nzinga a Nkuwa, fourth Mani Congo, Lord of Congo,
suffer a visitation not much less interesting for them, no
doubt, than the arrival of men from Mars might be for us.
Those of the great king's subjects who live where the river they
call Nzadi flows like a sea into the ocean — the river which the
Portuguese will call Zaire, and others will call Congo after the
kingdom of Nzinga a Nkuwa — witness the arrival of strange
ships and strange men. These ships, sea-stained and weather-
beaten, are larger than any before seen or thought of. Their
sails bear a large cross that is faded to the colour of crusted
blood. They are Portuguese caravels, and there are three of
them. Men come ashore with unknown weapons, wearing unknown garments, speaking unknown words. Nothing warlike
mars this first visit.

Though the people of Congo do not know it, this is the
great period of overseas discovery, the beginning of European
expansion across the world. It is less than fifty years since Gil
Eannes crept fearfully round Cape Bojador, which legend long
had held unpassable, and opened for the Portuguese a seemingly
endless route of onward sailing. It is three years before Barto-
lomeo Diaz will round the Cape of Storms and see the Indian
Ocean; fourteen years before Vasco da Gama will make a landfall on India; fifteen years before Columbus will discover the
continent of America; and eighteen years before Pedro Alvarez
Cabral, drawn off course to India, will sight Brazil. Across
these marvellous years the development of navigation will melt
the skylines of the world.

The captain of this expedition who had thus broken the long
isolation of the Congo sailed on a little further, went ashore

C   33

THE AFRICAN AWAKENING

again, and erected a monolith — a *padrão*, sign of overlordship — which declared that: 'In the year of the creation of the world 1681, and of the birth of Our Lord 1482, the most high, most excellent and powerful prince King Dom John the Second of Portugal caused the discovery of this land and the erection of this stone by Diogo Cão, squire of his house.'(3) Months later, in Lisbon, the King of Portugal listened to Cão and gave him fresh instructions.

Two years later Diogo Cão anchored once more in the mouth of the Congo and sent emissaries to the king's capital at Mbanza Congo, several days into the interior: these emissaries were four Franciscan monks, the forerunners of many missionaries who would follow in later years. They bore fraternal greetings from the King of Portugal to the King of Congo, as well as royal presents; and were instructed by their master to ask for news of Prester John. Having watched them depart for the interior, Diogo Cão sailed on again towards the south, returning for them in the following year. Not finding them at the mouth of the river, and not being able to wait, he seized hostages among the people on the river bank and bore them to Lisbon, where they were presented to the king and whetted the kingly appetite for further expeditions.

In 1487 Cão was back in the Congo estuary for a third time, carrying with him the hostages he had taken. These he sent to the king's capital, clothed as Portuguese and apparently in excellent heart. There followed an invitation for Cão to visit the king's capital, an event which occurred with much ceremony and entire success; and at Mbanza Congo Cão found his missionaries in equally good heart. Pledges were exchanged. The King of Portugal would treat his royal brother of Congo with the dignity and respect which were proper to kingship.

Through this small window into Africa legendary visions were now seen in Europe. The King of Congo's reputation became only less fabulous than that of Prester John, whom the Portuguese would go on seeking for another century and would think in the end to have found in Ethiopia. Tales of the Mani

34

Congo's wealth, power, and illustrious wisdom mingled luxuriously with the yearning for an earthly paradise.

This yearning has a strangely modern ring. Europe was sick, evilly at odds with itself: escape would be pleasant. It was not long after these events that Amerigo Vespucci, an Italian banker's agent who may reasonably be regarded as the father of popular journalism, caught the public sentiment with an epoch-making work thirty-two pages long. In this small work Vespucci, or someone who borrowed his name, faked the story of a voyage to the other side of the Atlantic and gave his name — baulking Columbus — to America. Whoever was the real author of this masterpiece of make-believe, he seems to have known 'what the public wanted'. He set a fashion in overseas reporting which would endure for many years, and even now is not quite passed away.

Lusty and desirable were the women of Vespucci's earthly paradise; and the men were complacent. These lotus-eaters, it was written, were 'lascivious beyond measure, the women much more than the men', while 'a father or mother considered themselves highly honoured when they brought us a daughter, especially if she were a virgin, that we should sleep with her'.(4) There was plenty of everything a tired European could want; moreover, it was free.

Such tales, sometimes decorated with griffins, monsters, 'and of the Cannibals that each other ate, the Anthropophagi, and men whose heads do grow beneath their shoulders', persisted for a long time: in more subtle form, they persist among us to this day. Over half a century after Vespucci, the Portuguese poet Camoëns refined them into the Ninth Canto of his *Lusiads*. Da Gama's 'stalwart Portuguese', hastening to an idyllic beach somewhere far beyond the Cape of Storms, are greeted by the nymphs of Venus herself. These nymphs prove more than welcoming. 'With many a smile and cry', they allow themselves to be overtaken by the stalwart Portuguese. 'As they ran, the breeze caught up now one's golden tresses, now another's delicate drapery, and desire, battening on the sudden glimpse of lovely flesh, grew more ardent still. One stumbled, by design, and her show was rather of complacency than indignation . . .'(5) Only an abyss of vulgarity, no doubt, separates the *Lusiads* from our celluloid and tabloid wish-dreams of today.

What lay behind the idyll was something different. Already in 1444 the Portuguese had taken their first slaves from the Guinea Coast: by the first decades of the sixteenth century there were regions in Portugal where the number of African slaves exceeded the number of native Portuguese. Discovery became plunder, and plunder mass enslavement.

The world of Diogo Cão, as the stone he erected on the Cape of Wolves bore witness, believed that God had created the world some two centuries before the birth of Christ. Pre-history had no meaning for these Europeans. They had no understanding of any but the most obvious implications of what they found, and these, following the spirit of the time, were the most commercial implications.

Even today, pre-history still has only a partial meaning. We are nowhere near a reasonably full certitude of what happened to mankind in Africa during the centuries and millenia before Cão's hard-driven caravels put down anchor in the waters of the Congo.

But we know a good deal. We know enough to be sure that mankind is of ancient origins in Africa. There are those who say that the human story first began in this continent, and spread across the world from here. Thus Professor van Riet Lowe, of the University of Johannesburg, thinks that during hundreds of thousands of years which flowed between the appearance of man in Africa and his occupation of a part of Europe towards the north and of Asia towards the east, Africa remained the greatest and most important stage on which the drama of human evolution was unfolded. He is not alone in thinking this.

'It seems more and more likely,' the Abbé Breuil has written, 'that, even from times that are hundreds of thousands of years distant . . . Africa not only knew stages of primitive civilization that are comparable with those of Europe and Asia Minor, but is also perhaps the origin of these civilizations in the classical countries of the north. . . .'(6)

The evidence of common cultures reaching from the Cape of Good Hope to France and Spain and beyond is various and reasonably complete. Numberless years earlier than the crucial third millennium before Christ, when the civilizations of Mesopotamia recorded themselves in writing and laid foundations for all that was to come, cave-dwelling peoples were drawing pictures on stone all the way from the Dordogne to the Transvaal. The techniques of these primitive Europeans may have differed from those of primitive Africans: they do not seem to have differed very much, and they were not superior. Which way did this imperceptibly moving tide of culture go: from north to south, or from south to north? No doubt it went both ways through the timeless years before history began; recent evidence suggests that its origins were possibly in the south.

So much for prehistoric times. Yet the world into which Diogo Cão sailed was a world entirely different from his own. What had occurred to isolate the one from the other? Why did these African peoples fail to shake themselves free of the 'Stone Age' while Europe and Asia went ahead?

Traditionally, Europeans have answered according to their interests: they have seen in Africans a necessarily inferior kind of humanity who might reasonably be enslaved, exploited and generally worked at will. This was what Nassau Senior meant when he described the Africa Company of 1567 as being founded 'to kidnap or purchase and work to death without compunction the natives of Africa', about which 'the English and the Dutch, at that time the wisest and most religious nations in the world . . . had no more scruple . . . than they had about enslaving horses'.(7) This was Lord Dartmouth's justification when, as Secretary for the Colonies in 1775, he resisted any check upon the slave trade on the grounds that: 'We cannot allow the Colonies to check or to discourage in any degree a traffic so beneficial to the nation.'

Nobody says anything like that nowadays. Even if millions of Africans are still treated as members of an inferior humanity, the justification for doing so is invariably couched in the noblest terms. We do it, nowadays, not for our good but for their good. Yet it is progress, no doubt, that the theory behind the slave trade is no longer thought admissible.

There remains the central point of African stagnation. Over ten thousand years ago Bushmen in the Transvaal painted wonderfully on stone: peoples in the Transvaal were still painting like this almost within living memory. In the museum at Johannesburg you will find a lump of stone which is painted with the picture of a man in recognizably European dress and a woman with the long skirts and head-dress of a Dutch settler's wife. And yet Dutch settlers reached the Transvaal only in 1840. The arts of the Stone Age reach into our own times.

It is only in our own times that we begin to have enough knowledge to attempt an outline answer to this central question. It is tolerably sure, for example, that most of the present inhabitants of Black Africa arrived where they are in many successive migrations from the northward — migrations which seem to have resembled the eastward-moving migrations which furnished Europe with our own ancestors, and whose original impulse remains a matter for conjecture. These southward-moving Africans, Bantu-speaking peoples and other peoples, were set in motion by causes which are also beyond present knowledge: no one can say exactly where they came from, but for certain origins in Arabia and beyond, nor exactly why they came. The long slow movements of this dispersal, spreading west and south of the area northward of the Great Lakes, possibly reach back over several thousand years: their ripples continued until recent times. When Dutch settlers first reached the Great Fish river in what is now the Cape Colony of South Africa, they encountered peoples — Xosa, Zulu and others — whose arrival there may not have preceded them by much more than a century or two. It seems to have been much the same with the ruling peoples whom the Portuguese found in the Congo.

These southward-moving migrants were New Stone Age peoples who had learnt, perhaps from the more advanced cultures of the Upper Nile, the working of copper and iron, though not of bronze. Little by little, through unknown vicissitudes over many centuries, they pushed into the boundless lands which flowed away to the southward, overrunning the aboriginal inhabitants — the stone engravers and painters — and warring repeatedly with those who pressed upon their heels.

With a high capacity for adjustment and survival, intelligently, stubbornly, they adapted themselves to the equatorial climate, learnt new techniques of agriculture, grew food where none had grown before, mined and worked copper, gold and iron; made pots and wove fabrics. With them they brought a higher social organization than any they found: by the same token, they exterminated or enslaved or absorbed the aboriginal peoples with the same ease of technical superiority that Europeans would later exercise on them.

And yet their social evolution slowed up, came almost to a stop. Even when allowance is made for the burning rotting destructiveness of the equatorial climate, there is no reason to think these peoples ever succeeded in producing a civilization comparable with that of Mesopotamia, the Nile Valley, or pre-Chou China. Even the massive walls of Zimbabwe, of Monomotapa, come nowhere near suggesting this.

In default of exact evidence, one can perceive two or three probable reasons for their failure. These African peoples manifestly suffered much in moving and living where they did; and what is remarkable, perhaps, is not that they failed to evolve but that they managed to survive. Their real misfortune lay in their moving away from the cradles of early civilization, not towards them. One may contrast their destiny with that of the Dorian Greeks, barbarian tribes who came out of the European steppes around 1000 B.C., plundered the wealth of Mycenae and, in so doing, changed their own nature. Within three or four hundred years of the arrival of these wild and illiterate barbarians, Hesiod was writing his poetry: within five or six hundred years the Age of Pericles had flowered. Dorian Greece became the parent of our modern world. But where these early Greek barbarians had collided with the richly stimulating civilizations of Mycenae, Crete, the Near East, southward-moving African peoples were driving into a wilderness where they could find only savages who possessed a culture even earlier than their own. In that solitary land of central Africa, cut off from the Mediterranean and Mesopotamia by the great deserts, they found no superior forms of organization, no challenging examples, nothing to fertilize changes in their own way of life. Instead of the civilization of Crete, they found paleolithic survivals that were pygmies, Bushmen and their primitive kind.

These aboriginal peoples were rare, and the land was endlessly vast. Negro peoples coming from the north brought a higher tribal culture — they brought much the same kind of culture as the forerunners of those who had founded civilization in Sumeria in the third and fourth millennium before Christ. But they encountered a tremendous difference in governing conditions. Childe has shown how the civilization of Sumeria grew out of relatively dense settlement in relatively tiny areas of abnormally high fertility. A barbarian subsistence economy in Sumeria was not only impossible: it was also unnecessary. People could only stay if they learnt how to produce a surplus for exchange, eventually for trade; but this surplus was possible. Out of these conditions there came urban settlement, the diversion of labour, concentrations of wealth and power, knowledge of writing and thus a revolutionary break with the neolithic past.

In Africa, by contrast, there was always more land. Food growers and stock breeders as these African peoples generally were, they could always move on whenever they had temporarily exhausted the lands of their settlement. Tribes would hive off sub-tribes who would forage further on, settle elsewhere. They were doing this right into our own times: only European 'law and order' has prevented them from continuing to do it. There could seldom or never have occurred any lasting over-population on any particular piece of land. This method of ensuring food was effective, for it sustained these peoples under severely adverse conditions: no doubt it was their only possible means of survival. 'Any human beings that found a habitation in the tropics would have had to face the same conditions. As far as we can see they would have had to deal with them in much the same way as did the primitive African cultivators.'(8) Notions that African agriculture was inefficient or 'backward' in relation to its circumstances may be dismissed.

Yet this tribal economy was above all an economy of extensive cultivation. Across this inhospitable continent the Bantu and their fellow peoples spread themselves thinly, and survived. But the very thinness of their occupation set close limits on their chances of evolution. It meant that there could never be any real division of labour, nor systematic development of trade, nor growth of commodity farming out of subsistence farming. Each family group or clan would be self-supporting in all its needs.

This was the kind of African society which the Boer settlers clashed with on the Great Fish river in the eighteenth century, which the Portuguese had found near the mouth of the Congo much earlier than that. It was not an entirely stagnant society: copper and iron working, for example, had begun to throw up blacksmith specialists who formed 'mysteries'. But its social growth was exceedingly slow. It had to grow out of its own genius, having no superior culture to imitate and learn from; and it grew slowly. Its growth was further slackened by this plenitude of land: whenever economic problems gathered to a point of crisis which might elsewhere have induced a change in economic relations — and hence a growth towards higher forms of social organization — the Bantu simply moved to new lands, warring if necessary with others who stood in their way.

These peoples nonetheless were pioneers, and their achievements were not small in spite of their isolation from the rest of humanity. Whether for war or for peace, they proved capable

41

of a high degree of centralized authority, of common purpose, of shaping and changing their laws according to their needs. 'Their legal institutions had progressed beyond the primitive stage and showed many resemblances to the archaic laws of the Anglo-Saxon, Germanic and Frankish peoples before the rise of feudal society. Indeed, in some respects, such as the absence of self-help or the judicial duel, the existence of centralized courts with a defined jurisdiction, the compulsory submission of cases such as treason, homicide and sorcery to the courts, the African legal system had advanced to the stage reached in Europe during the early medieval period. . . .'(9)

They had no system of writing, and were ignorant of the wheel. Europeans sometimes adduce the lack of these as proof that African peoples have shown themselves inherently inferior to other peoples. Yet the argument is worthless. The earliest written records in Sumeria, Egypt, Crete, were records of accounting, traders' sums, the notes of temple priests adding up their stores: such was the birth of written language. The Bantu had no need of accounts, because they had no trade worth the name. They were beginning to have primitive currencies when the Europeans came — cowrie shells and the like — and in time these currencies might have acquired written symbols, might have sponsored early forms of arithmetic. But their tribal economy was subsistence economy, and growth out of this — just as everywhere else — was exceedingly slow.

As for use of the wheel, one may question whether the wheel could have given much service to migrant tribes moving through dense forest: in any case, the wheel was an invention always slow to move from a higher culture to a lower. Even in Egypt wheeled vehicles came into use only a thousand years after the Egyptians had acquired the potter's wheel.(10) And once again one may question whether peoples who made pots for domestic need, and not for trade, could have felt the want of any more efficient means of making them than the slow process of 'building-up' which the Bantu used.

Just as the Bantu-speaking and other peoples moved southward into regions which could teach them nothing in terms of social progress, so they were cloaked from contact with civilization by the deserts in their rear. Unlike the peoples who brought early civilization to Britain, they were spurred by no near examples of civilizing ferment at their back. They had behind them nothing but a waste land without humanity. Cut off from the future, they advanced into the past.

Then, dramatically, in 1482, there is an end to their isolation. Diogo Cão brings to equatorial Africa the impact of a Europe that is growing out of feudal society into early capitalism, brilliant with new ideas, with innovations, discoveries, the beginnings of modern science. Here, surely, is Africa's chance: the fertilizing influence of this Europe will stimulate new African growth, will enable revolutions to overtake the slow centuries while Africa slept, will bring these African peoples into the family of the world.

Nothing of this occurs. There is little difference to be noted between the social organization of the peoples whom Diogo Cão discovered and those who will be found again some four hundred years later, when Livingstone and others tramp across central Africa. If anything, there is decay, degeneration.

Why? Was it the fault of the kings of Congo and their fellow monarchs that they failed to penetrate the secrets of the European's power? They tried in every way they knew. To that hidden pool of knowledge, conferring new powers over nature and over man, these priest-kings and their peoples were never given access.

This quest for the knowledge which their own history and situation have denied them is the central drama of the peoples of central and southern Africa. Beginning with Nzinga a Nkuwa, whom Cão's missionaries baptized John I, it continued until the slave trade suppressed it. Only now, in these middle years of the twentieth century, does the quest revive again and begin to reach its destination. With this new impetus many African peoples reach at last a turning point in their history.

43

FOUR

LORD OF CONGO

WHEN the King of Congo welcomed Diogo Cão and his missionaries he evidently thought — and on this the Portuguese records are clear enough — that he and his subjects were sure to benefit from this new and important alliance. He and his elders hastened to accept the White man's god. He ordered his people to become Christians; with gratifying celerity, they became Christians overnight. Their traditional animism made no great difficulty of that: the Europeans had merely brought with them fresh symbols and manifestations of a Supreme Being in whom Africans already believed, and whom, after their comfortably sceptical fashion, they universally respected.

There was nothing new or conspicuously African in this mass conversion. No earlier than five hundred years before, at a time when Hungarian nomads had given up ravaging western Europe and settled along the Danube, their king, Vaik, was baptized and his people reckoned as Christians. King Vaik became Saint Stephen. King Nzinga a Nkuwa was not so fortunate. Yet he was treated as an equal by the King of Portugal.

Nzinga a Nkuwa was glad of this alliance not because the peoples of his kingdom were especially destitute — such evidence as we have suggests that they were fairly well off — but because he had powerful rivals in countries neighbouring his own, as well as vassals who might revolt from his overlordship. This was not yet feudalism as Europe knew it, but a system of regulated loyalties moving towards feudalism. Most authorities agree that the kingdom of Congo — a patchwork of peoples linked by vassalship to the ruling family — had probably arisen from the incursion of a powerful migrating people able to establish its dominion over already settled peoples. It had possibly

44

been larger in the century before the Portuguese arrived: soon after their arrival, there occurred a characteristic outbreak of dynastic warfare between rival cousins, and in this the Portuguese found an occasion to assert their own supremacy.

Oral tradition gives Nzinga a Nkuwa, the Mani of Congo whom the Portuguese first found, three predecessors. During their time the kingdom had grown into a centralized system of government resting on a clear line of chiefly hierarchy, established by strong men at the head of strong tribes who had subdued other tribes, made them pay tribute as vassal peoples, and sometimes bound them in domestic slavery. Much the same picture emerges from the little that is known of other central African kingdoms, of the various kingdoms of the Baluba group, including the Bashongo kingdom of Shamba Bolongongo, for example; or that of Monomotapa whose African founders — having come from Ethiopia before A.D. 900 — threw up the massive ruins of Zimbabwe in what is now Southern Rhodesia.(11)

Under centralized authority these lands were generally at peace. Dynastic wars appear to have left the bulk of people as little touched as the Wars of the Roses (taking place at about the same time) left the bulk of the English people. Sovereignty was more than haphazardly established and defended. 'There also speaks for close connection the fact that the King of Loango was obliged to marry a princess of the royal blood of Kakongo, while the Mani of Kakongo had been earlier obliged to choose his spouse from a princess of the blood royal of Congo.'(12)

Geographically, the Congo kingdom at one time or another embraced both sides of the mouth of the Congo river as well as the country for several hundred miles into the interior. Congo kings at various times exercised authority over Loango, to the north of the river, and over other and minor states established in what is now Angola. At no time, of course, did the Congo overlordship include more than a small part of the Congo as we know it today. The frontiers of its overlordship fluctuated, as with all these African states, but were never much wider than those of modern France or perhaps Germany.

Knowing no African languages and no history, and filled with medieval certitudes about the origins of man, the early Portuguese misinterpreted practically everything they saw and heard, and generally misunderstood its significance. They concluded that these people were made for slavery; but they also concluded that they were human, and should therefore be baptized and saved for possible entry into the kingdom of Heaven. They thought African beliefs either ridiculous or morally wicked, and did their best, though quite vainly, to abolish them. At this distance, however, it is difficult to see that African magic was half so ridiculous or wicked as the European magic which the missionaries brought lavishly with them. At least the peoples of Congo had never thought, so far as we know, that they had seen flaming crosses in the sky, nor a host of other miraculous appearances to which the Portuguese were firmly attached.(13)

The Portuguese also thought that these Congo peoples were given to eating human flesh for the taste of the thing, and wrote them down as cannibals. Yet it is reasonably sure that before the Europeans' coming no African peoples had ever eaten flesh for the taste of the thing, but always because the eating of human flesh was a sacred ritual — and restricted to the governing few. After the long ravage of the slave trade some of these African societies degenerated into a misery and ruin in which famine and moral degradation fostered cannibalism and wholesale human sacrifice: the best judgments we possess agree that this was never a function of tribal organization, nor a social custom. The familiar picture of the missionary stewing in the cannibal's pot is one of the clichés by which Europeans have justified their own cruelties. It has no foundation in the reality of African society before the coming of the slave trade, and surprisingly little even after that.

For even after that the eating of human flesh generally remained a strictly ritual function. Few African peoples were more active in promoting the slave trade than the Ovimbundu of inner Angola. And yet 'the Ovimbundu are not ordinary cannibals, if indeed that term may be applied to any people in Africa, nor do the commoners of the Ovimbundu ever eat human flesh on their own account, but no king may reign or be considered as regularly enthroned until he has "eaten Ekongo" . . . literally, to eat "the Old One". This is a ritual feast in which the flesh of a specially fattened slave is eaten mixed with the flesh of various animals'.(14) No doubt a nasty custom; but not cannibalism. Tales of cannibalism for long rested on the rough-and-ready story-telling of worthies such as Andrew Battell, an English mariner who sojourned in Angola for some twenty years at the end of the sixteenth century. This story-telling was swallowed by the public at home with an avidity which exists, under different forms, among us to this day. Rapidly, the legend grew strong that Africa was a wilderness inhabited by howling savages. And howling savages might reasonably be enslaved: indeed, they would be better off as slaves. . . .

African nationalists tend sometimes to rush to the other extreme, and claim that tribal society was a garden of sweetness and light. It is an understandable reaction, but equally without truth. Tribal society was stunted in its growth and flowering by the narrow boundaries of its condition. It could seldom get outside itself, was generally closed to new ideas. Only here and there, towards the north where Mediterranean influences could still reach out and take effect, could pastoral tribes move towards higher forms of organization not remote from Asian or European example. Ghana, Mali, Songhay . . . these are great names in African history: they were stable empires built between A.D. 900 and 1600 along the southern fringe of the western Sahara where social change found good soil. But they were not typical of tribal Africa. Their influence never penetrated in any lasting form into the great rain forests to the south of them.

At the same time, as we have seen, the peoples of Congo and its neighbour kingdoms were not the howling savages they were quickly labelled by invading Europeans. These were tolerably peaceful lands where people appear to have lived tolerably well — certainly far better than they would live for many hundreds of years after European slaving began. Congo kings were generally members of the metal-smiths' mystery, and they knew quite extensive uses for copper and iron. Their arts were memorable for fine carving in wood and ivory, for raffia weaving, for music and dancing; and all these arts were part of daily life.

Their religion was stable and well framed for tribal society, of which it was the guardian. They took for granted the existence of a High God, but thought his influence much more remote and dubious than that of familiar spirits in rivers and springs, or of guardian spirits living in the memory of their ancestors. Their laws were intricate and socially complete, the emphasis being always on the good of the collective, the group, at the expense of the individual; and their rewards and punishments were clearly set forth, widely understood and frequently effective. Their sanctions for violent crime, which is still a rare thing in tribal Africa, recall those of the early Norsemen. 'Among the Norsemen, the man who had killed a fellow clansman was cursed and cast out of his clan. He became an outlaw. Unless, as sometimes happened, he was adopted into another clan, he ceased to exist as a member of society. Cut off from the clan, in which alone he had had his being, he went mad and died of starvation. So in Greece.'(15) And so in Africa.

Established at the head of such a system, half-priest, half-king, the Mani of Congo saw in the coming of the Europeans an occasion for advantage. He took it as a blessing. They brought new knowledge; and knowledge was power. They had only to share this knowledge for the wealth and welfare of Congo to benefit a thousandfold.

He was disillusioned. He — but more especially his son and notable successor, Affonso I — lived through years of disillusionment. If missionaries seemed to promise good, others came who promised only harm. As Monsignor Cuvelier has put it: 'Under the flag of idealism the brigands also went aboard.'(16) They went aboard in great number.

Voyages to the East could bring back spices, silks, the envied luxuries of ancient civilization. When the *Golden Hind* returned to London Pool in 1580 after sailing round the world, the

48

venture is said to have paid a profit of £1,500,000 on an initial investment of £5000. So well-provided were these eastern civilizations that East India merchants were for long obliged to pay in bar silver: there was nothing else that Europe could offer.

In Africa, by contrast, the Portuguese and their rivals at once concentrated on taking slaves. Later their thoughts turned to ivory and silver and copper; but there was little of these to be had, and slaves remained their principal commerce. It was highly profitable. There was now an inexhaustible demand for slaves from the mines and plantations of the West Indies and America, a powerful source of this demand being precisely the call for silver from the Eastern trade.

Economic strains in Portugal itself demanded more and more tribute in the form of slaves. By the beginning of the sixteenth century, less than thirty years after Cão's first anchoring in the mouth of the Congo, King Manuel was instructing his emissaries that: 'Although the principal aim is to serve God and the pleasure of the king, all the same you will explain [to the King of Congo], and as though you were speaking in my name, what he must do to fill our ships in the way of slaves and copper and ivory. . . .'(17)

Instead of a pooling of European knowledge, Europe offered the slave trade. Seldom was there a more obvious case of people asking for bread and being given a stone.

This disillusionment can be traced movingly in the letters of Nzinga a Nkuwa's son, baptized Affonso I, of whose intelligence and good will the Portuguese royal emissary Rui d'Aguiar bore witness in a report to King Manuel in 1516, writing that Affonso 'expresses himself so well, and so exactly, that I think the Holy Spirit must be always in his words. I must tell you, Sire, that he studies ceaselessly and sometimes falls asleep over his books. . . .'(18) Enough of Affonso's correspondence with Lisbon and Rome has survived in Portuguese archives to suggest that this was not all high-flown language. He seems by any account to have had unusual qualities of understanding. His letters to

D   49

Lisbon were neither servile nor ridiculous. They have Othello's pride: 'I fetch my life and being from men of royal siege, and my demerits may speak unbonneted to as proud a fortune as this that I have reached. . . .'

For nearly forty years — reigning between 1507 and perhaps 1541 — this African monarch strove to make sense of European avarice, to secure the fulfilment of European promises, to call up the sympathy and friendship of those in whom he trusted, although he had never seen them. He was betrayed, bamboozled, fooled and sold time after time; and time after time he returned to the charge. He accepted the demand for slaves, but regretted it as soon as he had understood the difference between the European slave trade and the domestic slavery always practised in his own country. He pinned his faith to the coming of missionaries, for he saw the future in terms of winning over the European's God — the manifestation of superior power over nature and mankind: in letter after letter he calls for missionaries.

He sends his own people to Portugal so that they may be trained for the priesthood; sometimes they reach Lisbon, often enough they are waylaid by slavers from the robber island of São Thomé. He persists in spite of every conceivable disappointment. At his capital of Mbanza Congo, which he renames San Salvador after the church he helps to build there, missionaries intrigue against him, become corrupted, think only of the wealth they can accumulate. Traders rob and kill. Slavers become more numerous. The Portuguese king seems deaf to all appeal.

He turns to Rome, seeking to find a way round the Portuguese monopoly of contact with the Congo; succeeds in 1518 in having one of his sons consecrated as a bishop in the Eternal City itself; goes over the King of Portugal's head in direct appeals to the Pope. They are fruitless. He excludes all Portuguese from his dominions and is forced to re-admit them. In 1539, making a final appeal for help against the Portuguese, he tries to send another embassy to Rome, for Pope Paul III has written him, in 1535, that the Holy See will aid and support his pious wishes. But he cannot send an embassy unless he has a ship to send it in; and this time the King of Portugal, scenting the wind of discontent, will not let him have a ship.

Faced with this refusal, Affonso beseeches John III 'by the Passion of our Saviour' that the Portuguese king may give him 5000 cruzados in exchange for 5000 Congo cowries so that he may cover the costs of the voyage. With these 5000 cowries, Affonso explains, slaves may be bought, and John may sell these slaves in Lisbon at a good profit . . . At last Affonso finds passage for his son, who embarks for Rome. But at São Thomé he is turned back: the Portuguese will hear of no such embassy. The Congo monopoly is theirs; they will not share it even with the Pope.

Soon after Affonso's death the Portuguese began turning their monopoly to good account. Contact became conquest. Having come as allies, they intended to remain as masters. Yet it was not until the latter part of the seventeenth century, after the death of Alvarez IX of Congo, that they succeeded in establishing their supremacy to the point of nominating the Congo rulers, and of ruling through them. Through all this time, and the years that followed, they had little permanent hold on the country except in their forts of Loanda (1576) and Benguela (1617); their influence in the interior remained fragmentary until the early years of the present century. Until about 1900, too, the Congo kings succeeded one another in more or less unbroken line, so that from Nimi a Lukeni, supposed founder of the kingdom in the fourteenth century, until Dom Martin, the last Congo 'king' who died less than fifty years ago, there are listed no fewer than fifty-five kings of Congo.

Their Portuguese titles date from soon after Cão's arrival. In 1512 Manuel of Portugal sent out a *regimento* which decorated the tribal hierarchy of all the ruling families in Congo, as well as of Loango and other sub-kingdoms in what is now Angola, with the whole gamut of aristocratic titles then current in

Portugal, so that the king and his vassals became dukes and counts and marquises; and all were presented with *Dom* before their names. Manuel also insisted on Portuguese as the official language. There at San Salvador, a little settlement tucked amid green hills to the south of the Congo estuary, 'chanceries with many secretaries appeared ... and the outward forms reflected down to the smallest detail the forms of the Portuguese court'.(19)

San Salvador was little heeded by the world at large, for it yielded only slaves; and these years saw the widening of horizons to India and the Americas. Portugal declined, rotten with human loot. For a century and a half after about 1700 these African lands retreated once again into their silence, broken only rarely by brave little bands of missionaries whose efforts proved vain. Through all this time African slavers from the interior delivered African slaves to the coast, where Europeans bought them and carried them to Brazil; and the impact of Europe was limited, almost literally, to this. When Adolf Bastian entered San Salvador in 1857 he found the place scarcely recognizable: its church was in ruins, overgrown, forgotten, and its greatness in African history totally obscured.

A year or two after Bastian's passage through San Salvador the Portuguese, fearing European rivals, moved a garrison from the coast, and began spasmodically to reassert themselves in the interior.

They found little to show for their long connection. Animism had long since absorbed Christianity and its symbols. 'The Congo kingdom', Ihle concludes, 'was subjected to the influence of Christian missions and European culture uninterruptedly for over two hundred years. But when one looks for the results of all this missionary endeavour one only concludes that there emerged from it neither moral nor material advantage for the negro.' It is a severe judgment, given the number of Portuguese who had left their bones in this land; but it is not unfair. From its earliest manifestations, the potentially fertilizing influence of Portuguese penetration of these lands was fatally sterilized by the slave trade.

Much has been written of the slave trade; and the more one reads the more terrible its shadow grows. 'How great was the moral damage of this hunt and traffic in "black ivory",' Ihle writes of its effect on tribal society, 'it is difficult to say. Gradually, the last social links were broken, and the whole structure utterly destroyed. Certainly there had been slaves in the Congo before the coming of the White man. They had formed an organic part of the social framework, however, and had in it their clearly determined place. But after the growth of the slave trade the possession of slaves was transformed into a savage manhunt. Not only did the stronger man sell the weaker, but even the bonds of family life were broken, and parents sold their children or children their parents as generally worthless objects to the Portuguese, who branded them with a hot iron as if they had been sheep.'(20)

It is above all the slave trade which has dominated, twisted, denied the humanity of Africans. Without understanding what the slave trade has meant to them, there is no understanding of what they were and of what they have become.

FIVE

A BISHOP'S CHAIR

'ON the wharf at Luanda as late as 1870,' the Reverend Tucker records, 'there could still be seen a marble chair in which the bishop had sat and baptized by boatloads the poor wretches as they rowed alongside the ship. The Government collected its tax, the pious ecclesiastic received his fee, and the slaves had their first introduction to the White man's religion.'(21)

The chair is gone from this pleasant Atlantic harbour sheltered from ocean storms by its long spit that is green with tropical plants and trees. All that is obviously reminiscent of the oversea slave trade is the flat-topped palisaded fort on the promontory above the town, brooding in primrose shadows among ancient muzzle-loading cannon; although, as I found in 1954, there are plenty of people inside Angola who still live and work as slaves.

Slavery had soon become endemic to this country. The customary subjection of a weaker tribe to a stronger, traditional to Africa and involving little or no social disintegration, nor even much cruelty, was transformed disastrously into commodity slavery. Men became currency. They were stripped of their humanity and reduced to the level of branded goods — divided into 'categories' according to their size and weight and temperament, and sold in the way that horses, dogs and cattle were sold. For a long time their best quality, fetching the best price, was known in the trade as *pièces d'Inde* — Indies pieces: these consisted of strong young men between the apparent ages of fifteen and thirty. The busy commercial world of Europe did good trade with Indies pieces.

The brigands, as Monsignor Cuvelier has called them, soon made all the running; and the Church ran fast behind them.

54

Once Affonso had thoroughly involved himself in this traffic his successors had no chance of extricating themselves, even had they wished to do so. Generally, they were content to ensure that their own families and dependents were left in peace: anyone else became fair game for the slavers. There set in that long process of African degradation which was not to end for several hundred years, and which dragged down these relatively strong, peaceful and energetic societies into misery and ruin.

Neither Affonso nor his successors had any real help from the Church. At the scene of these horrors the Church from time to time protested, but generally was content to take its share of the loot. New research in the ecclesiastical archives at Luanda, conducted lately by the Abbé Jadin, confirms an earlier judgment that the Church 'was content to demand that slaves collected for America be first baptized, so that at least their souls might be saved. Otherwise the affair was thought regular enough . . .'(22) The bishops, it is true, insisted that each slaving ship should carry a chaplain for the Middle Passage — the murderous sea journey which intervened between the march to the Atlantic coast and the march to the plantations and mines of America: unhappily, 'the charms of this voyage tempted few chaplains, and recourse was had to poor priests and others who were often of the least desirable kind'.(23) Even in the Church's own terms, its succour failed.

Having got so far, the Church evidently felt that it could do no more. The bishop sat in his marble chair and baptized the slaves; and took his share of the export tax.

This export tax on slaves was an important revenue of the government of Angola (whose authority spasmodically reached a little way along the coast to the north of the Congo's mouth but far along the coast to the south of it, scarcely ever penetrating the interior). In the seventeenth century, the Abbé Jadin finds, 'the baptismal tax of 300 reis a head that was payable by the slave traders was at first given entirely to the parish priests of Remedios and Benguela'. But after the end of the seventeenth century, with the export of slaves become an accepted institution, the bishop secured 150 reis of this tax for his own coffers. He refused, however, to impose the tax on infants. 'Children at the breast paid no export tax . . . and for the ports of Luanda and Benguela their number rarely exceeded 50 to 80 for every 15,000 to 20,000 slaves exported each year.' This was not exactly a crowning mercy.

Those who may be disinclined to accept the slave trade as the pre-eminently degrading influence of European contact should reflect on the immensity of the numbers involved. Millions were carried away. Nobody will ever know the exact number, nor does it matter. The number was large, the process continuous. A Portuguese historian has lately estimated, from Portuguese documents, a round figure of 1,389,000 slaves taken out of Angola (including the historical kingdom of Congo) between 1486 and 1641 alone, or an average of about 9000 a year.(24) But slaving intensified in the eighteenth and nineteenth centuries: the Abbé Jadin finds that slaves from Angola were transported at a rate of 25,000 a year in the eighteenth century, and up to 30,000 a year in the first years of the nineteenth century.(25) A conservative estimate must in any case conclude that several million Africans were seized in these now thinly populated lands and taken across the seas; and that perhaps as many millions more were either enslaved on European account in Angola or died in consequence of slaving. These millions were no small part of the whole population.

And they contributed by their labour, although it is unfashionable to say so, no small part of the accumulated capital which Europe and America would later invest in Africa. As to the impact of the slaves on Brazil — whither many of the Angolan and Congo slaves were sent — it was deep and many-sided. For these enslaved Africans possessed a generally higher level of social and economic culture than the Indians whom the Portuguese had first enslaved, or, in certain important respects, than many of the White colonists themselves. Above all, these African slaves came from a society which had already evolved a

stable and successful agriculture in tropical conditions not dis-
similar from those of Brazil itself. These men and women were
not only strong to resist the climate: they knew also how to
cultivate the tropical soil.

Thus the part that the Negro played in creating Brazil, notwithstanding his terrible hardships and his lack of liberty, was
'a most impressive one. Along the agrarian seaboard it was, in
my estimation, much greater than that of the aborigine.
Greater in a certain sense than that of the Portuguese'. Such,
at least, is the opinion of a leading Brazilian historian, Gilberto
Freyre, in his masterly analysis of Brazilian history, *The Masters
and the Slaves*(25a).

'The slaves that came from the more advanced areas of
Negro culture,' Freyre continues, 'were an active, creative, and,
one might almost add, a noble element in the colonization of
Brazil; if they occupied a lower rung, it was due simply to their
condition as slaves. Far from having been merely draft animals
and workers with the hoe in the service of agriculture, they ful-
filled a civilizing function. They were the right hand in the
formation of Brazilian agrarian society; the Indians and, from
a certain point of view, the Portuguese being the left hand in
the undertaking.'

When Africans come at last to consider their own history they
will learn much from the fate of their peoples sent across the
Atlantic. Far from passive savages resigned to their dismal
condition, these Negroes of Brazil — and not only of Brazil —
proved themselves capable of life-giving energy and intelligence
in bitterly adverse circumstances. They reproduced in modern
times the epic of Negro survival in the 'Stone Age' solitudes of
the equatorial forests of central Africa — and that, too, in face of
long-enduring slavery.

If the Portuguese were early in the field, they were soon
followed by others. 'From about 1730, Liverpool began for
various reasons to eclipse both London and Bristol as the chief
English centres of the trade. In the eleven years, 1783-93,

921 Liverpool ships were employed in the convoying of slaves. They carried 313,737 slaves of a total value of £15,186,850. After deducting 15 per cent under divers heads, the net return to Liverpool in those eleven years amounted to £12,294,116 ... It is computed that from 1750 to 1800, one-fourth of the ships belonging to the port of Liverpool were employed in the slave trade: Liverpool monopolized five-eighths of the British slave trade, and three-sevenths of the total slave trade of the world.'(26) Although most of these English slaves were taken from the Guinea coast, Liverpool ships regularly loaded slaves at Luanda.

Most slaves from this Portuguese-held coast — from Angola and Congo — were taken to Brazil, which dominated Portugal's West African possessions for over two hundred years. Though formally suppressed in 1826, the slave trade with Brazil continued for some years after that. By then the whole economy of these territories was linked so closely to the use of slaves that no real effort was ever made to suppress internal slavery, although the export of slaves came gradually to an end. This internal slavery continued until the last quarter of the nineteenth century, when it was somewhat modified into a form of slavery known as 'contract labour'. In this form, as we shall see, it continues in Angola to this day.

African kings and dignitaries were carried along on this wave of slaving profit. In time they lost all chiefly sense of protecting their own people and their own country. Often enough they could not even protect their own persons. They became little more than the miserable agents of European slavers, holding authority from the Portuguese on sufferance, always subject to despoilment and incarceration.

Abbé Jadin has lately turned up a case which illuminates better than anything else, perhaps, the helot misery into which these once independent and considerable kingdoms sank. In 1804 it fell out that the son and nephew of Garcia V of Congo, the 'princes' Pedro de San Salvador and Affonso, went to a seminary in Luanda to prepare for the priesthood. 'These young seminarists every year received three slaves from the king in order to pay for their studies. In 1812, the Prince Pedro sold his father's ambassador who had brought a number of slaves to Luanda. The Governor found himself obliged to cause this Congolese nobleman to be sought for in Brazil, and to send the two students back to San Salvador until the bishop could arrive and re-establish discipline.' No doubt the bishop did establish discipline, although that is not recorded; yet it is a dismal picture, this paying to the Church of an annual price of three slaves so that two young Africans may be taught to preach Christianity.

No sooner was the export trade suppressed along the West Coast — with men-of-war waiting to pounce on the slavers — than it expanded again, clandestinely, voluminously, through Arab slaving agents who had crossed the continent from Zanzibar on the East Coast. The Luanda archives date in 1852 the first appearance of Arab slavers in Angola, and Arab depredations were to continue until the turn of the century, when Belgian and British imperialism put an end to them at last. Yet it was often along these Arab trails into the interior that some of the early explorers of the mid-nineteenth century found their way across Africa. By then this middle continent had fully earned its name. It was Darkest Africa indeed.

Thus the coming of large-scale European penetration after about 1885 was in one respect a blessing for these peoples. The slavers were driven out, the evil trade reduced to little or nothing. And it seemed, for a time, as though the wrongs of four hundred years of despoilment would now at last be made good. That at least was Livingstone's hope, the vision which drew him onward until fever and the climate killed him.

After long years of silence these nineteenth-century explorers once again made contact between central Africa and the outside world. In 1815 James Tuckey went 300 miles up the Congo, when his escort refused to travel any further; in 1826 Owen followed him; in 1832 two Portuguese, Monteiro and Gametto, penetrated from the Moçambique coast as far as the river Luapula (which their compatriot, Almeida, had already reached in 1798, only to be killed there); another Portuguese, Graça, got even further in 1843, and touched the upper Kasai; and then there followed Livingstone and Stanley and other famous men, gradually mapping the whole outline of the lost interior.

If it remains uncertain why these Congo peoples had earlier failed to evolve a genuine Bronze Age and Iron Age, and to march along the same road towards civilization as Norsemen and Greeks and the rest of barbarian humanity, there can be no reasonable uncertainty why they remained stagnant, why they degenerated into chaos, between the time of Diogo Cão's arrival and the second quarter of the twentieth century. But the fault lay not only in the slave trade. There was also its aftermath.

The aftermath proved in some ways worse than the trade itself. Europe greeted the news of Victorian discoveries in Africa with fine talk of civilizing missions. Selfless idealists embarked for Africa. But once again the brigands also went aboard.

In 1885 the Congress of Berlin — the conference of the great imperial share-out in west and central Africa — recognized the sovereign right of a body called the International Association of the Congo to possess and govern the whole vast area contained by the basin of the Congo river. This Congo Free State, as it was called with unconscious irony, endured from 1885 until 1908, when it disappeared with the curses of humanity on its head.

Through these brief but terrible years this great continental centre of Africa was administered by a peculiarly vicious form of government known as the Leopoldian System after its founder and principal begetter, King Leopold II of the Belgians; and the Leopoldian System probably killed off more Africans in a couple of decades than the slave trade had succeeded in doing through the whole of the preceding century. It may not necessarily follow, of course, that Leopold and his principal lieutenants were especially wicked men, according to their own lights:

they had taken up much the same pious attitude as the earlier Protestant adventurers — men like Sir John Hawkins, whose slaving was all for the good of God's Elect and damnation to the pagans, and whose highly respectable coat of arms included 'a demi-Moor, proper, in chains'. Yet their lights were unusually dim, and their System unusually horrible. It was against this System that people so various as the Archbishop of Canterbury and Mark Twain, the great liberal humanitarian E. D. Morel and Lord Fitzmaurice, Booker T. Washington and the Marquess of Lansdowne, raised united and successful protest.

Once again, briefly, appallingly, the peoples of the Congo look for bread and are given a stone. And this time the bloody drama is enacted in the full light of the world of fifty years ago.

It was an American newspaper-man turned explorer, H. M. Stanley, who rang up the curtain on this drama. But it was Leopold, and not Stanley, who devised the plot.

SIX

RECONQUEST

WHEN Stanley reached the mouth of the Congo in 1877, after two years' Herculean wanderings across Africa, he was determined to give the benefit of his discoveries to Britain. He had something important to give, no less than the discovery that the whole central basin of the Congo was linked together by navigable rivers. No other part of Africa had anything so convenient; even the tremendous Niger was nothing by comparison. But London turned a deaf ear to these plans for colonial enlargement. Gladstone was in power, and wanted no more colonial adventures. Already the West Coast and troubles with the Boers and the tribes in the south were costing quite enough money without committing more in other African regions, and that without any clear assurance of profit.

Stanley had an obvious alternative. Landing at Marseilles in June 1878, on his homeward journey, he had found himself awaited by agents of Leopold II, who had begged him to return to the Congo on a secret mission as agent of Leopold's International Association, founded two years before. When he failed in London, Stanley crossed at once to Brussels and found a ready audience.

Leopold had long sought avenues to colonial expansion. 'From the high windows of his palace at Ostend, like another Henry the Navigator, he had allowed his imagination to run forth upon the waves.'(27) It had run a long way, but so far without result. Even the bourgeois timidity of newly unified Belgium could not hold back the royal imagination; and there were those who did not want to hold it back. Already in 1840 Belgian capitalists had reached a preliminary agreement with the Spanish Government for commercial monopoly and right of exploitation over the Philippines in exchange for 50 million

62

francs; unhappily, the Cortes had failed to ratify the agreement. Leopold re-opened the question in 1869, and was some way towards success when the restoration of the Spanish monarchy again frustrated him. He had also looked into the possibility of buying the Fiji Islands and of colonizing the New Hebrides, to which, he thought, skilful management could soon add the Solomons. Checked in all this, he turned his attention to China, and was busy drawing up plans for building railways there with Belgian capital (in anticipation of imperial concessions such as the Great Powers enjoyed) when his questing imagination made a landfall on Africa.

Then, as now, Africa was much discussed. Huge colonies were acquired in next to no time: rival expeditions hastened through swamp and jungle in order to set their flag over territories which automatically became theirs, in the international morals of the time, however carefully they might be referred to as 'protectorates'. Leopold knew that he could not simply send forth an expedition and follow suit: Belgium carried too little weight for that. Britain, France and Germany, the great military powers, must necessarily get the lion's share: but they were sharp and jealous rivals, and Leopold's chance came in turning these rivalries to his own advantage. It is the measure of his diplomatic skill and judgment that he managed to acquire the largest territory of all — and, as events would prove, by far the wealthiest.

He got it by the skin of his teeth. Putting a rod in pickle, he had formed in 1876 an International African Association with himself as president. The general idea was to bring civilization to the savages of Africa, naturally with the right of commercial exploitation for those who should bring it. The Great Powers had their hands full at the time: France and Britain in West Africa, and Germany in East Africa. When Stanley offered Leopold his knowledge of the Congo, Leopold seized the opportunity with both hands. He would civilize the Congo.

'But already this was no more than philanthropic pretext. Just as Henry the Navigator, five centuries earlier, had passed

63

from crusading against Islam to exploiting the riches of the African coast, so now Leopold subordinated his anti-slavery campaign to his plans for imperial expansion.'(28) In 1878 he gave Stanley a five-year contract to open up a route along the rapids which separated the mouth of the Congo from Stanley Pool, about two hundred miles inland where the river becomes navigable; to set up bases for exploring the lower Congo; and to induce African chiefs to recognize the 'protection' of the International Association. Stanley collected four hundred 'treaties' with Congo chiefs so that the International Association could 'prove' to the conference of Berlin, in 1885, that it was already in effective possession of the whole river basin. Meanwhile, diplomatic storms were blowing up.

Leopold knew that a notable French explorer, de Brazza, was penetrating slowly into the territory now called French Equatorial Africa — the territory which lies on the right bank of the lower Congo and Ubangui rivers — and might forestall Stanley in this noble work of 'protection'. Using his vast private fortune to good political effect in Paris, Leopold secured from the French Government an agreement that it would not interfere with the International Association's civilizing progress.

But he reckoned without Portugal, just then awakening to its possession of Angola, which lies on the left bank of the estuary of the Congo, and had traditionally included the coast of the right bank as well. Understanding Leopold's game, the Portuguese thought they had checked him when they declared their sovereignty over both banks of the mouth of the river. Portugal's traditional protector, Britain, thereupon rushed in with recognition of this Portuguese declaration of sovereignty — not indeed because the British Government cared anything for the fate of the Congo, but because it was deeply suspicious of French imperialism, and saw an enemy in Leopold.

What was bad for Britain was regarded in Paris and Berlin as excellent for France and Germany. Both Powers at once refused to recognize this Portuguese claim to the north bank of the Congo estuary; and the United States, believing that Leopold's aim was to put down slavery (as in one sense — of Arab slavery — it was) thereupon recognized the Association's flag as that of a friendly State. It was the first occasion of the United States' embroiling itself in Africa, and the effect was instantaneous. Only a few days later the French Government felt able to follow suit: being more practical than the idealists in Washington, however, the French did this in return for Leopold's promise to offer France, in case of later sale, an option on any territories the International Association might acquire. A few months later Germany recognized the Association as a sovereign State; and Leopold's game was practically won.

There followed the Congress of Berlin which recognized the Congo Free State. Portugal was bullied into acceptance; the British fell into line with a poor grace. Perhaps one may quote a dispatch from *The Times* that illustrates the kind of treatment Africa and Africans could hope to receive from this partition of their continent. 'Tonight', wrote the paper's correspondent at the Berlin conference, 'I have to announce what is probably the most solid result of the West Africa Conference — namely, the final settlement of the various territorial claims to the lower portion of the Congo . . . The Conference has only been kept waiting by the obstinacy of the Lisbon Cabinet, which seemed determined to have its own selfish way in respect to the Lower Congo, but after various remedies in the nature of *douce violence*' — oh, happy diplomatic language! — 'had been vainly employed by the Powers interested in the success of King Leopold's undertaking, the Portuguese Cabinet was at last induced to give way, under the pressure of identical notes from France, England and Germany. . . .'(29)

Leopold got his way. What was not the least remarkable aspect of this profitable affair was that the Belgians themselves had next to nothing to do with it. Overnight their sovereign became possessed in everything but name of a country far larger than Belgium; and neither they nor their parliament had control of the uses to which he might put it.

Transformed into the Congo Free State, the International

E   65

Association at once shed its camouflage. The Treaty of Berlin, true enough, had insisted that all nations should have equal trading rights in the Congo Free State; and this condition remains fragmentarily observed in the 'Congo Basin Treaties' of today. In practice Leopold was free to manage things as he wanted them. He wanted above all to make money; and his method of making it was of an unexampled directness even for the nineteenth century in Africa.

His first step, taken in July 1885, was to issue a decree whereby the Congo Free State declared itself the owner of all 'vacant lands', thus giving Leopold, the principal participant and initiator of this venture, a property about the size of western Europe. Most of these lands, of course, were not in the least vacant: they were lands either cultivated by African peoples, or left fallow by African peoples with a later intention to cultivate. They were lands whose property title, in so far as any existed in tradition, was vested in the chiefs of African tribes, since Africans in their savage and quite uncivilized innocence had no conception of personal property in land, but only in the fruits thereof.

Having 'legally' possessed himself of all these lands, Leopold proceeded to divide them among a small number of specially created concession companies, financed at first by Belgian capital and later by British, French and American capital, in return for a quarter of the shares in these companies. These shares were vested in the Congo Free State, whose arbiter and practical owner was Leopold himself.

There remained the problem of securing an appropriate 'return' for this selfless enterprise. For some years nobody could see how this might best be done, and it was not until 1891, when considerable sums had gone towards exploration and the establishment of commercial bases along the main rivers, that the problem was solved. Briefly, this solution was contained in a decree of 1891 (held secret for one year after its coming into effect) which said that the Congo Free State was also the owner of all the fruits of the 'vacant lands' — and notably of ivory and rubber.

To all this the Congo peoples, as they gradually understood the effects of what was happening to them, violently objected. Leopold raised African levies to fight rebellious Africans; and, as always seems to happen, one brutality led to another until all restraint was gone. But the concession companies also objected to the decree of 1891. They pointed out that the meaning of the decree was to make them pay the Congo Free State for all the ivory and rubber they might manage to secure by forced collection on the lands to which they had concessionary title.

An excellent business man, the king thereupon offered the companies a compromise which they felt bound to accept. He divided the Congo Free State into three zones, one for 'private trade', one for 'private estate' (*Domaine privé*, reserved to the State), and one which was closed for 'reasons of public security'. By 1895 the Congo, thus divided, began to 'deliver' in a monstrously profitable fashion; and in 1896, still hungry for cash, Leopold carved out a *Domaine de la Couronne* of about a quarter of a million square miles which he presented to himself.

What profits Leopold derived from this private estate (whose stock value, in 1908, was estimated at 60 million francs) may be seen by anyone who cares to visit Brussels and its neighbourhood. Many of those ponderous public buildings, constructed after the most solid examples of bad taste then available — the palaces and museums and places starred in the guide book, and others elsewhere, such as Leopold's holiday mansion at Cap d'Antibes — were paid for by the profits of forced collection of ivory and rubber in the Congo. For its first ten years the *Domaine de la Couronne* returned a profit, it is recorded, of about three million pounds, not counting Leopold's dividend from his quarter-share in the concession companies' profits. One of these corporations at the same period showed a net profit over six years of operation of about a million pounds on a paid-up capital investment of some £9000.(30)

If the profits were large, the methods left something to be desired. Lord Lansdowne called them 'bondage under the most barbarous and inhuman conditions, and maintained for mercenary motives of the most selfish character'; and it is hard to see that he exaggerated. But the truth of these methods was not immediately apparent to the outside world. The Congo State's foundation in 1885 had gone hand in hand with resounding dedications to humanitarian welfare. 'The new State', declared Baron de Courcel, speaking for France at the Berlin conference, 'has been dedicated to the exercise of every liberty.' The whole of official Europe plumed itself: here indeed was a triumph over the barbarians, a solid tribute to the values of Victorian civilization.

The truth was scarcely that. For the effect of the decrees of 1885 and 1891, and the method of their execution, was to make the African inhabitants of these lands into mere tenants on sufferance, forced to collect the ivory and rubber which grew there but prevented from drawing any profit or revenue themselves from this collection. 'If they interfered with that property they were poachers, and whosoever abetted them in that interference were criminals, receivers of stolen goods, and violators of the law of the land.'(31) The whole sordid and murderous story may be read in the crushingly full documentation provided by British consular reports, in publications of the Congo Reform Association, and in E. D. Morel's exposure, *Red Rubber*; and the epitaph of condemnation was duly read on the System by the Belgian Parliament itself in its debate on annexation in 1908.

Prohibited from trade, or even from pursuing their own peaceful agriculture, the native inhabitants were driven into forced labour as collectors of the ivory and rubber to which they no longer had any 'legal title'. European officers of many nations were called in to command levies of native troops; and gradually the whole crazy System began to deliver its goods to the mouth of the Congo. Brutality became the order of the day. So gruesome were conditions that the Italian Government later withdrew its officers seconded to the Congo Free State. Missionaries came home with tales of what they had seen and heard. Rival Powers grew interested.

68

In 1903, under pressure from humanitarian interests within itself and from the Congo Reform Association which Morel had called into being, the British Government loosed its first salvo against the System. This was a report which the Government had asked of one of its consuls in Nigeria, after sending him to the mouth of the Congo to inquire for himself. The author of this report would later acquire another kind of fame, for his name was Roger Casement.

Consul Casement's report was the first of several, and was very damning. People in Belgium began to awaken to what was being done in their king's name and to their king's profit.

Writing in *The Times* in 1895, an American Baptist missionary named Murphy described the manner of raiding that was carried on by native levies under European command against rebellious forced workers: 'The hands — the hands of men, women and children — were placed in rows before the *Commissaire*, who counted them to see that the natives had not wasted cartridges.'

In 1897 a Swedish missionary named Sjöblom, another member of the American Baptist Missionary Union in the Congo, appealed at a public meeting held in London for action against the System. His protests in the Congo had already earned him a threat from the Governor-General of five years' imprisonment, and one understands why. Extracts from his speech are quoted by Morel. 'The natives in inland towns are, as a matter of question, asked whether they are willing to gather india-rubber. The question put to them is not: "Will you live at peace together? Will you acknowledge the Congo Government?" It is, "Will you work india-rubber?" Well, many of the people are killed, and they try suddenly to disband, and refuse to bring the india-rubber. Then war is declared.'

Sjöblom went on to describe this singular warfare, saying that within his own knowledge forty-five towns had been burnt down. 'Describes' — I am quoting Morel's report — 'the sentry-system, the soldiers stationed in the village, living on the people, and driving the adult males into the forest to gather india-

69

rubber. Narrates how he visited a village at sunset. The people had never seen a white man and had returned from their hunt for rubber. As he was speaking to them, a soldier rushed in among the crowd, and seized an old man guilty of having been fishing in the river instead of gathering rubber; shoots him before Sjöblom's eyes. Right hand cut off . . .'

'From this village,' Sjöblom said, 'I went on to another where I met a soldier who pointed to a basket, and said to me, "Look, I have only two hands." He meant that there were not enough to account for the rubber he had not brought. He had several prisoners tied to trees. When I came back, some of the villages were in an uproar . . . When I reached the river I turned and saw that the people had large hammocks in which they were gathering the rubber to be taken to the Commissioner. I also saw smoked hands, and the prisoners waiting to be taken to the Commissioner. This is only one of the places in which these practices occur . . . In fact, the officers have always freely told me about the many who were killed, and always in connection with india-rubber . . .'(32) According to a British Government *White Book* of 1904, every cartridge spent by a native soldier required a right hand as tally.

The consequences of all this were to complete what the slave trade had begun. The country was depopulated, its tribal society appallingly degraded.

The civilizing mission to which Leopold continued to assert that he had set his hand was gradually revealed — the words are Joseph Conrad's — as 'rapacious and pitiful folly'. Of his journey through the Kasai in 1904, Frobenius records: 'And so we came to Kabeja, the most south-easterly post of the Kasai Company . . . And yet I had to ask myself more than once if that which lay before me could really be a company station. In a wide and quite empty forest clearing stood several little houses of thatch. In that place there was not a leaf, not a flower, not a garden to be seen — nothing, absolutely nothing, spoke of a civilized people having settled here. . . .'(33)

Like others, Frobenius told of the evils he had seen; and the point is perhaps worth insisting on because this, after all, was the handicap under which these Congo peoples were obliged to enter the twentieth century. Far into the interior he found that the miserable agents of the concession companies could not secure the rubber and ivory they were bound to produce unless they offered at least some small inducement to the forced collectors. They therefore adopted a kind of truck system, although this (for the benefit of distant humanitarians) was formally forbidden by the law. They gave their native sub-agents small quantities of cotton goods and told them to return in so and so many days with appropriate quantities of rubber. When these sub-agents failed to deliver, or else delivered too little, they would often be beaten to death. As Frobenius explains, these White agents had improperly used the company's cotton in order to obtain rubber which the company expected to receive free; and they therefore fell into debt to the company.

He describes in details the proceedings of a Monsieur Labryn in the upper Kasai. 'The Kaloshi Kapepulla had been taken on as sub-agent and was among the prisoners . . . He had been given a stock of thirty pieces of cotton and had brought in only 500 lumps of rubber. The man had two wives and a gun. Labryn took these. The wife Kaniba was sold by Labryn to the native Kassadi for ten pieces of cotton. The wife Chabu or Cahu was sold to the native Kasongo for ten pieces of cotton. The gun Labryn sold to the native Malaba for two pieces of cotton.'

But there was worse. 'On October 4th, during our second stay in Kabeja, a sixth unhappy negro, the Kaloshi Watebelle, was captured. He too was a Kapita [sub-agent] who had failed to cover his supply of cotton properly. He must have been an excellent fellow, was a Christian, and brought up at the mission of Luebo. He came in the evening and was seized next morning and held on the ground. On one side stood a Kapita, and on the other a European. Each held a stick. It sounded like a mill, *flip-flap, flip-flap*. And when one stick was broken, so another was quickly seized lest there might occur an interruption in the rhythm. And as the thing went on for some time I counted 53 *flip-flaps*, or 106 blows. There must in truth have been more than 150. And when it was finished the poor beaten fellow could not move. They took him away, bleeding in five big wounds. And this we saw with our own eyes . . .' Later on, Frobenius heard that this man had died. As was shown by an overwhelming weight of disinterested testimony, the case was typical enough.

Of all these score of years that Leopold's System endured, one may perhaps repeat the words that Conrad, in his *Heart of Darkness*, put into the mouth of the company agent Kurtz when dying of fever in the lost wilderness of the interior: 'He cried in a whisper at some image, at some vision — he cried out twice, a cry that was no more than a breath — *The horror! The horror!*'

72

SEVEN

DESCENT TO HELL

Y en a qui font la mauvaise tête
 A leurs parents:
Qui font les dettes, qui font la bête
 Inutilement:
Qui, un beau soir, de leur maîtresse
 Ont plein le dos:
Ils fichent le camp, pleins de tristresse,
 Pour le Congo . . .[1]

SUCH was the melancholy chant that a traveller in the Congo could hear from the lips of an 'old colonial' in 1898: the System was bad for everyone, even for those who held the whip instead of receiving it. Decent men would not serve here.

'We'd like to copy you', a Frenchman said to Colonel Thys at this time, 'on our side of the Ubangui.'

'Try it,' replied that experienced agent of the ABIR concession company, 'but I warn you that in the French Congo you've no king who does what he likes — and you've a Parliament in Paris.' The obstacles to extending Leopold's System to the north bank of the Congo and Ubangui rivers seemed at that moment insuperable: later on, these obstacles were overcome.

Inspired by a variety of motives, criticism of the System was

---

[1] Somewhat freely:
        And some there be who break the heart
         Of Mum and Dad:
        Who run up debts and act the goat
         Like any cad:
        Who of Fifi — on one fine night —
         Or else Bobo
        Have had enough, and get to hell,
         For the Congo . . . (34)

building up. In publishing its consular exposures, the British Government was not without thinking that it might do Leopold and his friends a deal of good to be shown that their success in using Franco-German pressure at the Berlin conference — to establish the Congo Free State against British imperial policy — would now end in their own frustration. And the Belgian Parliament, awakening to what was really occurring in the Congo behind the happy hand-outs of Leopold's publicity organization, awakened also to increasing British and American financial penetration. In 1906, it was noted, the Congo Government granted four big concessions to foreign, mainly British, capital: Belgian capitalists seem to have thought that a parliamentary control of the Congo they could influence to their own advantage would be much preferable to a royal control which they could not.

Yet the moral pressure to end the System was genuine and was widely felt. The world at large had seen nothing like it since the great campaigns to end slavery: bishops and factory workers, chambers of commerce, writers and politicians combined to attack the System, and the Congo Reform Association, formed in England by E. D. Morel but drawing wide support from the United States, became a force to be reckoned with. Not unreasonably could Morel claim in 1913, when the Association went into voluntary liquidation at the end of its task, that 'what all Europe should have taken in hand, what it was the duty of all Europe to have taken in hand, and what all Europe did not even attempt to take in hand, this Association, rising as a small cloud on the horizon of a tyrant's will, and gathering the force of a tornado which swept him from his African throne — this Association has been, in a large measure, able itself to accomplish'.(35)

In the end, of course, it was the Belgian Parliament which administered the final blow. Annexation was achieved in 1908, and with this the System lost its last means of survival. As the evidence of corruption, brutality and terror became overwhelming, the king's prestige was shaken to its foundations —

which by this time were well sunk in bricks and mortar, however, so that his wealth remained intact — and even his most sycophantic courtiers were reduced to angry silence. For the Socialists during the debate on annexation, Vandervelde denounced the systematic coercion and the huge profits which it yielded to the shareholders of whom the king was the most important. Colfs, on the Catholic benches, attacked the Belgian Government for constituting itself the 'systematic defender of the Congo administration'. He declared that 'from 1895 onwards the conspiracy against truth has been organized from top to bottom, under well-nigh unbelievable conditions, in order to hide the crimes which are committed in the Congo'. Everything which has emerged since then has shown that he was right.

The System had endured for twenty-three years: its consequences would endure as long again, and longer. Some of them remain in fragmentary life to this day. A former Belgian administrator, writing in 1952, could still urge 'suppression of the whip'.(36) Only in 1954 would the Congo Government apply itself to abolishing the last *administrative* forms of forced labour in rural areas. 'Negligent workers' in the Congo are still being sentenced in their thousands every year to prison with hard labour.

The condition of these peoples when the pressure was reduced after 1908 was sad indeed. They had suffered the destruction of much of their ancient tribal order; their chiefs were dead or dishonoured; their customs overridden; their pattern of social sanctions more or less completely wrecked. In 1885, the year of the Congo Free State's foundation, the German explorers Pogge and Wissmann could still sojourn with Kalamba, paramount chief or king of the Luba-Lulua group in the southern Congo, and find his capital a flourishing community of eight hundred huts.(37) In the years that followed there were tribal incursions from west and east. But there were also bitter revolts against Belgian authority, and Belgian punitive expeditions, as well as the exactions of rubber agents and their native levies;

and all this tore out and ruined the complex fabric of these relatively stable communities and petty kingdoms.

If the Arab slave trade was ended — the last of the Arab slavers were driven from their nests on the Lualaba by the end of the century — the System in its place had worked an even worse havoc. How many had paid with their lives will never be known: the number was certainly large. Writing in 1906, with the evidence of missionaries and others, Morel estimated that 'in the last fifteen years (1891-1905) the population of the Congo has been decreasing at the *minimum* rate of 100,000 per annum, or say 1,500,000 in the past fifteen years. I am convinced that is the very lowest computation compatible with accuracy'.(38)

Others thought the victims more numerous. Casement believed that the Congo population had declined over the decade before 1905 by nearly three millions. It is hard to know: earlier estimates of a total Congo population of fifteen or twenty millions when the Belgians had first arrived were probably too high. What seems certain is that the population was smaller in 1908 than in 1885; and probably much smaller.

Writing on the Bangala region a British Baptist missionary, John Weeks, who knew it well, thought in 1903 that: 'Without any fear of contradiction . . . the condition of the people is, to put it mildly, one hundred per cent worse than in 1893 . . . The entire population of the district is now 9400, and quite half has recently been driven from the bush to the river to re-populate its banks. Stanley, in 1885, reckoned this same district at 80,000 people. In 1890 Mr. Stapleton and myself, in search of a site, landed at a very large number of towns, and concluded that the figures of 1885 were too high, and put the population down at 50,000. The population has dropped in thirteen years from 50,000 to under 5000. . . .'

Casement's consular report of the same year 1903 remarked that: 'The population of the lake-side towns would seem to have diminished within the last ten years by sixty to seventy per cent. It was in 1893 that an effort to levy an india-rubber imposition in the district was begun, and for some four or five years this imposition could only be collected at the cost of continual fighting.'

These depredations might be stopped: they could not be quickly made good. As late as 1920 the British Admiralty Manual on the Congo is writing that: 'Compulsory work for Government purposes still remains legal, but the period of service has been reduced from five years to three. The policy of relying upon paid labour for such work appears to be gradually coming into force . . .'(39) One may still encounter Europeans who recall the Congo of the years after 1908: they speak of it invariably with a curious inflection in their voices and quietly call it *the old Congo.* 'When I first came out here thirty years ago,' a provincial governor said to me in 1954, 'the people were like skeletons.'

The snail-pace process of repair may be well enough followed in the reports of various meetings of the Permanent Commission for the Protection of the Natives that occurred at irregular intervals through these years.(40) Originally created in 1896 as part of Leopold's humanitarian smokescreen, this Commission had actually met a year later but had dribbled out of existence in 1901. Nothing more was heard of anything so radical as protecting the Natives until 1908, when the Belgian Parliament appointed a new commission. This met in three sessions of some days each in 1911, at the turn of the years 1912-13, and in 1919; with varying membership it has continued to meet occasionally ever since. Being made to the Belgian Parliament, its reports may be taken as saying the very least that could be said: they offer a discreetly worded but reliable glimpse into the sordid horrors of the place. From time to time, moreover, members of the Commission have spoken their minds in plain language: in later years, too, it would appear as though Brussels had sometimes taken notice of what they said.

The new government's first task in the Belgian Congo, if peace and an end to the worst practices of the Congo Free State were to be achieved, was to abolish the monopoly on the collection of natural products, and to break the trading monopoly of the big concession companies. 'The products of the soil, as everyone knows,' a British consular report had said, 'have been appropriated wholesale.' The life of the Congo Native, another British consular report explained, was one of 'perpetual labour for the State'. Even from the most orthodox colonial standpoint, change was imperative.

Yet only in 1912, four years after annexation to Belgium, were forced rubber and other collections in the interest of the concession companies brought finally to an end. 'Since July 1 last,' reports the Commission in 1913, 'natives throughout the Colony may now collect vegetable products, and trade in them . . . Since our meeting in 1911, negotiations entered into between the Government and the Company of the Kasai have happily reached conclusion. Thanks to this, commercial rivalry now exists where the Company had formerly exercised its monopoly.' With high-minded urbanity the Commission then proceeds to 'express its satisfaction in the measures taken by the Government to restore commercial competition to vast regions whose economic development was otherwise prevented by the monopoly of one or other Company'.

Thus the practice of forced delivery of rubber and other natural products, and their forced delivery to the concession companies, came gradually to a stop; and was displaced by a commercial system which, if anything but 'free enterprise', nonetheless supposed that the Congo peoples should benefit at least a little from the products of their own soil and labour.

But everything went slowly, and world war further delayed administrative change. Early attempts at rehabilitating tribal life by forms of 'indirect rule' through local chiefs and headmen were generally made nugatory by prevailing ignorance of tribal custom. In the rush for plunder, practically nobody had bothered to attempt any genuine study of these Congo peoples. No matter how well-intentioned the new administration might be, its knowledge of tribal life was rudimentary and mainly wrong (as elsewhere in Africa at that time); its attitude was generally indifferent or contemptuous; and its eyes were closely blinkered by a conviction of inherent superiority. And the administration was not always well-intentioned: too often it was bullying and ruthless, and conserved intact many of the tough methods of the past.

Thus in 1919 we have the Commission mildly drawing attention to the fact that forced recruitment to the *Force Publique* — colonial security troops — and long terms of enforced service were bad for the birth-rate and unfortunate for married men. 'Many militiamen torn from their homes scarcely support the trials imposed on them, and their transfer far from their places of origin is assuredly a serious cause of death.'(41) They were transferred from their places of origin, of course, because they were not considered reliable oppressors of their own tribes — as is still the case — and the Commission pleads for 'a reduction in recruitment of militiamen to the strictly necessary minimum'. It goes on to complain that however necessary it may be to have militiamen, the conditions of recruitment are unjust and arbitrary — 'either because the chiefs supply the men, or because the administrator, faced with the impotence or disaffection of the chief, must intervene himself, and seize the Natives he proposes to incorporate'.

In 1923 the Commission is complaining that although it accepts as necessary a maximum limit of sixty days' forced labour for every male adult, 'cases are reported where the Native has had to work for ninety or even for 104 days'; and it adds, respectfully polite as ever, that: 'These excessive exactions for work on roads that is often of doubtful value has evidently caused a genuine impoverishment in food crops necessary to village subsistence.'(42) Only in 1928 can the Commission agree with lively satisfaction that *portage* (manual carriage of goods) by women has been prohibited — a note which vividly illuminates the true condition of these forgotten forests of the Congo — and plead for a further reduction in *portage* by men.(43)

How little these pleas were heeded is shown by the Commission's repeated recommendations that women and old men should not be forced to build and maintain roads. In 1928 we have the Commission unanimously recommending that: 'There should be an absolute prohibition on the use of women, old people, and children in the construction and maintenance of roads.'(44) But in 1947 the Commission is again recommending the same thing, commenting that: 'There can be no doubt that it is the forced labour services (*corvées*) on roads which are the most unpopular, either because they entail long journeys, or else because they mean painful labour, often even for mothers of young children and for pregnant women.'(45)

There was slow improvement. If the number of doctors employed by the administration throughout the Belgian Congo — a territory, after all, as large as western Europe and one from which fabulous wealth had already been taken — was only 31 in 1919, the number had increased by 1923 to 63.(46) Attempts were made to tackle at least the worst manifestations of many of the new diseases which European penetration had brought into the Congo, some of the more devastating of which were tuberculosis, cerebro-spinal meningitis, typhoid, syphilis and influenza. On all this the Commission's reports oscillate between unrelieved gloom and an evidently baseless optimism.

Nowhere during these years, it would seem, was mortality much higher than among Africans forced into service with the security troops. In 1923 we have the Commission in a worried frame of mind on this point: the year before, official figures returned by the officer commanding the *Force Publique* had shown a mortality of 36.8 per thousand among recruits and 20.6 per thousand among the troops — among men, that is, who were young and physically sound when recruited, and who were generally well fed.(47)

Yet everything is relative. In the years 1917-23 deaths among migrant workers employed by the Union Minière company in the Katanga were returned as varying between 107 per thousand and 20 per thousand, while they were higher still for workers registered at the Bourse de Travail, a labour recruiting organization in the Katanga.(48)

And so it went on. Ending the brutally wasteful monopoly of the concession companies and of Leopold's *Domaine de la Couronne* was one thing: installing something better in its place was quite another. The Africans could trade, true enough: but what did that mean? They could sell their produce: but who fixed the prices? They could buy a few things they might need: but who decided what these should be, and how much they should cost?

Having drawn a lamentable picture of the ill health and malnutrition of whole populations in the Congo, the Commission reports in 1919, after years of redoubled forced labour during the war: 'But the picture is darker still. It is not only by the diffusion of existing diseases and by the introduction of new plagues that the mortality of the Blacks has increased through European contact. Our occupation and the introduction of trade have in many regions modified the conditions of life of the Natives, and diminished their vitality.

'At one time forced labour in rubber as well as forced labour in diverse foodstuffs, and today commercial exchanges freely consented in by the desire for gain, have submitted and still submit the Natives to conditions of life which obstruct their increase.' Out of twenty-two districts in the colony, reported a member of the Commission, 'we know of nine where the number of children does not attain half of the number of adults . . . and we find ourselves faced with a situation in which the adult population dwindles through many causes; in which the birth-rate, low in any case, is lowered again by sleeping sickness, syphilis, and abnormal conditions of life; and in which infant mortality, high in any case, is heightened further by causes which kill off the adults and reduce the birth-rate. Not only that, but direct exhaustion by the empressment of soldiers, and of workers for public and private use, continues and threatens to grow worse'.(49)

These extracts could be multiplied. If men who were entirely loyal to the colonial system could write like this, one may wonder what the full unvarnished truth could possibly have been. Yet even these extracts open a vista of misery and ruinous decay.

Now all this, and much else beside, these peoples of the Congo have carried on their backs. The climate and their historical misfortune in migrating not towards the centres of growing civilization along the Mediterranean but down into the isolation of the primitive forest; the wild beasts and the fevers and the gruelling need to find new ways of growing food and keeping live-stock; the coming of the Europeans and the slave trade and the Leopoldian System; the new diseases which followed in the wake of the Europeans, and the long slow aftermath of reassessment and gradual repair after 1912: all this the Congo peoples have managed to survive.

Those today who speak of Africa as 'decadent', of Africans as 'idle, feckless, immature'; those who see in sudden manifestations of long-provoked violence the stigmata of unnatural ferocity, and cry out in consequence, masking their real intention, that 'we must not go too fast'; and in general all who still feel able to enjoy a sense of inherent superiority over Africans and the continental slum in which Africans are obliged to live, might pause and ask themselves whether 'an inferior people' could have survived such a history.

The wonder in Africa is not that its peoples are backward: the wonder is that they are there at all.

EIGHT

CLIMBING OUT .

'I ASSURE you,' said my friend Monsieur P., veteran administrator of Congo countries much larger than Belgium or Britain, 'that in those grim days I had to kill in order not to be killed myself.'

He poured me another hospitable whisky and continued his memories of the years of the great slump which struck the Congo, as it struck the world, in 1930. He spoke of them with the wistful loathing mingled with affection of a kindly man who is proud of having kept his end up through times of which he is also ashamed. For the great depression found the Congo at its mercy. Raw material prices sank, and the Congo Government lived on raw material exports. Administration was cut to the bone. Improvements were shelved, bad old practices revived. The Congo slum was left to simmer in its discontent.

The kind of life which humanity in the Congo had to face between the two world wars was much the same, or worse, in neighbouring colonial countries. Little was attempted after 1918; less was done. Throughout these continental solitudes there reigned stagnation from which no way out seemed possible. What little was known of the state of the people's health and reproduction rate was gloomy, and what was suspected was gloomier still: not only was there no sure improvement, many signs pointed to a continued decline. Village agriculture languished. Men departed in quest of a bare living in the towns. 'There is no doubt,' the Protection Commission was writing as late as 1938, 'that certain villages are being emptied of practically their entire adult male population, which goes to the towns in search of a better life. There remain in the village only the old people, women and children: sometimes only the old people.'(50)

What was bad in the Belgian Congo had long been notably worse in the French provinces to the north of the Congo and Ubangui rivers. Here, in 1899, a French Government had installed a close copy of the Leopoldian System on behalf of French and Belgian capitalists, who were eager to reproduce in French territory the same opportunities for ruthless plunder which Leopold had found in the Congo Free State.

These hopes were realized. By 1900 the whole wide territory of these French equatorial provinces was parcelled out among forty concession companies enjoying a thirty years' charter. 'One idea dominates the system,' declared a French colonial decree of this time: 'All the products of the conceded territory, whatever they may be, are the property of the concession company . . .'(51) And the colonial court at Libreville in the Gaboon, when settling a dispute between these concession companies and British trading interests already established there, proceeded to confirm that 'the rubber belongs to the concessionaries, and not to the Natives who gather it'. Thus the peoples of the French Congo, like those of the Congo Free State before them, lost not only their liberty and independence, but also the greater part of all natural produce which grew in their lands.

Here in the French Congo — in the Gaboon, Ubangui and neighbouring lands — the concession companies behaved in the same way as the companies of the Congo Free State. And against this, too, decent opinion gathered in protest. In 1905 the *Cahiers de la Quinzaine* sent out Félicien Challaye to investigate; and the *Cahier*(52) which published his scathing report, a year later, bore an introduction by Charles Péguy. Many thought as Péguy did. Dying in bitter disillusionment in 1905 on his way back to France after a visit of inspection, the admirable de Brazza — first notable explorer of the French Congo territories — let fall his judgment in words which echo down the years: 'Ruin and terror have been visited on this unhappy colony.'

So it was; and so it continued. In 1910 the parliamentary

84

rapporteur of the French colonial budget, M. Viollette, told the Assembly in Paris that the colony 'is absolutely exhausted . . . The rights of the Natives continue to be violated with the connivance of the Administration . . . The concession companies are the most formidable enemy of this dependency . . . There is no law, no authority, other than that of the boards of the concession companies'.(53) There were 'terrible revolts', Challaye reported, 'cruel but justified'.

All this, once again, was the least that could be said. Later research proves it. In 1952 a French writer on French Equatorial Africa, orthodox and generally uncritical of the colonial system, pointed out that for many years the administration of these lands 'was subjected to a regime of double-truth': one should therefore be suspicious of official documents. 'And could one have known,' he asks, 'without the Toqué-Gaud case (trial of two officials accused of tortures committed at Fort Crampel in 1903), that for the first fifteen years of our occupation of Chad, verbal orders prescribed that administrative heads should make up false returns about chiefs, false accounts of taxation, false registries of information, in order not to contradict the optimistic declarations of those who had persuaded the central authority to support this undertaking?'(54) British patriots need not plume themselves: a French writer on British Africa would have all too little difficulty in turning the tables — although it is true that no comparably noxious system of concessions was ever imposed on neighbouring Nigeria or the Gold Coast.

These French charters ran their full thirty years. But they were not renewed. Too much had become known of their consequences. By 1927 no one any longer could seriously justify them, for in that year Gide published his *Voyage au Congo* after months of wandering in these lands. Even in 1926 Gide found that the concession companies were still using the Leopoldian method of exacting rubber from the Natives, and of causing their agents to hunt down and persecute Natives who should fail to deliver. Recalling the Congo Free State which

Conrad had painfully illustrated in *Heart of Darkness*, Gide wrote with the French Congo in mind that it was 'an admirable book which even today remains profoundly true, as I have seen for myself . . . there is no exaggeration in its descriptions: they are cruelly exact'.(55)

The end of this system coincided with the great depression. Even today the French Congo carries deeply the marks of its lamentable past. It is impoverished, perpetually in economic crisis, spending less money on education and social services than any other French colonial territory.

In the old Congo provinces of Angola, to the south of the estuary of the Congo where King Affonso and his forbears had once held sway, the African condition during the years was worse again. Portuguese decline carried with it an unexampled poverty and great oppression. Here, indeed, the 'old colonialism' exists in almost all its features to this day.

Things were better in the Belgian Congo, perhaps because the Belgians who governed it came from an advanced industrial country which possessed no other colony and thought itself extremely fortunate in possessing this one. They knew that they had by the neck a goose which was perfectly capable of laying golden eggs; and they cast about, industrious and orderly, for ways of inducing it to begin.

On the surface there was stagnation. Yet the surface, for all the poverty and unenlightened government, was misleading. Below it, in truth, this period of the 'twenties and 'thirties began to undergo the pressures and social impulse which ten years later would gather towards a tidal wave of change.

There was improvement in the administrative attitude towards Africans. 'The less intelligent a White man is,' Gide has remarked, 'the stupider Black men seem to him'; and the *mot* may serve as an epitaph in burying for the nonsense that it was the greater part of what administrators, company agents, settlers, and 'experts on Africa' had said. Understanding little of the lands they came from, these settlers and their kind generally understood even less of the lands of their adoption.

They freely took 'the African' for the wretched second-class copy of humanity which, all too often, European contact had turned him into. Those few who came to know him better would habitually temper their condescension with a statement of 'affection for the old African, you know'. Seldom would this affection lead to any real analysis of just why the African was poor, bedraggled, magic-ridden and generally in ruins.

Tribalism seemed usually a curious mumbo-jumbo which was silly and 'obstructive', and dangerous whenever (which was seldom) it was more than merely comic. Tribal rituals which had come out of the dawn of history, and had served their sensible regulating purpose through years beyond memory, were thrust aside as 'immoral', 'disorderly', or futile superstition. The distortions and accretions of the years since the slave trade began were taken all too often as the 'natural savage state' of people to whom individual violence was nonetheless known to be sharply repugnant.

Common judgments departed curiously even from Victorian sense. 'The standard of morality among the Batwa', writes the British Admiralty Manual with a most unnaval attack of prudery, 'is in general very low. Adultery is common, so common indeed that it is considered murder to kill the guilty party.' Such judgments were scientifically valueless.(56)

A more serious study of tribal structures began to be applied to the Belgian Congo in the 'twenties. With the passing of government by sheer coercion — Leopold's System — it was vaguely recognized as early as 1910 that peaceful administration would become possible only on condition that the people could be ruled through the traditional channels of authority of their own tribal system. 'Direct rule' should give way to 'indirect rule' — a system of ruling through Native hierarchies which the British had brought from India. A decree of 1910 attempted to introduce a measure of 'indirect rule' through chiefs and headmen, but was largely nullified by the profound ignorance of tribal hierarchies which prevailed among Europeans, and by the growing disintegration of tribal life. With the old hierarchies overturned by colonial invasion, chiefly systems had mostly gone by the board. 'At the end of the first Great War it was realized that Native society was drifting towards semi-anarchy. The number of independent chieftainships had risen to 6095, and some of these units were so small that they contained as few as 150 or even 50 adult males.'(57)

Progress was made between the wars in restoring a semblance of the old close-knit patterns of tribal authority. A decree of 1926 created 'Native tribunals' for a wide variety of crimes against tribal law and custom. Another decree of 1931 defined *circonscriptions indigènes* — areas of chiefly authority — and another of 1933 enlarged the sphere of chiefly authority. 'Native treasuries' were created, at any rate on paper, and care was taken to reduce interference in tribal ways of self-government to a minimum consonant with securing labour and keeping the peace. By 1939 the number of chieftainships had fallen to about 1500. Administration grew better equipped, better informed, more humane.

Involved in this process of 're-instating the African in his natural condition', there were many who thought — and in this the Belgians were no different from the British — that 'indirect rule' was not only of great convenience for the colonizing Power, but was also an effective way of restoring what invasion had destroyed or damaged. Tribal society, it was said, is natural to Africans: therefore we should do our best to conserve it. In so doing we shall protect the Africans from those disintegrating, disturbing, and potentially subversive influences which commerce, machinery and money bring in their wake. . . .

Arguing from this static view of history, some went even further and declared that tribal society in its 'natural state' had been something like an Age of Bliss. 'The native tribe', a Belgian exponent of indirect rule was writing in 1920, 'is neither autocracy, nor democracy, nor aristocracy. It has something of all three . . . Its authority is sufficiently centralized to be real, and sufficiently decentralized not to be a tyranny.'(58) An idyllic view, perhaps: and yet a useful corrective to the general opinion that life before the coming of the Europeans was benighted, short and servile. Perhaps a more balanced estimate is contained in Hailey's judgment, that it is 'rare to find in British Colonial Africa any instance in which the indigenous form of rule previously in force could be described as autocratic, and there are not many cases in which it could be described in a strict sense as authoritarian'.(59)

Now it might have been possible to restore the welfare of the rural areas and peoples of the Congo, if only indirect rule could have restored the self-administered authority and social coherence which had once made tribal society stable and secure. But this was exactly what indirect rule could not do, being, in fact, in absolute contradiction to the central requirement of tribal authority.

This central requirement was nothing less than *representative* authority. But indirect rule stood for imposed authority, however skilfully the imposition might try to hide itself behind the choice of chiefs from families traditionally chosen to rule. Indirect rule could not be representative. Whenever the selected chief diverged from administrative requirements because his people wanted him to diverge from them, he found himself deposed by an indignant District Officer, and a more complacent 'chief' installed in his place. And this, of course, was going on all over Africa.

The substantial point was that tribal society had not been autocracy. There had been, as Hailey says, few exceptions to this — and these only among militarized tribes like the Zulu of the nineteenth century and their offshoot, the Matabele. In the full flower of tribal life, government was broadly representative. The characteristic political institution of the Gold Coast tribes 'is the Akan stool or chiefdom, an elective and limited magistracy. The chief is elected by his people from the stool family, in which descent is through the female line. He is the judge and executive head of his community, but he exercised his function only on the advice and consent of the council of elders, of which he is president'.(60)

89

Destooling was and still is common form in the Gold Coast. Sir Alan Burns, who was Governor of that colony in 1942, records that 'within the last ten years no less than 22 Paramount Chiefs have been destooled, in addition to 22 others who have abdicated in that period — in most cases to forestall destoolment . . . seven stools of Paramount Chiefs are now vacant and . . . in many States no Paramount Chief has succeeded in maintaining his place on the stool for more than a very short time. . . .'

Nor can it be said that this turbulent tribal democracy was peculiar to the Gold Coast and the relatively advanced peoples of the Gulf of Guinea. Of one of the more numerous peoples of the Angolan plateau a Portuguese writer disgustedly observed in 1837 that: 'The government of Bailundu is democratic. These heathen mix with the infamous humiliations of the orientals, the unbridled coarseness of the English people at election time in England. The kings defer to and flatter their counsellors: these are they who elevate a king to the throne and also cast him down.'(61) Very disgraceful, no doubt: but not autocracy. *Vox populi* was also heard, it seems, in Africa.

But *vox populi* was largely silenced by indirect rule. It had to be. For the object of governing the Congo was not only to civilize it: a long way before that, the object was to make money out of it. There could be no making money out of it without securing abundant supplies of African labour, without subtracting large areas from African cultivation, without preventing tribal migrations: none of these and other desiderata could be satisfied unless the chiefs and headmen obeyed Belgian orders whenever a conflict of opinions arose between the Belgians and their African subjects. Inevitably, chiefs and headmen lost their representative quality in matters of key importance.

It is here that we encounter one of the root contradictions in all European administration of Africa: on one side, there is the desire to 'keep them quiet' under their traditional rulers — but on the other side there is a still stronger desire to 'make them work'. The two desires are mutually destructive, and it is the first, of course, which goes under. It is the African authority which dies and the European authority which prevails. Indirect rule may here and there slow up the process of tribal disintegration: it cannot possibly stop it. Historically, it has all too often served only to prolong the agony of Africans compelled by the consequences of colonization into trying to cross the bridge between tribalism and the modern world.

So it has proved in the Congo. 'The theories are brilliant enough,' a Catholic missionary was writing in 1923, 'but often they are no more than mere illusion . . . An administrator who was thoroughly consistent in his defence of Native custom would condemn himself to cease administering.'(62) It is well said; and British experience has everywhere confirmed it. In the South African colony of Natal, even before Union in 1910, the British executive had already arrogated to itself the function of paramount chief of all African chiefs — so that it might have the 'tribal authority', which it regularly used, of deposing African chiefs who failed in their imperial duties; and the Union Government has since continued in the same way. Thus did the British depose Seretse Khama; and the Kabaka of Buganda.

And one may note in passing that there is hardly more than one place in Africa where indirect rule can be said to have succeeded in prolonging intact a system of government which had existed before colonial penetration. But in this place, in Northern Nigeria, the ruling caste of Fulani emirs had already imposed *direct* rule on their Hausa subjects; and the British merely availed themselves of this utterly 'untribal' dictatorship.

Indirect rule has everywhere failed to conserve the reality of tribal government, and has shown itself, by that token, incapable of preserving the reality of tribal life. The very prevalence of destooling in the Gold Coast — let alone the emergence of parliamentary government — is another proof of this. And the last ten or fifteen years in the Congo, far from witnessing a restoration of tribal life through a more efficient rule, have witnessed its further disintegration.

Not only was the thing impossible. From the African standpoint it was also undesirable. Indirect rule might and often did mean an alleviation in their plight — a more humane and interested attitude by European administrators — but it also meant, as more and more Africans began to see, a frustration of their movement towards the modern world. To conserve tribal life, once its representative structure was gone, was to hold back Africans from understanding the logical conclusions of European presence in their countries. And European administrators who understand this often see in indirect rule a useful barrier to African advancement, and use it consciously for that purpose.

In this great transition stage, these subject peoples have never had more than two alternatives. Either they would linger in subjection to Europeans, conveniently shut away in Native Reserves, Tribal Areas and so on (except, of course, for the necessary migrant workers), and the future would more or less rehearse the past: or they would take lessons from European knowledge until they themselves could enter this world of new ideas. Either tribalism *plus* helotry — or the end of tribalism and a beginning of self-assertion. Nothing else is possible; and in the end, of course, only the second is possible.

The bogus character of indirect rule as a means of restoring tribal life can be seen in many territories. Everywhere it has meant that chiefly authority becomes increasingly transformed into irresponsibility; and peoples tend more and more to see in their chiefs the arbitrary instruments of alien rule. These instruments hold back the evolution of the masses, as a Belgian writer has pointed out, 'because its cadres are composed of chiefs, notables, judges who are opposed to progress, who are chained to old customs and submitted to the influence of sorcerers, clerks, secretaries, or teachers more or less trained but poorly educated, who make Native custom serve their own ends'.(63) Indirect rule, in short, has further perverted the chiefly system, and proved one more way of obstructing Africans from getting knowledge — and hence power.

Tribal discipline necessarily becomes more and more irksome. 'The young people go off to the towns, life dies out in villages which are sad and comfortless, without sufficient food, where forced labour services pile up without any hope of a man's seeing an end to them, where sickness is widespread without the European's fighting it, and where the old people, the sorcerers, and the beneficiaries of Native custom combine to prolong their tyranny.'(64) And when the young people return to their villages, nearly always with enough knowledge to understand the crucial importance of a modern education, they find their chiefs all too often enfolded in the darkness of total illiteracy, holding obstinately to the old ways which have lost their life and meaning.

'Give us educated chiefs!' the cry is heard from one end of rural Africa to the other. It is a crying after the moon, for tribalism and a modern education are opposed extremes, and the one necessarily destroys the other. Generally, throughout Africa today, the educated men of power and influence are not chiefs, but exponents of African nationalism. Even where they are chiefs — as among the Yoruba of Western Nigeria — they are also nationalists, and the expression of their power and influence takes increasingly a politically nationalist form.

From the African viewpoint, then, indirect rule as a necessary transition stage between tribalism and the modern world rapidly exhausted its usefulness, and became a sad obstruction better removed. Looking at the problem of colonial government from the European point of view, moreover, one can now see why the question of what to do next becomes acute. *Direct* rule has proved impossible, because impossibly brutal and therefore inefficient. But *indirect* rule — as a means of prolonging African inferiority, of course, and not a means of preparing for African equality — also begins to prove impossible: its tribal basis is crumbling fast. What comes next?

We have seen that Africans faced two alternatives. These alternatives have their European interpretation: *either* economic stagnation within the limits of the 'old colonialism' — of Native Reserves, Tribal Areas, migrant labour, and the rest — *or* industrial and commercial advance across those limits. In the Congo countries the Portuguese, reflecting their own pre-industrial economy, have held to the first. The Belgians, technically advanced, could not be content with this. They have chosen the alternative to economic stagnation — industrial and commercial advance.

In choosing thus they have notably enriched themselves. But they have also, however unintentionally, read a requiem over the 'old colonialism' — and, however reluctantly, over the whole pattern and ideology of indirect rule.

During the past ten or fifteen years the peoples of the Congo have felt increasingly that they could not go on living in the old way. Increasingly, they have abandoned their villages, trekked to the towns. And at the same time their European masters — seldom stopping to ask themselves what they were doing or where they were going — have increasingly wanted Africans to live in a different way. They have wanted Africans to come into town and settle there for good.

The tremendous history of the Congo in the years after about 1940 — reflected everywhere in Africa, and even faintly in the Portuguese territories — is the story of how millions of men and women have abandoned their old way of life and sought for another.

The problems of the Congo, of all Africa south of the Sahara, can no longer be discussed in the terms of the years between the two world wars. All the old landmarks are submerged in this forward-moving flood, and few will be seen again. Urban revolution, industrial revolution, has overtaken Africa. Upon this, more than upon anything else, rests the African awakening.

NINE

END OF THE NOBLE SAVAGE

SOME idea of the dimensions of this change may be had from a few figures. Already by 1946 no less than one-sixth of Congo Africans were living outside their tribal areas — were beyond the reach of their traditional chiefly authority. Most of these million and a half people were living in towns directly administered by European officials. But the townward flood during the war years, when the Congo enjoyed a boom in raw material prices, was nothing when compared with the townward flood which followed in the still greater boom years after the war was over.

In 1953 the total number of Congo Africans who were *hors chefferie* — outside the tribal areas — had risen to 2,350,000. Nearly one quarter of all Congo Africans were now living a more or less permanent urban life. Between 1940 and 1950 the African population of Léopoldville increased from 46,000 to 190,000, and to nearly a quarter of a million in 1954, when the flood began at last to relent. One or two other big towns — Elisabethville, Stanleyville, Coquilhatville — show much the same rate of increase; and everywhere the rate has been high.(65)

It has been high all over Africa. 'The problem of the hour,' an observer was writing of the French Cameroons early in 1953, 'is the problem of an emergent proletariat. To the south-west of Douala, the countryside grows empty.'(66) In Kenya the population of Nairobi increased from 53,000 in 1945 to 95,000 in 1952; and it was the same in the cities of Rhodesia, of French West Africa, of the Union of South Africa. Millions were on the move.

This move is largely irreversible. It is more than a mere change in numbers: it is a change in social relations. 'Changes

95

no less profound and extensive than those which accompanied the industrial revolution in Europe are slowly taking place in Southern Rhodesia,' a correspondent of *The Times* wrote lately: 'Africans are about to cross the frontier from a rural subsistence economy to an industrialized, urbanized money economy . . .' According to one study group in Southern Rhodesia, 'by 1980 the majority of the whole African population will be town-dwellers, as cut off from the rural subsistence economy they enjoy today as the average Londoner is cut off from the way of life of his forbears who may have come from the farms of Sussex or Suffolk'.(67) The verb 'enjoy' is strangely used; and the estimate is probably an exaggeration: never mind, the substantial point is made — this process is largely irreversible. It overturns all principles of colonial administration, poses problems of co-existence between racial communities that are insoluble along the old master-servant lines.

Parallels with Europe are obvious enough. Between 1801 and 1831 the wool towns of the West Riding of Yorkshire nearly doubled in population: and around all these new centres of manufacture the countryside was sucked dry of people — and of people, moreover, for whom rural life was rapidly being made intolerable. 'In Southern Rhodesia at the end of 1953 there were 1000 factories. In Northern Rhodesia secondary industries have been multiplying in recent years; and there are now over 200 factories.'(68)

Convulsive shifts of population on this scale have generally caused in all who witnessed or suffered them the sensation of a helpless chaos; and it was no different in the Congo. One need only consult the nostalgic lamentations of African townsmen who regret their village past, even though, when put to the test, they would not return to it. Administrators and missionaries have watched their subjects vanishing before their eyes, disappearing between the dusk and the dawn, and have known no way either of stopping them or of speeding their departure. Some of the more thoughtful had seen this coming for a long time. Others — especially the big mining companies — had more or less consciously willed its happening. But now that it was actually taking place counsels were often paralysed by a dividing of opinion between those who saw it as a beneficial exit from rural crisis, and those who believed that tribal disintegration on this massive scale could only drag still greater social evils in its train.

There is no doubt of the disintegration. It is patent in a thousand ways, in the breakdown of tribal custom, in the astonishing inflation of bride-prices, in prostitution. It has painful results for African agriculture. It speeds the ruin of village life. Formerly, the Belgians had tried to prevent more than a quarter of 'fit adult males' from labour recruitment outside their villages — or, more exactly, they had fixed a theoretical limit of 10 per cent of 'fit adult males' who might be recruited for work outside their tribal area, and another 15 per cent who might be recruited for work inside their tribal area. But these proportions were seldom respected. In many parts of the Congo they have long been far surpassed, so that the government has tried to apply an absolute ban on all recruitment in areas of exceptionally low birth-rate.

The townward flood made final havoc of these regulations. At the beginning of January 1952, the rate of absentees in villages around Pansi (to the south of Léopoldville) was said to be about 54 per cent of the adult male population. At the end of the following July there came another exodus, and absentees rose to 60 per cent. 'And even so, a recruiting agent then installed himself at Panzi where — apart from a few workers locally employed — there is practically no one but old people and women.'(69)

Nothing but the lively hope of a new kind of life radically different from and better than the old can explain this exodus. Everyone went who could, even the children.

'At the beginning of October 1952,' a missionary records, 'I was making my usual tour in order to enregister children for the regional schools. At Makakulu Tseke, a school which serves about twenty-five villages ... I had convoked 147 boys

G   97

now old enough to enter their first primary year. I was not a little surprised to discover that of these 147 boys, 34 were at Léopoldville — nearly a quarter of them. And not one of them was old enough to pay tax.'(70)

Recruiting agents who sought labour for their European clients and employers had to go further and further afield. 'Only in very remote districts, where fit adult males can still be traced down, are recruiting agents now active — well-paid, with lorries and attractive bribes, searching for whatever labour may be still available. And when they come back with their men, 30 per cent of these are refused on medical grounds — which fails to prevent them being taken on somewhere else.'(71) All this was entirely different from what had gone before.

In previous decades the European colonist who wanted African labour had generally needed to go and get it, by force, trickery, or other more or less disreputable means. Coercion had come first. Afterwards, in South Africa and Rhodesia, as in the Congo, ingenuity was shown in devising money taxes for Natives who lived outside a money-using economy — who grew or otherwise produced or bartered with each other all the things they needed. Forcing these Natives to pay money taxes — defaulters being generally sentenced to penal labour — meant forcing them to go to work for money. Along with this, recruiting agents would drive around the villages with promises of bicycles and blankets — promises which were never kept once the men were safely 'at the mine': or else, in more recalcitrant cases, the local administrator would come along, too, and frighten the chief or headman into 'finding' the required number of men. Long years of more or less openly forced labour have proved necessary in all colonies before the natural resistance of tribal society is overcome, and men begin of their own accord to go to work for a money wage.

This tribal resistance to wage employment is now more or less completely destroyed. 'Force is no longer necessary,' comments the authoritative Father van Wing: 'The young people troop of their own accord towards the towns — and children with them.' A few years earlier, another Belgian authority was pointing out that: 'Nowhere any more, one can say, does the chief really administer his tribe: nowhere does the grouping remain intact. The ties which once united members of the same tribe, both to one another and to their common chief, are everywhere relaxed and often broken.'(72) This opinion is of 1946: since then the broken ties have multiplied to a point where few remain intact. 'There are no longer any tribes in the Congo,' says the same authority, 'within which life unfolds today as it once unfolded fifty years ago. Everywhere and all the time the administration, the missions, education, industry and commerce have stimulated an evolution which overflows the narrow limits of tribal life.'

Already in 1928 a former governor of the Katanga Province, General Heenen, was noting that: 'The exodus of Natives towards the centres of European activity is inevitable: our cities, our enterprises of all kinds, our great lines of communication, attract and concentrate the most energetic and the most enterprising of the Native population.'(73) Even in the 'thirties there was little need for coercive recruitment: more and more men abandoned their sorry village life, their ruined tribalism, and departed for the towns.

If one can set a rough date at which this unhappy stream became an eager flood, and changed not only in size but also in meaning, the year was 1940, the beginning of the Second World War. Since 1940 the European problem is no longer to find means wherewith to bully and bamboozle Africans into employment: it is to house and feed these huge new urban populations, and to bring succour to a deserted countryside.

Many have deplored the change. They have pointed to the virtues of African tribal life, discovered now that they were disappearing: rightly, for the virtues were considerable. This was a society which approached, at its best, the vision of community where 'thine' and 'mine' had lost their compelling power for evil. 'Looking into the world from his own home, the Bantu child knows where he may seek hospitality and succour of every kind; where, also, he may of right be called upon to render assistance in case of need. The barriers of reserve shutting off human beings from one another are largely down so far as these classes of relatives [his kith and kin for many degrees on either side] are concerned, so that for economic assistance, for friendly counsel, in time of sorrow and in time of joy, these are the natural categories of people to turn to, the core of people with whom one is close-knit from birth in a way of reciprocal rights and duties.'(74)

This was indeed a happy barbarism. 'One of the values most stressed by the Nyakyusa,' writes Monica Wilson of one of the peoples of the Nyasaland-Tanganyika border, 'is that of *ukwangela* which, in its primary sense, means "the enjoyment of good company" and, by extension, the mutual aid and sympathy which spring from personal friendship. It implies urbane manners and a friendliness which expresses itself in eating and drinking together: not only merry conversation, but also discussion between equals, which the Nyakyusa regard as a principal form of education.' Although the Nyakyusa, Professor Wilson says, 'lay so much stress on geniality, and praise a man for being "a good mixer", yet they greatly admire dignity (*ubusisya*). To be *nsisya* (dignified, impressive) is one of the attributes of chiefs and village headmen . . .'(75) These admirable people, who could surely give lessons of deportment in clubs and pubs the length and breadth of Europe, have another lesson to teach. They were never subjected to the slave trade. They offer a glimpse of what tribal life can once have been, before that curse smote it.

But there is no point in arguing the case at length. Lamentation for the noble savage is futile. Once European mastery was riveted on these lands, the choice was no longer between conserving the noble savage or degrading him to a condition of more or less servile labour. One way or another, the noble savage would disappear: for the most part, European greed and stupidity have ensured that he should disappear in the way most painful to himself.

Ideally, no doubt, the choice was between degrading the African to a condition of more or less servile labour, or of raising him to a consciousness of dignity and equality in the modern world; but colonialism, true to its nature, was bound to prefer the first. Without excusing the stupidity and greed, one can still conclude that the process was a necessary thing. If Africans were to make good their backwardness, their long handicap on the road to equality, they would have to get into the modern world. European occupation has been excessively, needlessly, hatefully painful: but its end-result for Africans has been to force them out of a society that was barely capable of progress; and this is undeniable gain.

Once this is clear, the urban revolution begins to reveal its full and hopeful meaning. There is even the chance that Europeans in Africa will understand it for what it is, and will think about its problems and bestir themselves to solve these problems in a sensible way, which would also be good for Africans.

The urban revolution means that Africans who are deprived of their old way of life can now — although only, perhaps, through bitter struggle — acquire another. They can escape from more or less servile labour. So long as Africans were recruited for mining and other European enterprises by the system of 'migrant labour', this was impossible. They were denied entry into a new way of life. They failed to become free wage workers who could take fresh bearings in a capitalist world, and organize in their own defence. They had lost the past, but were denied the future. The navel cord connecting the individual with his tribe or community had been severed: yet there was offered him no other means of social nourishment. The foetus of a new African culture seemed bound to die in the womb of a civilization unable or unwilling to nourish it.

One may still watch this in its full drama at the gold mines of the Transvaal. To these goldfields, year after year for nearly seventy years, tens and hundreds of thousands of migrant workers have traipsed and trailed from every part of southern and central Africa. Whether they are recruited by mining agents or come of their own accord — and many come of their own accord, for there is always another bottom to hell — to this day they are herded into monstrous all-male compounds without access to the social stimulus of the modern world. Recruited on short contracts, they are forbidden to bring their wives and families, for the mining companies argue that proper housing would cost too much. They are in no real sense inhabitants of the towns where they live and work. From all this the moral and material consequences are deplorable; what is worst, though, is that these hundreds of thousands of migrant mining workers can belong neither to the old tribal world nor to the new industrial world. They must hang suspended between the two, frustrated, puzzled, often in despair, having the worst of both.(76)

Painful though it may be, the change to a more or less permanent urban life now begins to end this miserable oscillation between the old and the new, and to plunge millions of Africans directly and for the most part irreversibly into the same world as the world their employers inhabit. In doing this they take a long step towards their own salvation.

One can reach the same conclusion by another route. Essentially, the economy of practically all colonial Africa has been simple in the extreme. On one side there is the investment of European capital in mining enterprises and other forms of primary production, in which large numbers of migrant workers are employed. From this employment these labourers can gain nothing of enduring value for themselves: such labour leaves them, for the most part, much as it finds them. There is no real diffusion of ideas, no real transition of culture. On the other side, there are vast areas labelled Native Reserve, and in these the greater part of the African population is confined — behind a nice humanitarian signboard marked Indirect Rule — and lives on its old subsistence economy, growing or making or bartering what it needs.

This system looks stagnant, but in fact is not. It has meant for Europeans a steady flow of profit which is spent outside Africa.

For Africans it has meant a steady impoverishment. The Native Reserves, as a United Nations report has pointed out, 'by being maintained as areas of tribal life, are to a large extent cut off from the direct effects of the developments taking place outside them. With practically no internal capital resources, as they become increasingly unable with their existing techniques to support growing populations, they become exporters of labour'.(77) Whole territories, such as Nyasaland and Ruanda Urundi, have become little more than reservoirs of migrant labour; and their consequent impoverishment is visible for all to see. Nothing in all Africa is sadder to the heart and eye than the great Native Reserves of the Transvaal and the Cape Province.

Out of this system there has come the convenient European fable that 'Africa is poor'. Europe has found it possible to extract large profits with one hand, and yet gesture sadly at African poverty with the other. Someone has lately calculated, for example, that the revenue of the Government of Northern Rhodesia, a notably 'poor' territory, is no larger than the annual sums of money which quit that territory for investors oversea. In 1951 the revenue of the Congo Government was 5322 million francs; the exported profits of the Union Minière — not counting additions to reserve and reinvestment — were 2560 million francs. For the Gold Coast mining industry in 1949, a reliable official source calculates that 'of the £6.4 millions earned by the exports of gold, perhaps 3 million pounds can be considered to have been transferred out of the country'. In 1954 the Government of South Africa cut down the money it would spend on African education: yet South Africa's big corporations were making record profits. Thus it is obvious that 'Africa is poor' not in any inherent sense but only in its social heritage of industrial knowledge and experience, and in accumulated capital — 'poor', that is, because the colonial system keeps it so and makes it so.

Except in one or two territories where White settlers have succeeded in taxing these profits for their own advantage, nothing has availed to reduce this sucking of wealth out of Africa except potent *African* demands for 'a larger slice of the cake'; and perhaps nothing ever will. In the Gold Coast, Nigeria and Sierra Leone, African politicians have begun to make such demands, and not without success. In central and southern Africa, with an African share in government nowhere in sight, the only self-defence for Africans is to shed their tribalism — their condition of direct inferiority to Europeans — and to enter the European's world with bag and baggage, determined to sink or swim. It is this, precisely, that millions of Africans have done since about 1940.

The 'noble savage' was dying on his feet. But the African industrial worker, portent of the future, is not only not dying on his feet: he is full of new energy and new ideas, and he is multiplying fast.

This eventful fact is nowhere better seen than in the Belgian Congo.

TEN

TURNING POINT

I REMEMBER once meeting a British consular officer who expected to go to Elisabethville, in the south-eastern corner of the Belgian Congo. He had never seen Africa, having passed his career in palm-fringed splendour on a South American coast; but he had looked up Elisabethville on the map, found it lost in the middle of a continent generally believed to be given over to big game and little pleasure, and was near despair. He had got up in mind a picture of fever-ridden poverty, and wondered what firearms he ought to buy.

He was sadly out of date. Few cities in the world can offer as much creature comfort, to Europeans who can pay for it, as Elisabethville. There are broad tree-lined avenues through lines of well-built European houses, shops that are shaded from the sun by wide balconies overhead, and cafés where one may snooze *al fresco* under coloured awnings which recall the south of France. The sanitation is good, and there are few mosquitoes. Children thrive here.

Elisabethville is also a turning point for Africans, although their comforts are not exactly on this scale, for it is one of the cradles of the industrial revolution in Africa. One day in 1954 Monsieur Grévisse, who is the District Commissioner of Elisabethville and governs its African suburbs, offered to show me its factories.

We drove out past the central square with its general post-office where European ladies are learning to wait in a queue with African men and women, and even European gentlemen have been lately known to refrain from shoving automatically to the front; and through the managerial suburbs of fine bungalows behind bougainvillaea and jacaranda until we came to the outskirts of the city. Over to the right, carefully segregated

105

from the European quarter, there was now visible the bungaloid agglomeration which signifies a Native Township in any part of Africa, dust behind dust, dirty, dilapidated, thirsty for green trees and shrubs. Over to the left, one after another in a long-spaced line, there were new factories.

Product of a few years' economic growth, these factories make many useful things which formerly were brought from Europe or else done without: plastic goods, shaped metal sheetings, beer, furniture, and the like. Perhaps a third of Elisabethville's African wage-earners are now employed in this kind of industry.

The branch of a big firm from Brussels is making useful furniture, and employs twenty-four Europeans and 150 Africans. All but a handful of these Africans are casual workers learning simple skills on the job: its industrious Belgian manager says that he is far from satisfied with them, grumbles at their inefficiency, their slowness to learn, their unresponsiveness to 'ordinary incentives'. He thinks his best Africans may be only 'a third as productive' as an average European worker in the same trade, whereupon M. Grévisse, whose paternalism extends benevolently to Europeans as well as Africans, asks him whether he pays them a third as much as he pays his Europeans. No: he doubts if he pays them a sixth as much.

M. Grévisse nods affectionately, and forbears to score his point. Afterwards he says to me: 'You see, not only would this factory not exist without the market created by a widening circuit of wage-paying in the Congo — but it couldn't function for as long as a week without this African labour.' The European ideal, no doubt, is to have the African market without having the Africans.

Great cavernous halls, further along, show where the subsidiary of another Brussels firm will soon begin manufacturing cheap cotton goods for the peoples of the Katanga. Its machinery is piled in packing-cases: builders are laying the concrete floor. This will be one of the most up-to-date factories in all Africa; its labour will be almost entirely African. Its market will also be almost entirely African. 'All this,' says M. Grévisse with an understandable pride, 'one would have thought, when I first came here twenty years ago, entirely out of the question.'

The same is true of other urban centres. In Léopoldville there is a well-established cotton mill, Utexléo, employing 120 Europeans and about 5000 Africans: of these Africans, already a fifth are rated as specialized workers and another fifth as *demiouvriers*, or men who have already acquired an elementary skill. The river-barge and tug building yards on Stanley Pool, Chanic, have 1700 Africans of whom about a fifth are now reckoned as skilled workers. Starting from a point only a few years ago when none of these Africans was semi-skilled or skilled, the level of skills (even without much real attempt at technical training, and almost none at all at technical education) is steadily rising. In 1950 an inquiry into the productivity of African riveters at the shipyards on Stanley Pool showed that this was 'about 5 per cent higher than in 1939, and this in spite of the fact that riveting teams are composed as to about three-quarters of new personnel with only two years' service'.(78)

Most of these manufacturing companies have now adopted a system introduced by the big mining companies of grading wages according to skills and productivity. Such systems in Europe have often signified an attempt to get more work for less money; and they also signify this in Africa. But they carry nonetheless the cardinal gain of offering Africans an inducement and an opportunity to turn themselves into full-time industrial workers. Another gain is to educate Europeans in the potential ability of Africans to act reasonably, responsibly and consistently.

I happened to be present one day when the manager of an engineering workshop was asked by the foreman of the pattern-making office whether he couldn't 'increase the rating' — and hence the wage — of one of his best workers. This African, the foreman argued, was really something out of the usual: he was 'practically as good as a European'. The manager objected that the man was already rated at the highest level allowed for in the wages scale. 'Then you'll have to push the ceiling up,' the foreman said: 'He'll go elsewhere if you don't.' Already, that is, these Africans are beginning to be able to do what their fathers never could — bargain with their skills for higher pay.

The wages ceiling, no doubt, is very low; although it is higher than in neighbouring Northern Rhodesia. Yet here were two Europeans discussing an African worker as they would have discussed any other kind of worker: they accepted him as a man like any other — the only question was, could they keep him at the wage they were paying him?

Perhaps one may revert for an illustration of the change in attitude to that illuminating manual published by the British Admiralty. Here we have the bogus-scientific patter in its fine and full flower. 'The adult negro is, however, by no means devoid of intelligence ... The Congo negro is not devoid of reasoning power ... On the other hand, the members of some tribes are full of good sense.' And the learned naval authority, after a high-flown disquisition on the subject, discovers profoundly that: 'On the whole, then, it would seem that the Native is very much the creature of his environment.'(79)

More and more, as we have noted, this sort of patronizing flatulence is seen for what it really is: even in the most backward colonies there is progress to be noted. An official report on wages in Kenya, drawn up in 1954 by a committee under the Commissioner of Labour, reached the astonishing conclusion that Africans could not be expected to work well unless they had enough to eat. Solemn emphasis was laid 'on the necessity on moral, social, economic, and political grounds of moving as quickly as possible to a position where even an unskilled labourer can earn a wage sufficient to support himself and his family'.(80) *Even* an unskilled labourer!

This same report undermines the whole of British 'Native policy' in East and Central Africa, not to speak of South Africa, by observing that 'the basic conditions of the emergence of an effective African labour force is the removal of the African from the enervating and retarding influence of his economic and social background, and his permanent settlement outside the

Reserves'. What this is really saying, in short, is that the only path to peace in Kenya is by improvident White settlers abandoning their time-honoured policy of squeezing the last ounce of spade-and-muscle labour out of under-paid, under-fed, socially outcast Africans, and of treating them as human beings like everyone else. The recipe might seem obvious enough: among the settlers of Kenya, as the report's indignant reception showed, it was strong revolutionary talk.

Even so, this is the recipe which lies at the basis of economic advance in the Congo. With the practical exception of the Trusteeship territory of Ruanda Urundi, there are no Native Reserves in the Congo; and even in Ruanda Urundi the Belgians are trying to settle surplus people permanently outside that overcrowded land, and not *merely* to remove 'fit adult males' for migrant labour.

In 1926 Dr. Léopold Mottoulle, an officer of the Union Minière, succeeded in persuading his employers and the Congo Government to lengthen the labour-contract period for mining Africans from one year to three years. In the following year, having got his way, he sent 3000 migrant workers back to villages in the Kasai so that they should get married. He intended they should return with their brides. Most of them did return, though probably not without a good deal of administrative 'persuasion' such as was generally practised in those days (and, here and there, is still practised). Separate houses were built for them. The dormitory system was gradually brought to an end. Migrant labour dwindled.

Dr. Mottoulle's work was carried further by M. Ernest Toussaint, who is the Director of Native Labour for the Union Minière as well as being a member of the Commission for Protecting the Natives. Gains registered by Africans — we shall see a little later just what gains were registered by the Union Minière — are impressive and continuous in terms of building a stable working class in the Katanga.

In the years before 1926 the Union Minière had housed its migrant workers — men taken from their villages by bribery, trickery, or outright pressure — in big bachelors-only compounds on the model of the Transvaal mines: indeed, it was the Johannesburg Chamber of Mines which supplied the 'expert adviser' who designed these compounds and 'explained' how they ought to be filled and kept full. It was natural that the Johannesburg companies should render this service to the Union Minière because the Union Minière, within the highly concentrated framework of ownership provided by the Société Générale de Belgique and its related companies, was partly owned by British and South African capital. (Since the end of the Second World War, as a condition of granting 'Marshall Aid' to the British Labour Government, American interests have also secured a significant share via the British holding company, Tanganyika Concessions.(81))

These dormitory compounds were superseded by small family huts, some of which may still be seen. Later housing is much better, and the newest types of houses, such as I saw in these mining settlements in 1954, are better than anything else of the kind. What is more, the Union Minière is prepared to allow its more highly paid workers to quit their 'tied mining houses' and build their own freehold-tenure houses in the neighbouring Native Township — a big step forward in the urban revolution.

Messieurs Mottoulle and Toussaint are men of a kind that is rarely found, I think, in colonial services, for they are practical men who are familiar with general ideas. Very much 'old Africa hands' — Dr. Mottoulle's spade-shaped beard is only less in magnificence than the pictures show King Leopold's was — they met during the First World War while members of that small Belgian expeditionary force which fought the Germans in Tanganyika, and triumphed at the battle of Tabora. They are orthodox, entirely opposed to everything faintly radical, and strong upholders of paternalism. For all that, between them they have been largely instrumental in ending migrant labour in the Congo, and in establishing the principle of settled African residence in towns. Others have had a hand in this; but it was Mottoulle and Toussaint who started the ball rolling, and it is from their early efforts that later developments have flowed. These developments have proved highly profitable to European investors in the Congo; but now they also begin to show a solid gain for Africans — and that is really something new.

Their achievement is easily summarized. Between 1921 and 1925 the Union Minière had annually taken from bush villages as many as 10,000 men for mining work, or about 96 per cent of its total African labour force. Some of these would be men who agreed to sign on for a second year: most were raw conscripts who were new to the mines. Entirely unfamiliar with industrial techniques, they were good for nothing but spade-and-muscle work, and that is all they were used for. They left the mines knowing and understanding no more of the modern world than when they came. Diffusion of knowledge was nil. This was 'the Johannesburg system' pure and simple.

After 1926, as we have seen, Dr. Mottoulle began to alter this. Even so, between 1927 and 1930 there were sixty-three men recruited annually for every hundred employed; and the main reasons, of course, were that tribal resistance to wage labour was still intense, and the men could not take their families with them. Ten years later, between 1936 and 1940, only 11 per cent were recruited each year, and more than half had their wives with them. Ten years later again, between 1946 and 1950 — with tribal resistance to wage-labour practically dead, and conditions of mining labour much improved — the annual new recruitment figure had fallen to 3 per cent, with about two-thirds of the men having their families at their place of work. In 1952, nearly half the 20,000 Africans employed by the Union Minière had more than ten years' continuous service at the mines, and 3566 had more than sixteen years' service.(82) These men are permanently settled in town. Although many may still feel themselves sentimentally attached to their tribal background, diffusion of new ideas is rapid and continuous. The long Congo quest begins to reach a new starting-point.

Much the same process, it may be noted, was at work in the

Northern Rhodesian copper-mining settlements across the nearby frontier. Here, too, there was a high rate of 'detribalization', of 'permanent urbanization'. This process goes more quickly than many had thought possible or probable. Mr. Matthew Nkoloma, the general secretary of the Northern Rhodesian African Mineworkers' Union, was lately telling me that more and more of his union's 35,000 members considered themselves as townsmen. Many have given up returning to their villages even for their holidays. Children born on the Copperbelt regard these mining towns as their homes, and are conscious of no sure links with village life.

Migrant labour — the more or less forced recruitment of 'fit adult males' *without* their families — has everywhere told heavily on the survival rate of African populations. Stabilized labour — the transfer of whole families to urban places of employment — appears to be reversing this trend.

While rural populations in the basin of the Congo dwindle and threaten to die out, or else barely maintain themselves at the same level, new populations begin to appear in the sand and scrub of the arid Katanga. In 1925, the year before Mottoulle introduced his policy of stabilized labour, the Union Minière had 13,849 workers accompanied by 2507 wives with no more than 779 children. In 1940 these figures had changed to 11,200 workers with 6464 wives and 6634 children: almost exactly *one child* for each wife. In 1952 the Union Minière had 18,464 workers; but now there were 14,647 wives and no fewer than 28,000 children: almost exactly *two children* for each wife. In 1954 the number of children in the mining settlements of the Union Minière surpassed 31,000 children. No one interested in the survival of Africans can ignore the meaning of these figures.

The parallels with European industrialism are always interesting. Engels recalls how Josiah Wedgwood 'placed the whole manufacture of stoneware on a scientific basis, introduced better taste, and founded the potteries of North Staffordshire, a district of eight English miles square, which, formerly a desert waste, is now sown with works and dwellings, and supports more than 60,000 people'.(83)

Moreover, this industrialism in the Katanga offers a higher, not a lower, standard of living for Africans. If it was true in 1844 that 'in the working men's dwellings of Manchester, no cleanliness, no convenience, and consequently no comfortable family life was possible; that in such dwellings only a physically degenerate race, robbed of all humanity, degraded, reduced morally and physically to bestiality, could feel comfortable and at home', the comparison will not hold for the Katanga in 1954. It may hold for some of the slums around Johannesburg, Nairobi, Durban: in the Congo matters are otherwise.

Before the Union Minière stabilized its labour force it had lost an alarmingly high proportion by death, as we have seen from the reports of the Commission for Protecting the Natives: in 1929 the balance of births and deaths for every thousand inhabitants of the Union Minière's mining settlements was still *minus* 1.5. By 1937, however, it was *plus* 14, and *plus* 62 by 1952: already the Union Minière has younger generations coming up which are much larger than its own labour needs, and it is partly from this surplus that Elisabethville's manufacturing and other processing industries are now being staffed. These figures show the intelligence and foresight of a really big capitalist enterprise which is interested in the preservation and increased efficiency of its workers.

They also illustrate the change in working conditions for Africans which can flow from the large-scale investment of modern imperialism. With the Union Minière we are a long way past the old methods of direct plundering which sufficed for so many decades. The 'old imperialists' could be satisfied with spade-and-muscle labour, requiring no more intelligence or initiative from their African slaves than the ability to shift rocks and earth. This was the general method of mining in the Congo where underground work is seldom necessary; and it is still the method of the backward mines.

But the Union Minière has been rich enough and intelligent

enough to look a little into the future, a practice never much favoured by mining companies; and to see that mechanization of its labour force is not only likely to pay better — to yield an intensified rate of labour exploitation — but is probably the only way of ensuring the mines an adequate share of an always inadequate labour force.

With the decision to mechanize there necessarily fades away the familiar notion of an African worker as a half-starved urchin incapable of thought. The new imperialism cannot tolerate the wasteful indolence and inefficiency of the old. The spade-and-muscle Africans were 'expendable' — as they still are in many parts of Africa — but Africans trained to machines are worth preserving. They, too, have become capital assets.

And this, too, was part of industrialism in England. Looking back in 1892 on the half century which had passed since his famous survey of 1844, Engels noted that in proportion to the 'colossal and unparalleled' expansion of industry in England, 'in the same proportion did manufacturing industry become apparently moralized. The competition of manufacturer against manufacturer by means of petty thefts upon the work-people no longer paid. Trade had outgrown such low means of making money: they were not worth while practising for the manufacturing millionaire, and served merely to keep alive the competition of smaller traders, thankful to pick up a penny wherever they could. Thus the truck system was suppressed, the Ten-hours Bill was enacted, and a number of other secondary reforms introduced — much against the spirit of Free Trade and unbridled competition, but quite as much in favour of the giant capitalist in competition with his smaller brother. . . .'(84)

Growing concentration of industrial capital in Africa during the past twenty years has partly stimulated and partly served as instrument in shifting the economic basis from near-slave labour to more or less normal wage labour. Hand in hand with this shift there goes increasing mechanization, the breaking of industrial colour bars, the emergence of trade unions, the birth of a sense of common interest which is no longer the same as tribal loyalty — and, portent for the future, the growth of a true African working class.

More and more, the African worker becomes free to sell his labour in the market. In so doing, he opens up new possibilities of self-defence. He is exposed to the stress and strain of the acquisitive society: but something is given him in exchange. He is still a subjected person, making fat profits for people who care nothing for him and have never so much as seen his country; but at last he is given the opportunity of understanding the nature of this subjection. The conspiracy to keep him fooled and docile begins to fail.

Thus it is generally true in Africa today that the biggest employers are often — in this sense and in other senses — the best employers.

'What do you do in the Congo,' said the Prince de Ligne, *administrateur-délégué* of a big Congo company, 'when you get a black man and a white man doing the same job? Do you give them the same pay? We haven't solved that one yet.' The Prince subscribes, I think, to a policy also favoured by M. Toussaint of the Union Minière: that African workers suffering from no industrial colour bar should — eventually! — receive the same rates of pay as equivalent workers in Belgium, while European workers in the Congo would retain their wide differential through 'special expatriation rates'. Something of this kind is already practised in French West Africa.

'In my opinion,' the Prince also said, 'we shall have to rely on the Blacks for pretty well everything, and hope that they won't kick us out in fifty years' time — or sooner. If we treat them right, they won't.' This is the sort of long-range calculation which the small local investor and employer never makes, and perhaps cannot make: typically, in South Africa and Southern Rhodesia, as in the Congo, he sees the future only in terms of permanent White supremacy *on the spot*. The big investor, on the contrary, can allow himself to make many concessions so long as the inviolability of exported profit remains assured. Political concessions to the Gold Coast and Nigeria have not interfered, for example, with the profits of Unilever (whose interests include the United Africa Company), which were about £25 millions in 1952. One could argue that the desperate plight of Kenya today flows partly from there being no great investment ventures there: practically all European employers in Kenya are small local investors — emotionally as well as economically interested in 'keeping the Natives down', and consequently incapable of seeing beyond the end of their noses.

Sitting back in Europe and America, the big Congo investors can afford to take the long view. 'We sent out a bull-dozer to one of our projects not long ago,' recalled the Prince. 'When I went there I found it was standing ready assembled, although the resident European engineer was away on business elsewhere. Who'd put it together? George had put it together — a nice fat African who couldn't even speak French properly. But he'd looked at the illustrations, studied the plans, and fitted the parts together. Now, George gets 8000 francs a month and the European engineer gets 25,000. George doesn't want to work under the European engineer any longer, and I don't blame him.'

George is part of a great transitional process. With an almost miraculous power of self-adjustment, he has overleapt centuries and made himself into a tolerably good mechanic. It would be grossly over-simplifying matters to suppose that he sees himself as an altogether different kind of human being from his brothers and uncles in the village at home. In many ways he is still close to them. With 'first generation' townsmen the attraction of the tribal past is still very strong. But the ground shifts under his feet. If tribal customs are present in the towns, it is also true that in the towns they proliferate into astonishing confusion, become intermingled with quite other customs from other tribal areas, lose their old meanings and acquire new meanings, degenerate into commercial rackets, and universally show signs of luxuriant decay.

In this breathless rhythm of change, matters alter from one half-decade to the next. In the early 'fifties it was still possible, in these towns, to catch the meaning of the urban revolution for the older generations with whom it had embarked upon its course of upheaval. M. Grévisse recalls a richly typical incident of 1949. After thirty years' service, a certain skilled worker was to be honoured by a little ceremony, introducing his retirement.

'He came to the ceremony dressed in a European-style jacket, a *pagne* (cotton robe) and a leopard skin. He carried on his shoulders a pick and shovel. After receiving his medal, he knelt down and said thanks for it by beating his hands together, and then marched away to the sound of trumpets . . . Afterwards I was able to ask him what he had intended to symbolize. He replied more or less like this: "I left my village many years ago and made a long journey on foot. In the service of the Union Minière I did my best until I became a *moniteur* and, thanks to personal sway over my comrades, judge of the Native Township tribunal. In this sack I have my employment books and the proofs of my service. I carried two tools, those I had at the beginning of my service, to show how proud I am of what I have become through my work. Yet my heart is not changed . . . and this I showed by wearing the dress of the elders at home — the dress I shall wear again when I return to my village. Two loyalties I have had during my life — to my tribal group and its authority, and to my Whites and their authority. . . .'(85)

Born into a time which not only remembered slavery but also practised it, and which knew directly the horrors of the Leopoldian System, such men have built up new lives in the relative stability of well-organized mining settlements. They have accepted the new order because it seemed reasonable and not too harsh, but they have remained faithful to the old order. Yet the old order begins to pass away; and the younger generation will not come to ceremonies of this kind in leopard skins, carrying pick and shovel, but in swanky suits and with collar and tie — and thinking thoughts, perhaps, which privately explode the limits of an often suffocating paternalism.

More and more, the notion of 'returning to the village' becomes mythical, something one dreams of but does not really do, nor even want to do. 'Already, the return to the village is a solution [for retired workers] which no longer entirely satisfies the Natives. No doubt contact with their traditional surroundings may prick them with a momentary nostalgia. But where are those workers who, once their small savings are exhausted — and that is soon — do not see that the bush has somewhat changed? The bush reintegrates them in its community of mutual aid, but by plunging them once again into a common poverty. It releases them from European restrictions only to submit them to its own restrictions, to its own slow and monotonous rhythm. And all this contrasts painfully with the long experience of life in towns. Soon enough, these retired workers suffer, and suffer physically. They also suffer in another way, morally, for they are separated from their children ... Gradually, they creep back again into touch with the railway, or with a big road, or to the verge of the urban areas.'(86)

Between 1940 and 1948 the population of the Native Township at Elisabethville grew from 8301 to 33,486.(87) Inquiry a year later showed that less than 45 per cent of the inhabitants of the Township had resided in it for as much as five years. Yet a closer inquiry suggested that at least one-fifth of the adult population in 1949 had lived outside the area of tribal custom for twenty years or more; and as much as another two-fifths for more than ten years.(88) Perhaps 30 to 40 per cent could be regarded as permanently established in town, although most of these — like the elderly miner who received a medal — remained of the opinion that they would 'go home' towards the end of their lives.

This changes. With something between eight and ten thousand children born in the African quarters of Elisabethville every year, the proportion of permanently urbanized Africans grows rapidly: even an economic crisis on the scale of the early 'thirties, tending to empty the towns by sheer hunger, would send back to the countryside a large proportion of Africans more or less entirely strange to it.

For the younger generation, as these years abundantly show, the move to town and to industrial employment is no longer an individual compromise with White invasion — a means of surviving the exactions of a White master while remaining inwardly loyal to an African tradition. More and more consciously, it is a decisive break with that tradition, a leaping with both hands and feet into a new world of machines and money, where the law of the individual destroys the old law of the community, and every man's salvation seems to lie in his own hands.

In social stability and individual happiness the cost of this change is not small, for the naked cash nexus was never more naked nor unashamed than in these new towns. They are filled with people suddenly bereft of their tribal restraints on individual racketeering; and here our acquisitive society, as Tawney has called it, gets sharply back its own unlovely image. For all that, the change carries with it a surge of hope and energy which is not to be mistaken. The old disintegrates; but the new takes shape.

ELEVEN

INDUSTRIAL REVOLUTION

WE stood half blinded by the leaping flames of a black-smith's forge. White-hot bars twenty feet long were drawn from the fire by a European foreman and his African assistant. Two Africans seized the glowing bars in long forceps, set them squarely on the block of a stamping mill. Another African worked the mill, flicking a lever to raise and lower its half-ton hammer.

'Look up there,' someone said.

Above us, in the cabin of a travelling crane beneath the high roof, another African moved his levers so that the stamped rod should go gently forward as the mill did its work.

Four co-ordinated operations were required for this stamping of steel rods: six Africans and one European. I watched this clinical example of industrial revolution for a quarter of an hour: I could have watched it nowhere else in Africa.

No doubt it was not the latest thing in labour-saving organization: out here it needs comparing not with the latest thing, but with the gangs of spade-and-muscle labour, forced or free, which toil in this continent.

I watched this operation and others like it in the massive engineering shops of the Union Minière at Jadotville in the Katanga, two or three hours' hard driving by overworked roads to the north-west of Elisabethville. Here the Union Minière mines and processes copper, repairs all its machinery and makes new machinery, and has its railway link with the close-guarded uranium mine at Shinkolobwé in the sandy scrub to the south-west.

These shops are the cradle of the Congo's productive revolution. They employ 600 African craftsmen and a small staff of highly qualified European technicians. Their operations make finally an end to most of the myths and fallacies of African mechanical stupidity, 'absence of initiative', and so on.

In 1946 these shops had an average of one European foreman in charge of *five* African craftsmen each operating one machine tool: in 1954 they had an average of one European foreman in charge of *seven* Africans each operating one machine tool. A quarter of these 600 Africans, by 1954, were wage-rated as being skilled or highly skilled; and another quarter as being semi-skilled. The machine tools they are operating are complex and expensive: these men are fitters, turners, moulders, pattern-makers, casters, even draftsmen. They are cutting expensive metal to one-hundredth of a millimetre. They are performing most of the mechanical operations required in an up-to-date engineering shop, and, for the most part, with no more than routine supervision from their foremen. Most were born in little lost bush villages where the modern world and its machines could be glimpsed and heard only in the far-off passage of an aeroplane.

Most impressive, perhaps, are the electrical shops. Here the White-Black ratio is lower, because the work is more difficult and more dangerous. Even so, the ratio in 1954 was one European to four Africans. These Africans are winding spools, repairing motors, making circuits: over half of them are wage-rated as skilled or highly skilled. What is more, their European foremen (and it is apparently the same in the mechanical shops) are expected to pass on as much of their own knowledge as they can. There is provision for apprenticeship, though not yet on a sufficient scale. By 1954 the ratio in the machine-tool section of these electrical shops was as high as one European foreman with twenty Africans on twenty machine tools.

The manager of the electrical shops, a grave Belgian from Charleroi, explained 'the doctrine' of employment here. 'We think it is up to us,' he said, 'to bring out from Belgium the best workers we can find — those who will have the patience to pass on their skills.' He went on to complain to M. Toussaint of not being allowed enough apprentices — the only way, he argued, of ensuring a future supply of skilled workers. And he was greatly put out because of news that a big electrical manufacturing company from Charleroi would shortly establish a branch in Jadotville. 'They will attract away our best workers. The ones I've trained....'

All this was more than a pleasant picture for the visiting foreigner. I had read that each of these electrical workers was obliged to keep a small note-book in which he must record, as part of his qualification for higher wage-rating, the details of circuits he had made or repaired; and asked the manager if I might see some of these books. At random I saw half a dozen of them: they contained more or less clearly conceived notes of wiring jobs performed by their owners, together with sketches of the circuits involved in these jobs.

Now, this may sound tedious enough against a European background, where skilled labour is taken for granted. Against the African background it is exhilarating. In Southern Rhodesia, for example, or in South Africa — both countries of expanding industrialism — work-bench colour bars prevent Africans from doing skilled work except by the illicit connivance of European workers who are engaged (and paid) to do such work. Government, racially infected 'trade unions', and even employers have conspired to prevent Africans from doing the same sort of work as Europeans — from fear they would demand, eventually, the same sort of life as Europeans, the same rights, responsibilities and wages. In practice this discrimination hides behind high-minded talk of 'African immaturity': the reality is a fear by local Whites of any infringement of their absolute supremacy.

In these circumstances it is a major step towards African equality that the Congo companies — not being controlled by local Whites — do not tolerate industrial colour bars at the work-bench level. Their colour bars are of a different kind, and their constraint of African development just as severe in other ways (and notably in the ways of political repression and of higher education); but in this key field of industrial development they make an intelligent concession to African hopes of a better future.

Their results are formidable. According to the highly skilled managers of these shops in Jadotville, they are *already* getting from African craftsmen an average of about half the productivity of European craftsmen, while Africans who are wage-rated as 'highly skilled' are said to be producing an average of about 70 per cent of the production of highly skilled Europeans who have lived all their lives in a machine civilization.

All this means that the Union Minière is making a grossly inflated profit out of African workers who are paid far less than half the wage of European workers. But it also means that there is a gain for Africans in terms of self-development. The advantages, as we have noted, are not *all* on the European side: there is a genuine diffusion of culture. Here, the old barrier between master and servant begins to be destroyed. A gate is opened though which Africans may pass into the modern world: in the Congo they are passing in their thousands through this gate, even though they must pay heavily for it with the European profits of their labour.

Although ahead of other companies in this respect, the Union Minière is not the only Congo enterprise which practises this system. Manufacturing concerns like Chanic and Utexléo, already mentioned, are moving in the same direction. So are other mining companies. At important tin mines in the northern Katanga (the property of the Géomines company, itself closely linked to the handful of powerful enterprises which practically operate and govern the Congo), the policy of matching wage-rates to degrees of skill was introduced in 1951: before that, Géomines had recognized only unskilled and semi-skilled African labour, so that the process of specialization is still in a relatively early phase. Here, too, the system is more empirical and haphazard than with the Union Minière, for there seems to be practically no attempt at any consistent training of apprentices.

Haphazard though it is, and still depending greatly on the

whims and fancies of European foremen, this wage-rating by the Géomines in 1954 was already a long step forward on the old treatment of Africans as a crew of spade-and-muscle labourers. The latest open-cast working of the Géomines at Manono, where I spent some days, is now said to be as fully mechanized as the best American or Swedish examples. Here they have eighteen European supervisors and about 500 Africans, or a ratio of one to twenty-eight, with the Africans doing all the mechanical as well as labouring work and the Europeans restricting themselves to supervision and emergency repairs. Africans are drilling charge-holes, setting charges, firing charges, clearing debris with mechanical shovels, operating conveyor belts, working cranes . . . In South Africa and Southern Rhodesia they are not allowed to do these jobs. In Northern Rhodesia they often do them without its ever being recognized that they do them, so that they are not paid for doing them. And yet no investors complain, so far as I know, that these Belgian companies return low dividends. . . .

I was able to compare this latest achievement of the Géomines in the northern Katanga — its other open-cast workings have yet to achieve this high degree of mechanization — with the newest open-cast workings of the Union Minière at Kolwézi in the south. There are two 'quarries' here: at Kolwézi and next door at Musonoi; and in each case the ratio in the workings is the same — about one to twenty-eight, with a ratio of all Europeans to all Africans at one to twelve (including, that is, the office staffs).

Of the 4318 African workers at Kolwézi (and the proportions are much the same at the Géomines workings), 78 per cent were married in 1954 and living in separate houses with their families: these 4318 men were accompanied by 3381 wives and about 5900 children. Of these children, moreover, no fewer than 3278 between the ages of three and sixteen were at school or technical school. Thus, 2044 were at primary schools catering for the ages six to fourteen (having a total of five European teachers and sixty African *moniteurs* — or classes of an average size of

124

thirty-two). At an elementary technical school there were another 120 boys; while another 150 boys were at a secondary school (a secondary-primary ratio of about 5 per cent, which is very high for colonial Africa); and just under a thousand were at kindergarten. There are also 'housewife's' schools for girls.

The figures have another interesting side. It is thought at Kolwézi that the number of children between birth and three years old was about 1100 in 1954. Added to the 3278 at school, this makes about 4400 children. But the number of children in 1954 — up to sixteen — was probably 5700, which means that about 1300 either stayed at home between leaving school at fourteen and starting work at sixteen, or else went to visit relatives in the country. Urbanization is thus far a partial process: links with the tribal villages remain strong and frequent, and tribal customs generally rule the social habits of those who have come to town, even if they mean to stay in town. Which is as good as saying, no doubt, that this emergent African civilization will be specifically African, carrying with it much of its own past, and not merely a copy of European examples.

Public order? One thinks of the nightly terrors of Johannesburg. Yet the mining settlement of Musonoi has a total of seven African constables for its 2700 inhabitants.

The schools for miners' children are provided by the Union Minière, not by the Government. 'We prefer,' said M. Toussaint, 'to keep education in our own hands.' Why, in view of the high cost? There is a number of reasons. Partly, perhaps, because the Union Minière is rather in the position of a millionaire who inhabits a slum: he likes to be popular, and to do things which disarm envy of his wealth. But mainly, I think, because the Union Minière has resolutely turned its back on migrant labour, and is determined to build a skilled — and therefore educated — labour force. If it allowed the Government to educate its miners' children, the Government would hand them to the Roman Catholic missions; and this, as we shall see, would turn out children knowing a great deal of the catechism but precious little of arithmetic.

So the Union Minière maintains a big schooling apparatus for its 31,000 African miners' children, employing twenty Belgian teachers of whom each is said to have the assistance of about twelve African *moniteurs*. Perhaps 5 per cent of the most promising of these primary-school children are sent on to pass two years in elementary technical schools where they learn woodwork and metalwork, improve their reading and writing of French, and are taught more arithmetic and elementary science. Another 20 per cent or so are given two years of part-time courses in much more simple industrial techniques, so that later on, when they go to work at sixteen, they will be useful labourers for the Union Minière and its many sister-companies. It is a policy which keeps a firm eye on the main chance: but it also carries a gain for Africans.

There is another interesting development in this field. 'We simply cannot afford', one of the managers of the Union Minière explained to me, 'to allow the children of our European workers out here to grow up into Boers.' Formerly, the problem scarcely existed: Europeans in the Congo sent their children to Europe, intending to leave them there. Nowadays, with pleasant towns to live in and effective drugs against African fevers, there is no reason why European children should not spend their lives in the Congo: more and more of them are doing this. One sign of this change in habits is that the Congo Government has lately undertaken the military training of European youths who were formerly expected to go to Belgium: this training takes place at the new military base of Kamina, where a parachute-battalion is now permanently stationed. There begins to emerge the 'White settler problem' — easy enough to deal with so long as it concerned only settlers who were filtered through a careful screen erected in Belgium by the Congo Government, but much more difficult now that it concerns European children who are born and educated in the Congo itself.

Arguing always that they must avoid 'the South African situation', the rise of acute racial hostility, the Congo Government and the big Congo companies (and there is really little difference between the two, when it comes to matters of high policy) are now trying to educate European children — often against the inflamed prejudice of their parents — in the notion that they can live and work alongside Africans. Thus the Congo Government issued a decree in 1953 by which all secondary schools (they are few and far between) should be opened to 'children of all races'; and in 1954 it founded a university college near Léopoldville at which Africans may graduate and will in theory — for the practice has still to be shown — sit side by side with European students.

Meanwhile, the Union Minière arranges matters intelligently so that European apprentices receive their work-bench training alongside African operatives: to some extent, it seems, they are even encouraged to work *with* Africans instead of merely ordering them around. In the shops at Jadotville I actually saw a European and an African worker standing together inside a furnace they had taken down, and cleaning it *together* — an impossible 'lowering of White prestige' in other countries of White-settled Africa.

In 1953, moreover, the Union Minière opened an *école professionel* at which a few European and African youths will together receive a more advanced technical education than other schools can offer them. So far there is a careful segregation of students, partly because 'you mustn't go too fast', but also, in fairness, because the Europeans arrive with a much better educational equipment than the Africans. M. Beudels, its enthusiastic principal, hopes that 'in ten years' time we can have Africans entering the European class'.

What Jadotville shows, then, is a thoughtful effort by big European investors to plan for the future so that they may continue to profit from a peaceful and sufficiently numerous labour force, paid at rates notably inferior to any which might be paid to Europeans in Africa or to any Europeans in Europe, but increasingly adapted to industrial techniques. It is an effort which admits that to bring in European workers for these industrial jobs (the South African and Rhodesian ideal) would not only be hugely expensive, but would also be politically unwise.

Jadotville thus shows an intelligent anticipation of some of the needs of African development. More than that, it shows with unmistakable clarity just how adaptable these Africans can be. It refutes the familiar settlers' dictum that 'they will 'ake generations to catch up'. It illustrates the truth that circumstances, not any lack of intelligence or an inability to evolve, have kept Africans in tribal backwardness. The Jadotville shops, and other such demonstrations up and down the Congo, suggest that Africans can be fully-fledged citizens of the modern world not in a hundred years' time, nor in fifty years' time, but today and tomorrow. Perhaps that old King Affonso, sending vain messengers to Lisbon and to Rome in search of knowledge, of power, may at last have had his answer. What missionaries could not do, or would not do, machine tools are now accomplishing.

And although this process may not be comfortable, and certainly not beautiful, its core of meaning nonetheless spells regained dignity, self-respect, an opportunity of standing equal with the rest of humanity. An ideal world, no doubt, might accomplish the transition at a lesser cost in social confusion, with fewer drunks and fewer prostitutes, and nobler notions of common service. Colonial Africa is not an ideal world, but a continent out of which the colony-owning peoples are still taking great wealth that is spent elsewhere, a slum where men and women must live and survive as best they may, and where the curious examples of 'free enterprise' are mirrored — and strangely mirrored — in every act of life. In this colonial world, human progress does indeed recall that pagan idol 'who would not drink the nectar but from the skulls of the slain'.(89)

There is a familiar picture in England of the Victorian man of God who read family prayers at every meal, lived an upright life, was charitable towards the poor and humble — and made a fortune out of the labour of little children in dark Satanic mills. There is a contrast as wide, however different in its terms of reference, between the upholders of Europe's civilizing mission in Africa, and the products thereof. Not Pompeii in its prime could offer more luxuriant variations on a *material* theme than the great cities of the Congo today. This gay riot of bars and brothels, of 'free enterprise' in its most extravagant and wildest form, is not peculiar to the Congo. One may find it now in all the great towns of Africa. But here it achieves a degree of luxurious variety, of emotional syncopation, of fun and filth, hope, despair and sheer amazement, that practically defies description.

TWELVE

BY THE WATERS OF BABYLON

PRIDE and centre of Congo city life is the bar. It is the apex of this urban civilization that capitalist contact has brought into being, the peak of ambition for everyone with money in his pocket, and the envy of everyone without.

Inquiries conducted in 1953 found that 'officially there are 300 bars in the old Native City of Léopoldville and 400 altogether in the African quarters. We estimate there is one bar for every 500 inhabitants: in Belgium, there is one café for every 484 inhabitants'.(90) And this, of course, without counting the practically uncountable — the private reunions for the drinking of liquors other than legally permitted African or European beer. Even the indefatigable Monsieur Mons, who administers a good deal of African Léopoldville, admits that he is unable to keep up with *all* the combinations and permutations of alcohol consumption in the sprawling African suburbs under his care.

Full-flowering product of civilization according to European precedent and example, these Congo bars are nonetheless as far from Belgium's mournful little *bistros*, from her shadowy holes at the foot of six-storeyed cliffs of sooty granite, as the *Folies Bergères* from a Salvation Army meeting. Nor is there anything in common between these Congo bars and those cosy *salons de rendezvous* which pass by the name of bar in the more moneyed and less moral neighbourhoods of Paris: except, no doubt, in the making of *rendezvous*. Finally there is no remote connection other than the purely alcoholic between a Congo bar and a British pub. I doubt if there ever would have been. When my father was a little boy in Scotland he used to assist his village friends in carting home their fathers of a Saturday night as soon as the publican threw them out, dead to the world:

late in the evening but early enough, my grandfather fondly hoped, for them not to have defiled the Sabbath. They would turn up in kirk next morning, scrubbed and shamed, and enjoy a powerful and ennobling sense of guilt while my grandfather preached against their sins of luxury and drink. My grandfather was strong on the subject, I have always understood: even if he had not been, no doubt the sense of shame would have been satisfyingly general.

There is nothing sodden, sad, or shamed, so far as I can see, in the whirling swirling life of these Congo bars; and Monsieur Mons, who knows practically everything about this sort of thing, assures me I am right. Everyone spends to the limit, his own money or someone else's if he can only get hold of it: so that the night or so after pay day, which is generally once a fortnight, will attain a full tide of animation that ebbs thereafter to a mere trickle in the dog-days when everything is spent.

On the main road through the old township *Congo Bar* is as brilliant as its proprietor's lighting system can possibly make it. *La Joie Kinoise* does as well or better. Both are glowing — and most of the other two hundred and ninety-eight are glowing — in deep saffron light winking with particles of dust. All is as public and companionly as a widely open-fronted shed, mounted on pillars and furnished with a multitude of little tables and chairs, can make it. There is gaiety and light and noise, dancing and jiving, the making and taking of sentimental vows. There is the drinking of innumerable bottles of *Simba*, thoughtfully provided by a European brewery established in the city.

The girls of the town are much in evidence. At *La Délicatesse*, as I remember, they are banded together in an association of their own, a sort of prostitutes' co-operative, which is chaired by a European trader in cotton cloths. Everyone is satisfied: the trader has mannequins wherewith to publicize his products, the girls are assured of new robes every few weeks, and customers can rest assured they are paying absolutely top prices. Somewhere on the wall of one of these bars, I cannot remember which, there is even a picture of a group of girls, inscribed with their names and offered with the compliments of Monsieur So-and-So, who sells cotton garments and is making lots of money. Some of these bars have European financial backing.

Normal dissolution of city life? Not really. Nothing here is normal in the European sense: nothing is to be explained in familiar terms. M. Grévisse has estimated that a quarter of all the women in the African townships of Elisabethville are *femmes libres*, 'free women',(91) and M. Mons thinks that the proportion may be about the same for the African quarters of Léopoldville.

What are these *femmes libres*? They are not really prostitutes, although their way of life is to sell their sexual services to the highest bidder for a period of weeks or even, now and then, of months at a time. In a sense, they represent a kind of concubinage which testifies to the inevitable breakdown of African marriage customs once numerous populations shift into the towns. But they also represent something else. Even though obscurely, they represent a deliberate act of feminine emancipation. These *femmes libres*, more or less brilliantly dressed and made-up, with bold eyes and lacquered finger-nails, audacious, determined, frivolous, fickle, seizing life with both hands, dominate the city life of Congo Africans: on that everyone seems agreed. They flock to the bars, laugh the innocents out of their fears, initiate the village boys new to the city, corrupt the stolidly married husband, organize in their own defence, fleece the lascivious European, and generally carry on in gross defiance of Morality and Family Order.

But why so many?

'It's because of the money,' one of them has explained. 'Only a husband has money. A wife has usually no more than what her husband gives her.'

Not a very clear response; but she goes on: 'In the old days we women had possessions. We had our place, our work...'(92) Women in tribal life, that is, had and still have inalienable rights, both of work and of property; and these compel mascu-

132

line respect and ensure a measure of independence. But in
towns only men work for wages, for the women of the Congo
have yet to undergo the industrial revolution and take employment; so that the *femmes libres* represent a transition between the
urbanization of large numbers of African women and the utterly
different situation which may be expected as soon as many of
these women earn wages on their own account.

However that may be, all African males who have unbur-
dened themselves on the subject are at one in condemning their
wickedness. 'In these days,' writes M. Henry Bongolo, 'African
women are disgustingly emancipated from the severe restrictions which tribal custom rightly applied to them: and this
emancipation of our women is a festering sore not easily cured,
because it is gangrened with prostitution. At industrial centres,
where only men are employed, men are generally more
numerous than women. With money thrown at them from all
sides, these women soon acquire a clear notion of their "market
value", thanks to the prostitution by which most of them earn
their living. So they become contemptuous of marriage. . . .'(93)

'Another thing about Catherine,' M. Bonaventure Makonga
has written of an imaginary case which he regards as typical,
'is that she has been to school . . . Of course she has misunderstood and misinterpreted those destructive words, "equality and
emancipation" . . . Now she believes she is the equal of a man,
and as free to do what she likes as he is. At the least quarrel . . .
she abandons her marriage. She goes home, ends by joining
the ranks of the prostitutes — often to the vivid satisfaction of
her parents.'(94)

Whereas in tribal life, M. Makonga points out, it is customary
to say to a flighty young thing:

> Wanengena teka,
> Le buya badiaboo.

> You are beautiful; but learn to work,
> For you cannot eat your beauty.

The *femmes libres* know better: they do eat their beauty. Fifty years ago, in the days before industry liberated European women, Mrs. Warren put the matter squarely. 'The only way for a woman to provide for herself decently is for her to be good to some man that can afford to be good to her.'(95)

Disarray in marriage, in the social relations between men and women, is one obvious sign of tribal disintegration in these new African cities. In the African quarters of Brazzaville, on the French side of Stanley Pool, Professor Balandier lately found that no less than 60 per cent of legal cases over a reasonably long period were concerned with 'adultery, divorce, disputes over children, complaints over failures to carry out sexual duties in marriage, and even incest'.(96)

When young, Professor Balandier notes, the African girl in town 'prefers to go with bachelors who pay her rather than get married: for then she has nothing to do but prepare meals, take part in sexual intercourse, and *faire toilette* — she gains by a complete upsetting of society. This sort of situation costs a man perhaps 2000 colonial francs a month (about £4) and the usual present of a piece of cotton cloth. Sometimes it may lead to marriage and a family: but that seems to be rare until the woman begins to feel herself growing old.

'These expensive women are accessible only to men who are economically strong — the rest go with prostitutes. Prostitution is often with the complicity of parents who speculate on their daughters as they would on rare goods. Such is the burden of a song one may hear in the streets of Poto-Poto [African quarter of Brazzaville]:

> Listen, my friends:
> God has given us mothers . . .
> Mothers who are killing us
> For money and for more money . . .'

At Brazzaville, as in the Belgian Congo, 'prostitution is institutional. "Associations" conduct it, more than a dozen of them: Dollar, Diamond, Brilliant Star, Lolita, Violette, etc.: and these' — as in the Congo — 'curiously mingle mutual aid (aid to each other and to their parents) with amusement and with prostitution'.

M. Bernard Mambeke has made a collection of their songs. One of them runs:

> Come along, why be afraid?
> I'm married no longer.
> For I married too soon, you see.
> Thinking there were no other men.
> But if only I'd known!

'Free enterprise' could scarcely go further. 'Everything', laments M. Bongolo, 'is dominated by money . . . In this way, so far as marriage goes, the value of the bride-price [traditional in all tribal Africa, being a dowry paid by the man to his bride's tribal group] rises higher and higher in Léopoldville where it is no longer rare to find parents asking six, eight, or ten thousand francs [between £45 and £70] in hard cash, without counting certain payments in kind which the would-be bridegroom also has to make. . . .

'Take, for example, this or that pretty girl who, being in regular relations with a European, or a Gold Coaster, or a Senegalese, carries back to her parents five or six hundred francs a month . . . Far from shameful, prostitution becomes rather the ideal of many parents of young girls. In these conditions, to ask the hand of such girls in marriage is like asking for the daughter of a Maharajah. . . .'(97)

'Let us consider', writes M. Boniface Mwepu(98) in a mood of reasonable indignation, 'the various devices which these women use in order to seduce their victims.' Note that we are dealing not with a handful of sluts, but with a big proportion of the feminine population of any of these new cities — women who are by no means weakened in their grip on life.

'For instance, instead of dressing properly, they dress in the fashion called *Jibula*. This fashion allows the woman to show her thigh, and very often her groin, when she is walking. The object', complains M. Mwepu, 'is to disturb the man and more easily seduce him.

'Or these women wind round their buttocks, under their robes, a *jikita*. This is made of the little cork fillets which are found in the caps of *Simba* bottles, or else is simply a dress rolled tight round their haunches. So that when they walk, these women make their haunches waggle more than they should, and that, too, is done to seduce you. . . .'

All this is common enough and painful enough, although M. Bolongo and his friends are perhaps inclined to exaggerate its relative importance. Certainly it is endemic to African urban life under present conditions. Dr. Busia's survey of the coastal city of Sekondi-Takoradi in the Gold Coast, carried out in 1948, included inquiries of 127 known prostitutes. 'Many of them said they had no ties with home, and had changed their names. They neither shared any family obligations, nor were wanted by their kinsmen. Some of them said their relatives did not even know where they were. To make up for this, there is a strong comradeship amongst prostitutes, and their "union" provides the security of a befitting funeral celebration and burial. Fifty of the 127 interviewed had been to school. . . .

'Some of the girls said they were driven to prostitution through sheer poverty. Their guardians could not provide for them with food and clothing, and they had to leave home to fend for themselves. Some prostitutes make their living by remaining mistresses to Europeans who pay them a fixed salary every month. Nine in our sample lived with the Europeans in their bungalows; others lived in town and slept in the European quarter at night. . . .'(99)

There is plenty of excuse for M. Bolongo's pessimism. The African life of Congo cities is wild, disturbing, extraordinary. Old customs, once meaningful and efficacious, acquire fantastic overtones, become frenzied opportunities for removing other people's money. New customs, Christian customs, suffer the same distortion. Never was the anarchist accent of capitalism more wildly celebrated. Everywhere the link between men and women, cause and effect, the past and the future, appears to reduce itself to one of sheer and simple cash.

Consider various forms of marriage, complains M. Bonaventure Makonga.(100) 'For example, the religious marriage celebrated with pomp . . .' — bridegroom in black coat and pin-striped trousers, bride in flowing white dress fussily stitched with lace, both facing the camera with stolid faces, aggressively 'civilized', deliberately 'aping their betters' . . . 'It's the copy of the European conception. And it is followed by festivities which profit those who organize them. If Jules gets married this morning he invites everyone in a *cabaret* that evening to pay fifty or sixty francs for the "right of entry" . . . The number of guests has no limit. . . .'

Everyone comes, apparently, who can. 'It matters nothing to the host if he should have a hundred, two hundred, or three hundred guests, provided there be enough for him to see a profit for himself of five or six thousand francs . . . He invites for four o'clock in the afternoon next day, but he is careful not to begin the feast until nine o'clock. Like that, he can calculate his profit. If he sees that his hopes are being realized, he tries to put off his guests with immensely long speeches. Do not forget that closing time is midnight. He begins handing out beer at half past nine. But hardly have his guests started drinking than they are called on to dance. Midnight comes before they have had time to empty the bottles that are due to them. But now the owner of the bar is afraid to remain open after closing time . . . So he turns out the light as a signal for everyone to go. Often enough the beer remains untouched and will be sold on the morrow to the profit of the organizer of the feast. . . .'

Alongside this kind of high finance, elementary devices for helping money to go further, such as *likilimba*, seem quite beneath notice. *Likilimba* (*Chilimba* in Northern Rhodesia) is a common practice all over Africa, and is typical of the associative tendencies of tribal Africans beginning to live an urban life: it consists in several men or women grouping themselves together so that one of their number may receive the sum of all their tiny wages for any one pay period — and therewith may buy a sewing machine, or a bicycle, or a wireless set, or a new dress, or something of the kind. M. Bongolo would recognize the essentially tribal origins of *likilimba*, which is always a means of making very low wages seem to go a little further. Admittedly, it is difficult for him to recognize ancestral burial feasts in the *matanga* that is practised in town.

Matanga is a wake-feast. Tribally, it is an appropriate pro-pitiation of the spirits of ancestors on the fresh arrival among them of the latest addition to their number. In Elisabethville, however, it is the occasion of a grand set-to and a shindy with-out parallel. According to M. Makonga — and M. Mons and other authorities would agree with him — the customary period of 'active ceremonial' is now lengthened to two or three weeks, and during this time as much may be spent on beer and music as can possibly be mustered by everyone involved. It will end with another big party at someone's favourite bar. 'Like the marriage celebrated with pomp, the end of mourning takes place in a bar for everyone who can afford it. Entry is by special invitation after payment . . . The relatives of the dead person profit from this at the expense of others, the occasion is marked by traditional dances and songs that are often quite scandalous. Nowhere may one find a memory of the deceased on the faces of relatives staggering noisily out of the bar. . . .'(101)

It is natural and understandable that M. Bongolo and his friends should doubt whether this kind of civilization can be worth having: isn't this perhaps another occasion of Africans asking for bread and being given a stone? M. Bongolo and his friends tend to see their past, which they are now learning to evaluate in new terms, in a roseate light. What is more, re-acting against European chauvinism (present all around them all the time, whether in the kicks of the farming settler, the con-tempt and trickery of the trader and store-keeper, or the suave denial of responsibility that is returned to African demands by the administration), they begin to see it as a possible future, too.

No doubt this may be one of the germs of African nationalism in the Congo — increasingly, as we shall see, a live force. It carries with it a tendency to see the pre-European past as pure, noble and independent; and the disintegration of tribal life as the entirely negative consequence of European presence. This romantic attitude has had obvious European parallels: it lies at the root of much of the obscurantism which is now at work within the nationalist movements of central and southern Africa.

In this there is evidently much delusion. Yet it is not difficult to see why the delusion exists. Instead of the higher civilization they are asked to believe in, many Africans see in reality a Stygian mess of disbelief and dishonesty. Instead of something better, they see what is certainly much worse. They see the venerated tribal links of group and kinship loyalties displaced by an arrant individualism which overrides every frontier of decency. All too often the values they are preached and taught become travestied by the lives they are obliged to lead, and the European examples they are given. They observe that the wicked flourish like the green bay tree, while the upright are diligently fleeced.

When M. Bongolo and his friends look around them they see an African reflection of European custom: they see no reflection of the traditional dignity of their tribal milieu — of that milieu in which the tribal chief, celebrating their ancestors, will exhort his people:

> Master your hearts.
> May each respect his brother:
> Money is nothing,
> Passion is evil. . . .(102)

They know as well as M. Grévisse, careful administrator of Elisabethville, how greatly 'certain bar owners prosper', how 'their declared earnings may exceed 20,000 francs a month (about £150), and there is no trick they scorn in making them larger still. Most Native associations are promoted by them. They patronize the bands, all the festivals, all the dances, everything that calls for heavy and pointless expenditure in clothes and that sweeps off the African world in a torment as bad for its health as it is for its future. . . .'(103)

And is it not M. Grévisse himself who calculates that as much as 55 per cent of the tax-produced revenue of the African townships of Elisabethville 'derives directly or indirectly from the social *malaise*'? What is one to make of a civilization which not only appears to foster mass prostitution, but even makes an institution of it by taxing women known to follow that trade?

The anger of M. Bongolo and his friends is understandable: it is shared by many decent Europeans. They observe the disintegration of tribal life, obvious and many-sided; that the emancipation of women leads to mass concubinage and prostitution: that women's associations such as the *Jeunesse Malade-Monnaie* — Youth Sick-for-Cash, and was ever the acquisitive society more festively named? — the Opera, the Diamond and the rest play on what M. Bongolo calls the 'well-known vanity of women'.

Seldom do they see this as a liberating step towards a new social synthesis more capable of matching the African woman (and hence the African man) to the struggle for equality in the modern world. They do not see that there is evidently no other way for our capitalist society — for the civilization which colonialism reflects in Africa — to make this liberating step. In a word, M. Bongolo and his friends see the collapse of the past, but they do not see the signs of a different future. They see the trees, but not the wood.

For an understanding of this positive side to the disintegration and decay of tribalism, one needs to turn in another direction. And then, for all its initial hesitance, its half-formed consciousness, its immaturity, the reply becomes strikingly clear. The real beneficiaries of momentous change over the past ten or fifteen years — of the possibility for Africans to sell their one great possession, their power of labour, on a more or less open market — are not the *évolués*, the privileged clerks and teachers and others whom the European has tried to 'bring over to his side'. The real beneficiaries, in spite of very high levels of profit-making by Europeans and very low wage-levels for Africans, are the wage-workers of a growing industrialism. It is at this point that the story takes on its fuller meaning, the skylines widen and retreat, and much is possible that was inconceivable before.

141

THIRTEEN

NEW WORK, NEW WAYS

IF the public life of African cities makes an impression of spendthrift mania, their private life has other things to show. Beyond the squandering in bars and cabarets, there are other signs of change entirely new to African life.

The dusty little slums on the outskirts of European Elisabethville now begin to disappear. Even the old Native Township, dating from Elisabethville's foundation half a century ago, scarcely resembles any longer the typical 'location' of central and southern Africa — a huddle of sties and straw-made huts thrown together on the outskirts of a town — and begins to look like something better.

A few years ago, newly arrived immigrants from the countryside were packed and pressed together in these 'Native quarters'. Everywhere else it was the same: the townward-moving flood had overwhelmed the petty sums and subsidies which European administration had made available for housing Africans. Conditions went rapidly from bad to worse.

Just how bad housing conditions were (and in a lesser degree still are) was shown by Father van Wing, who destroyed a great deal of Belgian complacency in 1951 with a powerful speech to the Royal Colonial Institute that he roundly called 'The Congo Off the Rails'.(104) Berating the authorities for more or less completely failing to build cheap housing in Léopoldville, Father van Wing pointed out that while a typical plot in that city should normally be large enough for four persons, the average in 1950 was twelve persons, and sometimes twenty. 'The great majority of proletarians in Léopoldville are thus lodged in conditions which are a challenge to morality and hygiene. Their food situation is no better. . . .'

Such conditions would soon provide a powerful threat to law

and order; and after 1951 a marked effort was made to improve them. A government-financed housing authority, the *Office des Cités*, began building African housing at several places in the Congo; and some of this new housing, as I saw, is of comparatively high quality. The position at Léopoldville has notably improved.

It has also improved at Elisabethville. In 1949 the District Commissioner, M. Grévisse, introduced off his own bat a well-designed plan by which the administration gave would-be African householders the concrete foundations and wooden window-frames and doors for a simple three-roomed house, provided that the recipients then built houses for themselves. House-building being a living tradition among these people, the 'Grévisse system' caught on quickly, and by 1954 as many as 6000 African householders in Elisabethville had completed their dwellings.

Effectively, these are *freehold* houses. The householder puts down perhaps a tenth of their cost (the lowest cost being about £300 altogether) and the rest is paid off over ten or fifteen years from the equivalent of the householder's housing allowance — each Congo employer being obliged by law to provide housing for his employees or to pay a housing allowance, and most preferring to pay the allowance.

These early 'Grévisse System' houses, owner-built, were shabby enough. I saw many of them: they are built to pattern, and their owners have been content to follow the simplest path to completion, adding nothing from their own experience or fancy or preference, perhaps because they had nothing to add. These are rows and rows of poorly built shacks, their main distinction — and yet not a small one — being that their owners may really own them.

Penetrate a little further into these African suburbs, and you notice that the huts and shacks are beginning to turn into decent little bungalows. They begin to differ from one another, to lose their compound-like uniformity. Administration has also learnt a useful lesson, and allows the foundations to be set more widely apart. Thus the self-built houses of 1950 are better than those of 1949; and those of 1951 begin to be contractor-built — African contractor-built — and even individually designed. Adjustment to urban life can be noticed, year by year, almost like the age-rings of a tree. Early in 1954 African contractors were building the first two-storeyed houses which Katanga Africans had ever owned.

M. Grévisse took me to the house of an African whose profession is the cleaning and pressing of clothes. He is evidently diligent and well-liked; his business prospers. His house has four rooms, is shiningly clean, and would match for house-pride with the neatest European equivalent. Its owner came into possession about a year ago. His account book, which he showed us, noted that he had paid off 33,000 francs out of the 42,000 francs (about £310) which he had borrowed from the administration.

Further along there was the house of a skilled worker at the mines. Something of a show-piece, it is individually designed but also individually decorated in lively colours which are variants of some remembered tradition. Unhappily, we found the family in mourning — wife and sisters and brothers all decamped into the scullery for the period of *matanga* — and the house at sixes and sevens. 'There you are,' M. Grévisse observed: 'The man is a skilled mechanic, thoroughly urbanized. But his wife and relations are still more than half in the village. It's difficult for him — he lives in one world and his people in another. Aspect of transition. . . .'

We visited the wife of a clerk in the employment of the Union Minière. Their house was not yet finished: the ceilings and the plastering had still to be done. Yet it was a decent house on African standards, clean and light and relatively spacious.

'Does your husband give you regular housekeeping money?'

The woman is large and comfortable and full of decent pride: hasn't she five children and a house of her own? Yes, her husband gives her 2000 francs (about £15) a month. A large sum, perhaps an exaggeration: never mind, it is clear that the 'conception of family responsibility' is vividly present here. The children look well nourished, well cared for. And this is another aspect of transition. In place of the old clan loyalty there begins to emerge a narrower family loyalty. More and more in practice — no matter if overlaid with heavy traces of older and wider loyalties — urban Africans begin to behave as though their children and their natal parents were their nearest and most influential relations.

This is where the Belgians reveal their administration at its most intelligent. Having accepted the need for permanent African residence in towns, they are prepared — short of political concessions — to aid in property-owning, and generally to assist in the transition from tribal inheritance to family inheritance. Under tribal law, a man's possessions in Elisabethville might be properly inherited by uncles or cousins inhabiting a village five hundred miles into the bush. In practice, succession now begins to pass directly from husband to wife, or from parent to child. Decrees of October 1953 sought to provide a legal framework for this new kind of inheritance.

Behind this benevolence there lies a careful thought that property-owning may be the best way of diverting Africans away from rebellious nationalism and radicalism: a reflection of the same Catholic policy which can be found in Belgium itself. 'Let each man own his own house and garden', runs the theory, 'and there will be no revolution.' Whether the calculation is likely to work out in Africa — and the evidence suggests on balance that it will not — the valuable consequence for Africans at this stage is to enable them to acquire a relatively high degree of security of tenure in their new urban lives. This in turn stimulates an even more rapid process of urban adjustment.

House building is one sign of this. In many Congo cities you may come across Africans building their own houses, or causing other Africans to build them. Thus one counterpart of the 'immorality and vice' of feminine emancipation — of all the evils which M. Bongolo and his friends rightly deplore — is not

K   145

a falling birth-rate and a decadent family life, but quite the reverse. Alongside the bars and prostitutes and beery gatherings there is a flourishing domesticity which could never exist before, only a few years ago, because the physical requirements for it were never present.

For the 65,000 inhabitants of the African townships of Elisabethville, early in 1954, there were 120 licensed bars. But the police force was no more than eighty men, and violent crime almost nil. On the credit side there were several thousand African house owners, a flourishing birth-rate, a multitude of children — places in mission schools already found for about half of them — and a significant number of artisans. In 1954, trading licenses were already held by 42 building contractors (each having his own work-team), 99 carpenters, 14 housepainters, 13 plumbers, 4 electricians, 3 blacksmiths and 2 welders — or 177 altogether.

I met one of these building contractors. An energetic man in middle-age, he had obtained his training in the employment of a European builder; for two or three years now he had employed his own team, and built houses for Africans. At the moment — he pointed to a nearby site — he was building two model houses intended by the administration to act as a 'building exhibition' for local house designers — for Africans, that is, who are on the way towards becoming practical architects.

Next door to these model houses was the Hotel des Congolais, which is another initiation. This hotel is a smart new building on one floor with twelve rooms which should let for a sum of 3000 francs (about £25) a month. In whose benefit? Still another initiation: the Hotel des Congolais was mainly built with the capital of the house-builders' *Mutuel* — a sort of insurance society, presided over by the District Commissioner, which ensures that loan-repayments may continue to be made on self-built houses after the death of the original borrower, so that inheritance of self-built property may be reasonably assured. Most of the *Mutuel's* capital is invested in real estate: it is the embryo of an African bank.

NEW WORK, NEW WAYS

All this reflects prosperity, full employment, an economic boom which has brought the European owners of the Congo's wealth unprecedented dividends in these years. There are one or two statistical indications of African buying-power that bear witness also to the permanence of this urban revolution. Here and there Africans own motor cars, but that is rare: African urban transport — there being practically no public transport — means the pedal cycle. 'The cycle population has increased from 56,000 in 1946 to 426,500 in 1952. The current rate of import is at the rate of over 200,000 cycles a year, the 1951-52 import being valued at about £2 millions compared with a valuation of under £3½ millions for the import of private cars.' (105) These African townships are awhirl with bicycles during the busy hours of the day and evening.

In spite of a generally low standard of wages, a State savings bank was opened in 1951 with marked success. After little more than two years of operation — in November 1953 — the total number of savings books (almost all African) had risen to 176,754 with an average saving of 2711 francs (about £20), or a total saving of about 479 million francs (about £3½ millions). This is a tribute not only to the African capacity for rapid adjustment, but also to the probity and paternal carefulness of Belgian administration. There is apparently no distrust of this method of saving. Yet next door, in pre-industrial Angola, how different things are! The Union Minière, for example, regularly pays the pensions of a large number of its retired Angolan workers through the Belgian administrator at Dilolo, on the frontier with Angola — simply because these retired Angolan workers, settled in their tribal homes just beyond the frontier, could not otherwise hope to receive their pensions after these had filtered through the muddle and corruption of Portuguese colonial government.

This comparatively wide distribution of money is having its expected result: there is an increasing stratification in African urban society. The Belgians favour this. For reasons which will become clear later, they have had little enough success of the

147

kind they were after in forming a class of *évolués*, of literate Africans designed to act as link between the 'civilizing Whites' and the 'uncivilized African masses'. Now they hope to do better by arranging economic and social privileges for artisans, small businessmen and other 'middle class elements'. They use the term 'middle class' as synonymous with the individual ownership of property, and hope from the growth of an 'African middle class' to find conservative allies in political struggles which most thoughtful Belgians in the Congo now accept must lie ahead.

It is difficult to assess the amount of property-ownership in the Congo. By far the great majority of all urban Africans are wage-earners and will remain so. Prospects for a middle class in the European sense — a capital-owning and investing class which is politically dominant — are extremely slender.

Most Congo wage-earners are poorly paid. They live badly, possess little or nothing. Far from being able to save, they cannot easily make a tiny budget match their pay-packets. 'We know personally of dozens of families with several children where the father earns 200 francs (say 30s.) a month and 50 a week, or less than three francs a day for each person in his household. If it were prohibited for the mother to earn a few francs every day in selling fermented maize (for beer) or in manufacturing every Saturday or Sunday her 36 litres of *pombe* (Native beer), the children would go hungry. . . .'(106)

Small family allowances are paid by all employers. It is also compulsory on all employers to provide a daily ration for each male employee, a half-ration for his wife and a quarter-ration for each of his children. These ration scales vary with local prices: according to the regulations, they (or their equivalent in cash) ought to provide a male worker with about 3300 calories a day. In practice they are often insufficient, as M. Grévisse showed in his masterly survey of social and economic conditions in Elisabethville, for a minimum standard of living. He found in 1950 that 78.5 per cent of all workers in Elisabethville failed to earn enough to feed a wife and child — even allowing for rations received — and must withdraw from their wages (which are not supposed to allow for basic food requirements) a weekly sum between 43 and 121 francs each.

The years of the war were especially hard. In speaking of the 'tremendous war effort' of the Congo — when European profits soared from the relatively low level of the 'thirties — Father van Wing recalls that 'wages and prices of Native produce were kept so low that only coercion enabled us to reach the end of the war without too much damage . . .', and he goes on to complain that the inhabitants of the Native townships — of the *Centres Extra-Coutumiers*, as the Belgians call them — suffer acutely from continuing shortages of foodstuffs and consequently rising prices.

Income stratification — it is too early to talk of class stratification in this emergent urban society — is powerfully aided by the relatively high rates of pay which are possible for clerks and skilled workers, but also by the extremely low wages paid to unskilled workers, who are still the majority of workers. Even in this time of boom there can be little doubt of the progressive impoverishment of many town-dwelling workers, although its impact is cushioned by the distribution of rations and, on colonial standards, of relatively good housing.

At a time of sharply rising prices, in 1947, the Congo Government published figures for a minimum cash wage which it recommended to employers: this cash wage, together with rations and allowance for housing and in some cases for working garments, constituted the recommended minimum wage. It would appear that the bigger and wealthier employers have generally adhered to this minimum, which was low on colonial standards and, of course, abysmally low on European standards. It would equally appear that many other employers have not. Thus at Kindu in the Maniéma — not an especially backward area in this respect — actual wages in 1949 stood at four francs a day, and the government's recommended cash wage at six francs. In 1952 the same figures had risen to five francs and seven and a half francs respectively, and in 1954 the gap was scarcely narrower. Only in 1956 was it thought that actual wages in the Maniéma would overtake recommended wages. Most workers, that is, were receiving a wage which the government recognized as being inadequate to support a minimal standard of living. In Léopoldville, however, where a number of large employers — promoting semi-skilled and skilled labour — tends generally to push up the average real wage, a Belgian writer estimated that in January 1951 the recommended wage stood at an index of 470 (based on 1938), while the average cash wage stood at 490.(107)

While it is probable that wages in the skilled and some of the semi-skilled grades have kept in step with the rising cost of living, and have at times exceeded it, there is evidence that the mass of unskilled workers have suffered a steady fall in real income. This does not always come out of the official and orthodox figures; but what is written in the Congo — and the Congo is hardly unique in this respect — is not always what takes place. The level of wages at Elisabethville in 1950 meant 'much poverty, much malnutrition — a heavy mortgage on the young generation now coming of age. On one doctor's view, cases of infantile malnutrition are numerous: in his opinion, they are generally present in families with two or more children. . . .'(108)

This gap between the ideal and the real is common to all colonial Africa. Excessively low wages are part of a hang-over from the days of full-scale migrant labour, when it was reckoned that employers did well enough in paying a wage capable of keeping life in one man, not counting the man's need to support a family. Often enough, in those days, the man's family was at home in the Reserve: they supported themselves, it was argued, and there was no need for European employers to provide for them. Now that men have brought their families to town, they find employers persisting in the old attitude — with the result that hundreds of thousands of unskilled African workers are having to support *a family* on wages calculated as the minimum required to support *one man*.

In the African townships at Brazzaville Monsieur Soret has shown the pernicious effects of this system.(109) He found from detailed investigation in 1953 that 90 per cent of people in the township of Poto-Poto, and 88 per cent in the township of Bacongo, were living on less than the government's recommended daily minimum, although only 14 per cent and 10 per cent of workers respectively were actually earning less than the minimum. Intense poverty results. The French authorities at Brazzaville have calculated that a worker needs a minimum of 120 French colonial francs a day (about 5s.): yet 74 per cent of the people in Poto-Poto and 42 per cent of those in Bacongo had less than 60 francs a day. In 1954 a government report on Kenya returned much the same picture of disgracefully low wage levels.

Even so, given the nature of the colonial system, the gains of industrialism are not small from the African point of view. By 1954 the Union Minière had nearly 12 per cent of its workers in the skilled and élite categories, and another 32 per cent in the semi-skilled categories. Most of these partially skilled men could earn significantly more than casual labourers had ever earned: if a casual labourer with two years' service could earn between 11 and 14 francs a day, a semi-skilled worker could earn from 21 to 30 and a skilled worker from 41 to 133 francs (137 francs = £1). To these basic wages there would be small additions for every year of service above the initial two years, as well as various bonuses. About 40 per cent of all underground workers of the Union Minière were on piece-work in 1954: at the Kipushi mine, for example, the actual level of underground earnings in 1954 was said to be running at about 160 per cent of the basic wage.

A comparison of the mining wage structure in the Katanga with that of the Copperbelt in neighbouring Northern Rhodesia after the general strike of African mineworkers and the Guillebaud award of late 1952, shows that in the Congo there is a much wider gap between the bottom and the top levels of wages. Perhaps this is the only comparison which can usefully be made, given the widely varying costs of living, but it is a significant one. It shows that the Belgians have accepted the logic of their own industrialism in a manner which the industrial colour bar has so far prevented Northern Rhodesian employers from doing.

Wages are only one indication of the gains of industrialism for semi-skilled and skilled African workers. The abolition of industrial colour bars at the work-bench level means an act of liberation in terms of more than mere working power. African skilled workers produce more and earn more: but they also feel themselves more or less permanently and positively installed in the modern world — the world of machinery, individualism, and 'what happens outside the Congo'. Those who have watched this process over a number of years say that skilled workers are tending more and more to take the lead among their fellow Africans: they are the leaven in the chaotic urban multitude, pointing a way ahead and leading towards it.

Much the same thing is noticeable among African mineworkers in the Rhodesian Copperbelt. Although usually less educated than the clerks and 'supervisory staff', the mineworkers are often more confident of themselves, more conscious of their strength both individually and together, more hopeful of carving out a better future for their children and their successors. It is perhaps no accident that this process should first crystallize among miners, who are trained and shaped by the demands and dangers of their work into self-reliance, self-respect and an understanding of their dependence on one another. Europe knew the same thing.

The wage-grade definition for a first-class mines locomotive driver in the Congo shows something of the qualities which work of this kind is likely to develop. In order to achieve wage-grade 13 (all grades being from 4 to 21, ranging through unskilled to highly skilled, and each grade carrying a wage improvement on its predecessor), a mines locomotive driver must show himself capable of 'driving for traffic in the mines all types of locomotive — diesel, battery-electric, steam, etc. . . . Is responsible for greasing and upkeep. Has much responsibility in case of accident. Does exacting work on lines which are often difficult. Must thoroughly understand all signalling devices and conventions, and be capable of working by himself with no more than the general directions of a European. Will also have passed the two previous years, without accident, as a second-class driver. . . .'

Or consider the mental effect likely to be produced in an African responsible for a drilling team (with wage-grade 11). Although he works always under supervision of a European, 'he himself supervises his drilling team, and takes care of all they do. Must be able to estimate the depth of charge-holes and warn the European supervisor of all anomalies. Carries out charging of drill-holes. Must therefore understand which type of charge to use, and know how to make fuse and detonator connections under the general direction of a European. Must understand different kinds of explosives and explosive devices. Takes all necessary precautions . . . checks on detonators . . . may fire all non-electrical charges. . . .'

And what thoughts about himself and his life will come to a first-class electrician (with wage-grade 18) who must be 'capable of making any kind of repairs, of drawing up plans, of taking down and reassembling motors of any type, of constructing special tools . . .'?

Or compare the idle underfed indifference of the 'normal African worker' — consult the nearest White settler — with the man who is capable of achieving wage-grade 16 as a skilled foundryman employed by the Union Minière: who 'must be able to read, to weigh exactly, to manage his team without directions or supervision from a European. Must be able to conduct major furnace repairs: must know welding, brick-laying . . . must be able to conduct, appreciate, and turn out "heats" of steel, pig-iron. . . .'

Such workers are appearing not in dozens and in scores, but in hundreds and in thousands.

They are held back by their women? So it is said: and we

have noted the curious revolt of the *femmes libres*. Yet even this begins to change with the growth of secondary industry.

Not far from the centre of Léopoldville, a little way down river and nearly opposite the unforgettable rapids where the Congo goes wild in its seaward-running chase, there is the textile mill of Utexléo. Its employees are nearly all men. Until 1953 they were all men. Then the management decided to open a modern laundry, imported the latest boiling and stirring and pressing machines from the United States — and, finding itself short of men, embarked upon the experimental employment of women. Not many, true enough: the laundry is a small one. But here, one day, Monsieur Mons showed me twenty-seven African women in regular employment.

'They are better,' the young Belgian manager said, 'than men would be.'

And why should they work? Perhaps one was prepared for 'curious answers' — after all, the first African women in the Congo to 'go into industry' might well be eccentric. M. Victor Brébant, Director of Native Affairs for the Government-General, asked one of them at random why she should work for wages. Because, she explained, her husband had deserted her, had gone away to Elisabethville, leaving her with a child to care for and no means of support . . . The choice, that is, was the laundry or prostitution: she had chosen the laundry.

Such are a few of the hopeful things that are growing in the Belgian Congo today. They give the lie to those who deny Africans a capacity for rapid adjustment to urban life.

And yet a doubt obtrudes itself. How is it possible to reconcile these striking and splendid advances with the Belgian formula of strict imperialism, with the paternalism which 'always knows better' and guides severely from above? If an industrial worker becomes efficient in the measure that he becomes a self-conscious thinking individual — and common sense, as well as experience, shows that he does — how reconcile his promotion to skilled labour with this rigid Belgian denial of all political development?

This is where we begin to run into the limitations of Belgian colonialism; to meet the contradictions of a system which gives with one hand only to take back with the other; and to see why the very African workers apparently most advantaged by Belgian industrial policy are those who tend to be most dissatisfied with Belgian political policy — no doubt because it is they who understand it best.

To reconcile the training of skilled African workers with a refusal to allow these workers any means of political organization is a difficulty of the same order as that of reconciling 'indirect rule' with the preservation of African tribal life. The thing is impossible. It cannot be done. And because it cannot be done two contrary policies exist at one and the same time, the one promoting African development and the other obstructing it; and these two contrary policies begin to throw up conflicts in the Congo which are of the same order as the conflicts which exist, or have existed, in the Gold Coast and Nigeria, in French West Africa, in Kenya and the Union of South Africa.

These limitations in the Congo reveal — just because the Belgian administration of the Congo is better and more efficient than that of most African territories — the colonial dilemma in its full magnitude. They explain why the Congo, for all the stifling completeness of its paternalism, has political problems which its administrators cannot solve.

FOURTEEN

NOT EYELESS IN GAZA

OUT of the equatorial jungles of the Maniéma in the eastern Congo there erupted, in 1943, two warlike columns whose intention would be easily understood in Kenya today. So far as could be discovered in the inquiry which followed the fighting, these columns meant to overwhelm the few European inhabitants of nearby Lubuta and Masisi, 'take over the government', and thence pass on to bigger things. They marched through hidden paths and were stopped not far short of their first objectives. A few Whites narrowly escaped: none was actually killed.

Seventy-three of the rebels were condemned to death, although only two were hanged: the names these two had given themselves were Jesus Christ and Hallelujah. They believed, according to the findings of the inquiry, that God had chosen them to put down the mighty from their seats, and generally to ensure that the meek should inherit the earth — in this case, that they and their followers should inherit their corner of the Congo. God in his heaven would welcome Africans: and Hell would be filled with presumptuous and prideful Whites.

About a year after that, African troops in garrison at Luluaborg in the Kasai revolted one morning and held the town for a number of days. In this case several Europeans were killed before the fighting ended; and other Europeans were forced to do manual work and otherwise 'degrade themselves' in obvious ways. A Roman Catholic padre from the Katanga was telling me the other day that a similar revolt would have erupted in Elisabethville at the same time, but for a lucky accident.

Official statistics for 1952 show a total of 3818 relégues politiques (political prisoners exiled to distant villages) in the Congo; and of these 612 are labelled as 'dangerous' and held in

156

special penal settlements. Of those at Belingo, the 1952 report comments: 'The Kibanguist fanatics remain fiercely attached to their beliefs, and there is little hope of changing this.'

Belgians in the Congo speak with alarm of what is happening in Kenya: some have offered me the opinion that 'one of these days it will happen here'. I was motoring one day over a bridge which links together two mines in the northern Katanga, when the security officer with me — he was with me by chance — remarked that the bridge was 'very convenient, because you could always put a machine gun on it, and cut off one mining camp from the other', a further point being that all Europeans at this mining centre lived on one side of the bridge.

A wandering sociologist, elsewhere, asked me whether I had reflected on the parallel between the friendly attitude of Africans towards African prisoners, and the attitude of Belgians during the war towards Belgian prisoners? 'Anyone seized by the Germans — the occupying forces — became a hero in the public eye, didn't he? Even if he was really quite a scallywag. Of course, you don't want to push the parallel too far, but there's something in it, you know. Africans here attach no social stigma to prison. Rather the contrary.' One could multiply these chance impressions.

Does this mean that the Belgian Congo hides something in the nature of incipient revolt? Belgians in authority are inclined to answer this question in the affirmative, although convinced that they will in practice be able to remove the detonator before it goes off. They have been extremely careful about studying their 'Native situation' (unlike the Government of Kenya); and they know a great deal about it, even if they show few signs of actually understanding it.

These revolts at Luluaborg and in the Maniéma ten and eleven years ago, and the 3818 political prisoners of today, all appear to derive from two main strands of thought and feeling, both of which are more or less obvious in many other African territories. They constitute, between them, one African answer to European oppression at a time when that oppression is more and more understood by the oppressed for the noxious thing it is. The first of these sources of discontent takes the form of literal interpretations of certain Biblical teachings; and the second of tribal and more-than-tribal nationalism — even, perhaps, of a vaguely felt Congo nationalism. Where these two strands diverge or intermesh is exceedingly hard to say: the 1943 rising seemed to derive from the first and the Luluaborg revolt from the second, but with no very sure division between the two. Both followed years of redoubled *corvées* — rural forced labour imposed by 'war needs' or, more honestly, by the opportunity of inflated war profits — and both were surely exasperated if not provoked by that.

Jesus Christ and Hallelujah, hanged in 1943 for armed insurrection, were leaders of Kitiwala. The word itself is a corruption of the English word Watchtower; and Watchtower, of course, is a religious sect given to the teachings of primitive anarchism that is allegedly stimulated by funds from a parent body in the United States. Now, the odd thing about Watchtower — severely chased and repressed in the Congo — is that it exists in many parts of Africa without giving serious trouble. I have run into its adherents both in the Gold Coast and the French Sudan (where a youthful American mulatto pressed an explanatory pamphlet into my hand while dining one day at the *café de la gare* in Bamako); and the Manićma rising, in the Belgian view, was instigated by Watchtower propagandists who had come across the border from Northern Rhodesia. Yet Watchtower in Northern Rhodesia is not a banned society, and so far as I know it has given the administration no trouble (other than the occasional seizure of pamphlets which advise adherents not to obey orders from any government at any time) since early in the 'thirties, when there occurred an insignificant outbreak of civil disobedience which was quickly settled. In the Congo, by contrast, Kitiwala is 'bad medicine'.

Not only that. Alongside this potentially eruptive Kitiwala there exist other prohibited societies devoted to the furtherance of the idea that the Congo belongs to the Congo peoples, and not to anybody else. 'In the countryside and in the big towns and workers' settlements,' Father van Wing has commented, 'hatred of the White is propagated mainly by the politico-religious sects called Kibanguism, Kitiwala and others, which can operate only in secret.'

In the Lower Congo region the powerful Bakongo are much given to Kibanguism. 'We have dozens of prophets in this region,' observed an experienced administrator in the province of Léopoldville. The language of these 'prophets' is not always poetic, yet it recalls unmistakably the baleful fury of the more revolutionary prophets of the Children of Israel, and it occurs in temperamental circumstances which are not perhaps so very different.

Did not Amos castigate 'the bulls of Bashan, which oppress the poor, which crush the needy', the rich men who sell 'the righteous for silver, and the needy for a pair of shoes'?

'But I will send a fire on the wall of Gaza, which shall devour the palaces thereof: And I will cut off the inhabitants of Ash-dod, and him that holdeth the sceptre from Ashkelon, and I will turn mine hand against Ekron; and the remnant of the Philistines shall perish, saith the Lord. . . .'

Some hundreds of assorted African Daniels are arrested in the Congo every year. They are not much maltreated, I believe: on the contrary, a puzzled and well-meaning attempt is made to show them they have misunderstood their true interest as well as the teachings of Holy Writ. These attempts generally fail: Kitiwala and Kibangui remain successful in winning new adherents. These adherents do not come, moreover, from the dregs of the population but precisely from those who might otherwise be looked to for some kind of political lead in defence of their own people.

Speaking of these 'prophets' of Kibangui, an administrator at Léopoldville remarked to me that: 'What's disconcerting is that they are often among the most reliable and persistent workers.' He went on to recall an indignant complaint from no less an employer than the Union Minière, not long ago, to the effect that the police were arresting as Kitiwala suspects 'some of the best workers we have'. After we had visited a well-to-do clerk whose material prosperity was in evidence with a wireless set, a gramophone, a refrigerator, and no fewer than thirteen pairs of shoes, he added that 'even that man, secretly, may belong to one of these proscribed associations, these dissident churches. And it's our fault, in a sense. We give such energetic people no chance of playing their part in society'.

The Belgians, in short, are long-sighted investors but short-sighted politicians. There notably lacks among them a frank reckoning with what may not unreasonably be called the Great Factor — the factor which has queered so many pitches, made so many colonial experts eat their words, upset so many plans and programmes and constitutions these last ten years: the dynamics of African development. The last ten years have shown this factor as a geometric progression; yet most Europeans in Africa are still adding it up in simple arithmetic, and they are repeatedly getting the wrong answer. Policies are continually being devised for situations which have ceased to exist.

The Congo African is more and more an African thinking in terms of the modern world — and hence of national rights, democracy, human equality. But the politics of the Belgian Congo remain those of yesterday or the day before. The political situation in the town of Jadotville, wrote its District Commissioner exactly twenty years ago, consists of 'the direct authority of one colonial official, who is chief of the place, assisted by 12 counsellors of whom one is secretary and two are policemen'. The description can be generalized, and is quite up to date.

Only in 1954 were plans being made for a gingerly groping towards elementary forms of municipal self-government, while the notion even of municipal elections still seemed impossibly and wickedly radical even to more enlightened members of the administration. Meanwhile, too many of the coercive habits of yesterday remain in force. There are sanctions against

Europeans who hit Africans; but there are also sanctions against Africans whose European employers may accuse them of 'rudeness' or 'slacking'. And perhaps one may recall the question which a Jesuit missionary, Father Charles, said lately that Africans were beginning to ask 'with a certain impatience': 'Are negligent workers in Europe condemned to imprisonment with hard labour? No? Then why are we?'(110)

Persuaded of the need for change, the best brains in the Congo administration are looking for ways of persuading this unmanageable Biblico-nationalist enthusiasm into manageable outlets. Unhappily for them, the strictly clerical paternalism of the Congo together with the vested interests of a handful of most powerful companies, though strong on the side of welfare, are highly obstructive on that of political development: and there are few Europeans in the Congo, I think, who see the connection — obvious at a distance — between political stagnation and the popularity of African prophets. It should be clear enough that the logical result of Belgium's promotion of 'property-owning middle-class Africans' ought to lead to a situation not unlike that of the Gold Coast and Southern Nigeria, where British policy tends to hand over local authority (within careful limits not extending to economic control) to a 'local middle class'. Yet there is a complete unwillingness to learn from this British experience in West Africa, where Belgians appear to see nothing except that the British are 'dangerously forcing the pace'; and most Belgians I met refused so much as to discuss the Gold Coast on the courteous grounds that they could not possibly have done so politely.

The trouble seems to be that their paternalism, though benevolent and thoughtful of African welfare, is also badly scared. It is scared of letting go even a tithe of its authority. Although Belgians admit literate Africans to the title of *évolué*, they laugh at the literate wretch behind his back and are still a thousand miles from that pleasant intellectual companionship which is now possible in West Africa. I found it difficult to meet *évolués* except in the nervous presence of Belgian administrators.

This Belgian refusal to match intelligent economic advance with intelligent political advance is likely to exact a heavy price in terms of political and social peace. Belgian paternalism seems determined to allow skilled African workers, now emerging in their thousands, no means of understanding their position of inferiority other than the arid chantings of the mission school, and no means at all (no matter how peaceful) of objecting to that position.

Unlike European workers in the days of early industrialism, these Congo Africans have as yet no social thinkers to tell them how and why the world goes round, to explain to them the real mechanics of their condition, to bring them into intelligent contact with the rest of struggling humanity. Great sums of security money are expended every year in making sure that no 'unhealthy' political influence comes near them. Stanley Pool is watched by day and night to prevent 'subversives' from crossing into the Congo out of the 'nightmare liberty' of French territory. The bags and grips of sailors landing at Matadi are searched with astonishing diligence to ensure that no wicked pamphlets come ashore from workers in other parts of the world. There is everywhere an atmosphere of acute suspicion. Two Africans were lately arrested on board a river steamer at Elisabethville on charges of carrying dynamite for 'terrorist activity', and great were the rumours and the repercussions thereof: subsequent inquiry revealed that they were carrying a small quantity of 'trading powder', which is harmless and legal.

But Africans are no different from other kinds of humanity: deprived of access to a reasonable explanation of their inferiority, they tend to arrive at an unreasonable explanation; and this unreasonable explanation may easily carry them, at any rate for a time, into extremist positions from which retreat — even without the influence of European stupidity and greed — would always be difficult. A strong and healthy tree which is prevented from growing straight may otherwise grow crooked.

The Congo situation can be generalized. Of Brazzaville in the French Congo, an experienced French writer has lately said

that: 'If the citizen reacts confusedly to an unfavourable economic situation, he reacts to the religious and political dependence
created by the old colonial position in a manner which is
organized even if not effective', and refers to 'the prophetic
movements (Matswanism, Kakism) and to the independent
African churches' which are present on the French side of the
river.(111)

Throughout South and Central and East Africa, Professor
Gluckman has said in this connection, 'there has been a
proliferation of separatist Christian sects, sects led by Africans,
for Africans, against White domination. Some are modelled on
the sects of missionaries: others draw both on Christianity and
on indigenous belief. Many are revivalistic, and believe in a
Heaven where the colour bar is reversed, and the White skin is
a signal for exclusion. These churches are based on the Old
Testament and the coming of a Messiah: they cleanse from sin
and witchcraft, and they heal the sick. Some are rackets. But
all are political movements. . . .'(112)

Europeans have usually sought in manifestations of this kind
the proof of their wearisome reiteration that 'the African is no
good, the African is decadent'. Yet the truth is evidently elsewhere. There is everything to suggest that the positive aspects
of these more or less vaguely defined nationalist or proto-
nationalist movements are the tardy harvest of European
stimulus. At long last, the fertilizing influence has begun to
take effect. They are linked closely to a growing industrialism,
to a growing literacy, to a growing understanding of the Africans' position in the world; and they should obviously be understood as a sign of growth by all who acknowledge common
humanity with the peoples of this subject continent.

But why violent, why anti-White? Not, certainly, because
violence and racialism are 'natural' to Africans — all the
evidence suggests the reverse — but because Africans in their
awakening everywhere encounter the violence and 'anti-
Africanism' of White supremacy. There is convincing evidence
that the negative aspects of these movements — outbursts of

terrorism, perversion of tribal oaths, and the rest — are the product of what Professor Gluckman, writing of Mau Mau, has called 'a nihilistic movement of desperation'. The oaths of Mau Mau may be revolting and obscene, and an utter distortion of the old tribal sanctions on murder, theft, adultery: but the distorting hand is not African. The distorting hand is the nature of European occupation. Colonialism begets its own unlovely image.

Many foresaw what must happen in Kenya if policy were left unchanged. It was almost elementary that a growing nationalist movement must have extremists on its wing, and that these extremists could gain control of the movement in the measure that its moderates and radicals found legal progress always dammed by European obstruction. And yet Europeans in Kenya were blind to this, changed their policy not by a single line; and their immediate thought when the explosion occurred was to lay violent hands on every moderate and radical they could suspect or find, and clap him into jail. The field was left to the wild men; and the wild men were not so easy to capture.

It is hard to see anything especially mysterious in all this. And perhaps it is mysterious only for Europeans whose hidebound conservative orthodoxy is blinkered further, if that is possible, by direct money interest in the *status quo*.

Belgians in the Congo are free with their criticism of Kenya settlers: they rightly say that 'a situation such as existed in Kenya' could not for long remain peaceful. But they seem quite unwilling to turn the same argument against themselves. The 'bulls of Bashan', as Amos so rudely called the Philistines, were no doubt just as blind.

FIFTEEN

ARE THEY CHILDREN?

A MODEST Franciscan missionary, devout, obscure, living long years in the bush, published in 1948 a book which was harmlessly entitled *La Philosophie Bantoue*. It was a revolutionary book, and involved the author, Father Placide Tempels, in severe ecclesiastical sanctions. He was removed from his mission, sent to Belgium, obliged to do long penance in a monastery, and finally restored to the Congo only through the influence of powerful friends in Elisabethville. When I met him for a moment in 1954 he was the almoner of M. Beudels's technical high school at Kolwézi — a sadder and much chastened man.

Father Tempels had no intention of appearing as a revolutionary. And at first sight the central idea in his book might seem harmless enough. This central idea is that Africans are not children. Far from being children, he argues, they possess and have long possessed an ontology, a theory of knowledge, of their own; and this theory is capable of a reasonably coherent explanation of the world within the limits of primitive society.

'Every day', he writes, 'there is fresh evidence that these primitives are something other than children afflicted by fantastic imaginings...'(113) The Bantu, suggests Father Tempels, are not 'backward' within the limits of the social organization possible to them in the equatorial forest and the high savannahs: they have in truth evolved workable explanations of life, consistent systems of belief... in brief, their own appropriate philosophy.

Innocently springing his mine, Father Tempels goes on to say that Europeans have usually placed themselves before Africans 'as All before Nothing. In our educating and civilizing mission, we had the impression of starting from the bare ground — so that it was necessary only that we should sweep away a pile of rubbish so as to lay healthy foundations on the naked soil. We were convinced that we ought to make short work of stupid customs and empty beliefs which were completely ridiculous, essentially evil, denuded of all sense.

'We thought that we were educating children, "big children" . . . and that seemed easy enough. And then quite suddenly it seemed that we were dealing after all with an adult humanity, conscious of its own wisdom, penetrated by its own universal philosophy. At this point we began to feel the ground moving under our feet. . . .'

In the light of this changed angle of vision, 'the false image of the primitive man, the savage, the anthropomorph left behind the full development of full intelligence, vanishes irrevocably . . . and one feels the need to speak "from wisdom to wisdom", "from ideal to ideal", "from one conception of the world to another". . . .'

Father Tempels's mine was sprung. The doctrine of Church and State in the Congo is the doctrine of paternalism: but what becomes of paternalism when the children disappear?

More ink has flowed into those evidently magical and all-conjuring words, 'civilizing mission', than water from the Congo into the sea. So long as it was accepted that Africans were children, then it would be right to withhold the rights and privileges of adult equals, to defer until the Greek Kalends the day of maturity. . . .

And now came a Catholic priest to say that the doctrine was mistaken, the 'civilizing mission' hopelessly misconceived. No wonder they bundled him off to a monastery in Europe.

'The colonizer must never lose sight of the fact that the negroes have the spirits of children,' Dr. Mottoulle has written in an authoritative work,(114) 'who are moulded by the methods of the educator: they watch, listen, feel — and imitate.'

Dr. Mottoulle, it is worth remembering, was the man who perhaps more than any other in the Congo was responsible for ending the curse of massive migrant labour. It was Dr.

Mottoulle, furthermore, who introduced some thirty years ago the first sanctions against Europeans who hit Africans. 'You should have seen the effect of that,' Monsieur Toussaint recalls: 'It was unheard of. A week off work for the first time that a European employee hit an African employee. Two weeks off for the second time. And the third time — repatriation to Belgium or South Africa.' But all this, be it noted, not primarily from any sentiment of human equality, but because the educators must not give a bad example to the educated.

Others with a far less liberal and indulgent attitude than Dr. Mottoulle echo the same opinion. The 'raw native', a Portuguese authority says, 'has to be looked at as an adult with a child's mentality'.(115)

Yet Dr. Mottoulle remains faithful to this opinion. I asked him some months ago why Belgium allowed no Congo youths to study in Belgian universities. 'I am entirely against their coming here,' he replied. 'The reason is that here these Africans would be treated as friends — whereas in the Congo they are not. They would become a political nuisance . . .' They would, that is, 'misunderstand' the great teachings of humanity on right and justice: like so many children, they would think that what was sauce for the goose must be sauce for the gander. Stupid children! How could they be expected to know that they were not yet grown up, not yet ready for equality, not yet mature members of the human race?

Dr. Mottoulle, surely enough, is conscious of no dishonesty in arguing as he does: a man who has wrought much good in his life, he is convinced that he is working for the best of both worlds, African and European. Yet the argument on which his whole philosophy is based, that Africans are children and Europeans their necessary guardians, will no longer stand up to serious dispute. If it was possible in a pre-industrial phase to treat Africans as children, it is possible no longer. Father Tempels may not have Authority on his side: he has the facts.

The heart of the matter lies in the kind of economic relations which bind these colonial communities together. These are more simply defined in the Congo than elsewhere, perhaps, because this colony is dominated by a handful of interlocking companies, always in close liaison and agreement with the government; and because the distracting presence of European settlers is relatively unimportant.

No one has defined the traditional economy of the Belgian Congo more clearly than Father van Wing, doyen of Belgian experts and president of the Royal Colonial Institute in 1954. 'The Congo economy', he has written, 'makes two essential requirements of the rural population: to provide labour: and to provide this labour with cheap food.'(116) Cheap labour: and hence cheap food.

It is the same elsewhere. In Southern Rhodesia, to quote a British example, one may note that much of the food consumed by Africans in that colony is grown by African cultivators, while most European cultivators prefer to grow more profitable crops such as tobacco, which Africans are forbidden to grow. What imperialism has required and still requires over most of Africa is that Africans shall work in mines and other European-owned sources of exportable raw material; and that they shall also provide the food with which to feed themselves.

If anyone should object, 'But it is unjust to take without giving an equivalent in return', it was answered that Africans were not yet ready to receive the equivalent — they were not yet ready for equality, for a share in government, for other attributes of civilization. All that should come 'later on': meanwhile, it was justifiable to extract huge profits and at the same time to leave the standard of living of Africans low enough to be satisfied by African cultivation — inadequate and inefficient though this cultivation necessarily was, once subsistence economy had been abandoned. If Africans objected, then they were 'bad boys', 'agitators' — they were the product of evilly subversive influences creeping in from abroad. Properly, they were arrested, confined, banished. . . .

All this continues possible, with only occasional outbreaks of protest and repression, so long as Father van Wing's two requirements can be met; and so long as the prevailing economy puts no other and more complex requirements. There may be temporary shortages of labour, temporary famines: all these things are 'understandable' in a continent so 'poor' as Africa. That mining companies should be doubling their capital every few years or so on the profits of this 'poor' continent is irrelevant, apparently, to the issue: there is, it seems, no connection between the great wealth of mining shareholders and the great poverty of Africans. The first may live on princely dividends in Europe and the United States: the second, apparently, must fester in their misery until they grow 'old enough' to know better.

But with industrialism there begins to be a change. The second requirement, as Father van Wing has noted, can no longer be met: the standard of living of African industrial workers, and their town-dwelling families, must tend to rise above the absolute minimum previously afforded to migrant workers. Food shortages in towns mean rising prices: rising prices, with static or with falling local food production, mean malnutrition. There occurs an acute food shortage precisely in those places where the Europeans most need their workers to be reasonably well fed.

Not only that. Migrant workers — single men more or less driven out of their tribal areas — may with relative impunity be treated as 'children', paternally condescended to, and pushed around as their 'guardians' think proper or convenient: stabilized factory workers cannot be treated like that, or not for long. Even in the evil mining compounds of Johannesburg, the mining companies have lately had to abandon their prohibition on literacy classes for migrant workers. And how can the Belgians, industrially efficient and advanced, afford to treat as children the men who drive their crack electric locomotives on the Katanga railway, who cast and mould their steel, who turn their lathes, who command their river tugs and steamers?

Even though they would like to go on treating these stabilized workers as children, the Belgians in the Congo Government and the big Congo companies begin to see that the thing is after all impossible. They need the reassuring sense of contact with these workers upon whom, more and more, they are directly dependent. Yet all too often they find themselves speaking to a blank wall: no echo returns from those careful and remembering African faces. Instead, they find that 'some of our best workers' are precisely the most discontented with the system, most eager for change, most demanding in their claim to maturity.

'The Africans', wrote Dr. Mottoulle in his treatise, 'are big children of whom one will obtain more by a kindly word . . . than by an insult or anger or brutality . . .' But it turns out that after all they are not children. It seems that they are capable of work as exacting as the work which is done by Europeans. In Nigeria and the Gold Coast they are capable of completing university courses which are of the same order of difficulty as the courses which European students complete. In Northern Rhodesia they are capable of building and operating a large and efficient trade union, effective enough to double African wages in the first four years of life . . . The ground, as Father Tempels observed, begins 'to move under our feet'.

And the colonial dilemma is complete. For the colonizers are no longer faced, as always in the past, with a simple situation in which they could continue to make money with one hand and deny it with the other. So much could easily be done, in the past, at the cost of a little political ingenuity and a substantial police force. They are faced now with the accumulating consequences of an industrial revolution in which the relations of production become different from those described by Father van Wing — in which the 'solutions' of the pre-industrial past cease to answer.

The Congo economy of today is required to produce growing supplies of semi-skilled and skilled workers whose detachment from their rural origins is increasingly complete; and, secondly, to change rural conditions so radically that continued decline in the countryside may be averted. To prolong the old system much longer will be to pass a death warrant on this colonial golden goose. For the flood into the towns of the past ten years has left the rural areas in a parlous state: denuded of labour, as they were always denuded of capital for essential services and improvement, they slumber in a deepening poverty.

So much is officially and formally recognized. One of the primary tasks of the Congo Government's 'ten-year development plan' is to construct a peasantry which shall be economically strong enough to survive the strains of the past ten years and the likely strains of the next ten. 'We must save the rural areas': the cry goes up from administrators, missionaries, agronomists, experts of every stripe.

That is one aspect of the dilemma: to blunder along as before or to accept the consequences of industrialism. Kitiwala, Kibangui — all the evidence of growing political ambition among Congo Africans — presents another aspect. If it is true, as the Prince de Ligne said, that those who operate the Congo 'will have to rely on the Blacks for practically everything', then it is also true that these political ambitions will have to be assuaged with something more imaginative than timid trials in municipal self-government and a reinforcement of the security service.

Many Belgians certainly recognize what is happening in the Congo, even if they are generally slow in admitting it to visitors: but they rarely seem to draw any fresh conclusions. They talk at length on the need to evolve an African 'middle class' — a property-owning class which shall defend the *status quo*; and yet they avert their eyes from the logic of their own thought. They seem to imagine — in default of all the evidence, which is abundant by this time — that 'their' property-owning Africans in the Congo will be able and content to remain subservient to a paternalism which is too scared of change to take its head out of the sand of administrative repression. They want to have their cake and eat it.

From the African viewpoint, this wears a curious garb of stupidity. For it promotes its opposite, as we have seen: the doctrine of necessary White supremacy provokes the doctrine of necessary Black supremacy. 'European racialism', as Father van Wing has said, 'is the father of African racialism.'

Even if that were not so, the evidence suggests that the African 'middle class' of Belgian dreams can never be strong enough to act as the regulating dominant in a compromise with inequality, such as the European middle class has generally supplied since the beheading of King Charles I. The stronger this African 'middle class' grows, the more irksome will it find its subservient position, the more strongly will it feel the pressures of a new nationalism, of new radical strivings pushing up from below — pushing up from the masses who own no property and can never in the nature of colonial things own any property worth the name. Hence the more clearly will this 'middle class' stand for a specifically African liberation, just as it now stands (no matter, at this stage, with what limitations) in the Gold Coast and Nigeria and in parts of French Africa. More evidence of this may be found in South Africa, where the continued imposition of White supremacy, whether under Smuts or under Malan, has found no sure allies among African 'property owners': on the contrary, the bulk of these now find themselves obliged to follow the lead of an African National Congress standing boldly for racial equality and an end to White domination.

The making of political concessions to Africans is not synonymous with the end of the colonial system, as British experience in West Africa already shows. There are many steps on the road; and the road takes many routes. But it *is* incompatible with a refusal to disburse a portion of the takings. The price for peace which the British have paid in their West African colonies — genuine and in some respects far-reaching political concessions of high importance to Africans who have fought to get them — has so far added up, in economic terms, to no more than a willingness to disburse a small portion of the takings. All that new African governments have so far done to modify the economics of imperialism is slightly to raise the level of mineral duties, to claim a small share in the profits of foreign operators, to ensure that the myth of 'Africa's poverty' is at least partially exploded. So far, for their part, the Belgians appear unwilling to unbutton even to this small extent. They make the impression of being determined to hang on to their money bags to the last moment, and if possible beyond the last moment — even though many of them now believe that they are heading for explosions in the not distant future.

Is this mere short-sightedness, mere greed? If one looks a little closer, other elements appear. These other elements, part of the structure of Belgian society, are generally resumed in the word 'paternalism'. They draw their strength from an institution powerfully equipped to defend itself. The Roman Church, so far as I know, holds no shares in the Union Minière: but its share in the government, administration and policy of the Belgian Congo is large and cannot be ignored.

SIXTEEN

THE ROMAN ROAD

IN the trembling heat of an African afternoon, hoses sprayed on green lawns. Wide french windows offered a view of abundant grass and scarlet flowers. We were in the far interior, and everything was peace.

Only the high administrative officer was violently at war. He vaulted the memories of twenty years of service: 'It is the Vatican which rules here. They want to build a Church like the church of the Middle Ages, monasteries and all.' Had not 'the fathers' grossly inflated the true number of children in their schools in order to win higher subsidies from the State? Was it not the case that they had admitted girls to their schools only after the State had promised special subsidies for educating girls? 'They did nothing for the women before that.'

And what education would they give? This high official, Walloon and Protestant and smarting under years of Flemish clericalism, exploded into protesting scorn. The 'fathers' provided an education *par trop livresque,* much too bookish, which dealt bravely with the catechism and Bible fables but neglected life. As for technical training for school-children — he shrugged away the question as not being worth reply — 'they hoe the Reverend Father's vegetable patch'. Technical training in the Congo, much vaunted in official statistics given me in Brussels, 'is worth nothing'. He jabbed a furious finger vaguely towards the garden, towards the church beyond the leafy gum trees: '*They* don't want it.'

Political representation? Not a shadow of it. 'Oh yes, we have put two or three Africans into our Consultative Council. They sit on their bottoms at the top of affairs, and represent nobody. But why shouldn't we have elections — if only at the local government level?'

Others in the Congo speak otherwise. His next-in-command, another high official, was severely Catholic, authoritarian, and opposed to elections of any kind. 'Let me assure you,' he said, 'that nobody here is thinking about elections.'

This second opinion has carried the day. This is the opinion of the Roman Church, which does not welcome the urban revolution. Catholic missionaries and authorities appear to see in the urban revolution only the negative and disintegrating factors which M. Henry Bongolo and other Mission-educated *évolués* so understandably deplore. 'Our "money philosophy"', says Father Tempels, 'has shown itself incapable of civilizing the Bantu.'

'We are developing the economy of the Congo', writes another Catholic, 'to the detriment of its peoples. We must put a brake on the appetite for gain.'(117) Father van Wing laments the rootless existence of the detribalized African: 'In these surroundings he learns nothing good from us. If he considers the Europeans, the honest labour and the dignity of life of some are eclipsed in his eyes by the opposite conduct of others. If he compares his standard of living with the comfort enjoyed by Whites employed by the same company as himself, the marvels of our industrial technique inspire him with no admiration. When he sees Whites, who earn thirty times more than he does, going on strike in order to earn still more — and succeeding in this instead of being punished, as he is, for every unjustifiable absence from work — his notion of labour and society is overturned. . . .'(118)

Understandably, the Roman Church would prefer a completely rural Congo where the souls of 'children' could be saved without having to do battle with the doubts and difficulties which multiply in an urban world. Perhaps that is why the Roman Church in neighbouring Angola seems rarely to suffer misgiving at the continuance of slavery there. For slavery goes hand-in-hand with rural 'innocence'. Slavery for thirty years, which is probably a generous estimate of the average African expectation of life in Angola, may be a mere bagatelle when compared with an eternity of heavenly bliss.

Apart from saving souls, the Roman Church in the Congo has placed its 'civilizing mission' in the production of a group of literate Africans, of *évolués*, many of whom are trained for the priesthood. In Ruanda Urundi there is now an African bishop, the first African bishop of the Congo since the son of King Affonso was installed in 1518 at Rome itself. Seminaries have provided thousands of young Africans with more than elementary education; many of these earn two or three times as much as an industrial craftsman.

Évolués were intended not only as a Christian leaven in the Congo, but also as the vanguard of a Europeanized class of Africans who should 'mediate' between the European and the Black man — who should act as lightning conductors of discontent, earthing the sparks of popular unrest in the safe 'superiority' of their educated condition. Until 1953 (and even after that with only rare exceptions) higher education for Congo Africans was available only in priestly seminaries: they could not and they cannot learn to become engineers, lawyers, doctors, or quantity surveyors, soil scientists, and so on — but they could become priests. The Congo should be Belgium's, but it should also be the Virgin Mother's. 'The Congo for Mary' is still the Church's best-loved slogan in this battle for the heart of Africa.

An African bishop, a wonderfully skilled church organist, thousands of more or less well-trained clerks, a number of priests and aspiring priests — the results are of this kind, and, within their narrow limits, they are not small. But success in the main endeavour, of channelling African ambition towards a conveniently safe acceptance of European supremacy — this seems to have eluded the Church. Signs of intellectual disarray, of disloyalty, of scepticism, of whoring after strange gods, of deepening hostility to European domination — these are evident on every hand.

'A real *évolué*', according to another Jesuit missionary, Father Coméliau, 'is one in whom we may have confidence for the building of the Congo of tomorrow.'(119)

176

The man, it seems, is rare indeed. In 1948 Father van Wing calculated that the Congo might have 40,000 *évolués* out of 750,000 wage-earners. Since the second figure had grown by 1954 to nearly 1,200,000, the first is certainly much bigger than in 1948. But the attitudes of this 'evolved group' leave something to be desired. 'In spite of their religious formation, most do not live as good Christians. In some of the big centres, there may be as many as 90 per cent whose matrimonial union is irregular: consequently, they no longer practise their religion. In the prisons, the proportion of *évolués* exceeds those of common prisoners. Most are individualist, avid of gain and sensual pleasure. And towards the Whites there grows a smothered hostility — mixture of a complex of inferiority, of jealousy, and, with many, of resentment.

'It is a fact which will surprise many people,' Father van Wing goes on, 'that *évolués* who have dwelt longest in our seminaries, small or large, undertaken noviciates or attended training schools, do not constitute an *élite* among the *évolués* as a whole . . .'(120) Those, in other words, who have most nearly sought the apparent instrument of the European's power, as King Affonso and his contemporaries had once sought it from the Portuguese, do not seem to feel rewarded. They react away from Catholic teachings, begin to search elsewhere. . . .

There is little difficulty in discovering the evidence. Monsieur Mons, diligent administrator of Léopoldville's African townships, is positively killing himself with overwork, mainly through having to preside over some thirty apparently harmless African 'associations' — boy scouts, saving clubs, tribal unions, and the like. So long as he or one of his subordinates is chairman or president or treasurer, he feels sure that nothing much will 'go wrong'; otherwise, good heavens, what sort of subversive wickedness might not emerge between one evening to the next?

When I asked to spend an evening with a group of *évolués*, I was accompanied by two high officials of the administration and confronted, formally and suspiciously across a table, by a

M   177

score of Africans who sat politely on benches, but privately, no doubt, cursed the waste of their time. There was available, it seems, no other 'safe and proper' way of meeting them. M. Léopold Senghor in French Senegal may preside over the grammar of the Constitution of the Fourth Republic. In the Gold Coast Dr. Busia may compose a brilliant factual survey of social conditions in Sekondi-Takoradi. But the best that the safely assimilated *évolué* may safely do in the Belgian Congo, it seems, is M. Antoine-Roger Bolamba's *Problèmes de l'Evolution de la Femme Noire*, a garland of moralizing platitudes as far removed from the 'social study' it claims to be as could well be imagined. For most Belgians the *évolué* is not only a pitiful caricature of an educated man, an *évoluant* as they contemptuously call him: he is also an enemy, and it pays to keep a careful watch on him.

Regretting industrialism, the Roman influence is necessarily at odds — though at carefully veiled odds — with the big companies, which welcome industrialism. One sees this most clearly in the Union Minière's retention of control over the schooling of mineworkers' children, already noted: the Union Minière has no objection to the catechism, but it knows the value of arithmetic.

Yet this contradiction between the Roman solution of the Congo's future — a clerical paternalism prolonged indefinitely across the years, sublimely indifferent to the outside world — and the more realist views of the big companies, is nonetheless subordinate to a greater contradiction, to the contradiction between the totality of European ambitions and the nascent dreams and needs of Africans.

The lesser contradiction has helped to delay and damage the chances of African secular education, and to confuse still further the confusion which has attended this great flood of people to the towns. It has darkened counsel, particularly on the true nature and purpose of 'indirect rule', and nullified a great many good intentions. But when it comes to the basic problems of government — to questions affecting the existence of colonialism, rather than its method of operation — Church and companies close their ranks. Both know, when it comes to the point of choice, which side their bread is buttered on; and they know that for both of them it is buttered on the same side.

Determined to exclude politics, Church and companies (making the State between them) have placed their hopes of 'keeping the Africans quiet' in the production of *évolués* and of a property-owning 'middle class'. Neither, by the early 'fifties, looked like yielding firm ground for a prolongation of the colonial system indefinitely into the future. Both showed signs of growing instability. The *évolués* were dissolute or unreliable, quick to resentment, affected by nationalism: the property owners (when they were not *évolués*) seemed more closely linked by their property not to the Europeans but to their own people, among whom they now began to feel themselves taking a lead.

Belgian helplessness in this situation is typified in the reply of a highly qualified and intelligent administrator when asked how the Congo Government would deal with Kitiwala and other anti-White secret societies. 'It is necessary', he answered me, 'to ensure that the priest and the administrator should live more closely and intimately with the Natives. The Natives must be helped through their problems of transition by the sympathetic guidance of the European.' Even from this man there emerged in its purest form the cliché that the African is a child. And yet it is clear enough that Kitiwala is by no means the consequence of any failure in 'guidance', but one kind of African answer to European suffocation of all legitimate political activity.

If Africans in Léopoldville may not gather together for almost any regular purpose without having Monsieur Mons or one of his assistants for their chairman, then obviously they will take their ambitions underground, where even Monsieur Mons and his numerous spies will not easily be able to follow them; and that, as the security records show, is what they do. If they cannot reasonably object to their position of permanent inferiority, they will object to it unreasonably; and they do that also.

Belgians who see and say this carry little or no weight with government. Arguing in 1947 for gradual moves towards 'racial partnership', a former District Commissioner pointed out that 'evolved Africans' would 'increasingly wish to compete with us'. The higher education for which Africans were asking would throw up 'strong individuals, young and progressive, driven by contemporary ideologies, who will rise above their fellows and will lead them'. Detribalization would create a racial cohesion. 'And at that point, whatever may be the good will and the intelligence we deploy, it is sure that we shall enter into conflicts with our subjects. There is no room for illusions: once set in motion, these basically racial aspirations cannot be suppressed. . . .'(121)

This forecast has proved its value. In the few years since 1947 the sense of Congolese unity — even of an incipient Congolese nationalism — has developed among a widening section of people. Colonial conquest reaps the harvest of its own unifying and centralizing tendencies: and Congo peoples increasingly find in French a common road across their language barriers.

In the high old days of the Conference of Berlin the central 'problem' was to know whether this or that European Power should 'have' the Congo. It is already possible, today, to see through the appearance of things to another central 'problem' — that of knowing whether the Belgian Congo can remain a viable unity in the eyes of its inhabitants, or whether it must break down into ethnically more consistent parts. One may note the same trend elsewhere. Are the Yorubas of Nigeria, or the Ibos or the Hausas, members of their own 'nation', of their own nationality, or are they Nigerians? Which will prevail? Little by little, imperceptibly, control of the future slips from European hands — even while the full panoply and apparatus of European domination remains apparently intact.

But it is one thing to talk sense, and another to apply it.

Politically, the Congo is no further forward than in 1947: only in 1954 could one perceive nervous moves towards the shadow of a 'racial partnership'. A measure of the potent interests which fight against all such moves could be had from the ultra-cautious statements of the Governor-General, Monsieur Pétillon, himself a man of liberal persuasion. All that this thoughtful governor had felt able to do, by the middle 'fifties, was tactfully to prepare the ground of European thought — or perhaps one should write of European *feeling* — for severely limited concessions to African educational and political advancement.

The inertia of heavily vested interest is as powerful here as anywhere else. Habits of 'kicking them around' die hard. The manager of a Belgian marketing agency showed me records of African employment at his branch in one of the towns of the interior. Against quite a number of the dossiers there was clapped a slip of paper marked with the words: *In prison.* For what reasons? Lateness for work, absence without leave, insolence while sweeping out the office . . . 'A strong hand is needed.'

Penal sanctions for 'negligent workers' are the rule in the Congo as in neighbouring territories.(122) For 'negligence' or 'desertion', these sanctions allow fines and imprisonment with hard labour. They date from an earlier time when it was still necessary to force tribal Africans to take wage employment, and when 'the sack' meant only that the victim was gratefully free to go home again. Thus it was useless to sack a man whom you had more or less forced to come to work: he was only too delighted. Indeed, you had to stop him running away, and if he ran away you had to bring him back. So when you took him on you made him 'sign a contract' allowing you to do all this to him, and you sentenced him to 'hard labour' whenever he offended. This doctrine has often degenerated into a convenient administrative practice of 'finding prisoners' whenever a road was to be built or improved, or something of the kind. Penal labour today is still an important means of administrative effort.

THE AFRICAN AWAKENING

Urban revolution and the emergence of a 'free labour market' on lines familiar to Europe must logically put an end to this. Some Europeans see this; but not yet many of them, as the following will show. In 1951 the various Provincial Councils of the Congo — consultative councils composed of settlers, administrators, missionaries, one or two isolated Africans — voted on whether to prolong or suppress these penal sanctions.(123) In the Province of Kivu — rather surprisingly, settlers being strongest there — the council was mainly for suppression. The Province of the Equator opposed total suppression, but would 'make exceptions'. The Eastern Province rejected suppression by seven votes to two, with one abstention: it recommended lower prison sentences but higher fines.

Most revealingly, perhaps, the council for Léopoldville Province passed a resolution to the effect that 'the educational character of these sanctions is still necessary in the state of evolution of the mass of Congo workers': it added, however, that penalties should be applied to offending employers as well as the workers. The Province of the Kasai was unanimously against suppression, except for holders of the *carte de mérite* or *médaille de service* (badges of 'reliability' awarded, but rarely, to *évolués* and others). In Ruanda Urundi — a United Nations Trusteeship territory, be it noted, but little more in practice than a vast labour reserve — the council was for maintaining penal sanctions. So was the council in the Katanga, which added a unanimous opinion that 'it is absolutely premature to envisage the complete suppression of sanctions for all workers', but admitting 'certain exceptions'.

These votes reflect the slow movement of European opinion. It begins to be understood that industrialism makes these penal sanctions out of date even from a narrowly employer's view: for all that, most employers want to be sure they still have the whip hand. They only partially, reluctantly, fearfully, accept the logic of their own development. As someone has said, the 'African problem' is all too often a European problem.

182

SEVENTEEN

WHITE MAN'S GOD?

WHAT marks of change would an African skipper, steering up and down the waters of the Congo and Kasai in fair weather and in foul, traversing the length and breadth of this equatorial immensity which is increasingly his land, his home, the source of his nationality, make out to guide his thoughts? What do he and his friends say on all this when through long quiet days and nights their talk comes round to the perennially interesting subject of themselves, their past, their present and their future?

It is difficult to know what they say, for they are careful to say it to themselves, and European listeners are little welcome. It is only certain that they say a great deal. The proverbial 'bush telegraph' of news currency through Africa is more than a myth: Africans talk incessantly of themselves and their neighbours. They also talk about their employers. Many Europeans live in Africa among African faces they do not really see or care to see, among African opinions they do not hear or care to hear: with Africans it is the reverse. They inspect their masters with a wry and careful interest, noting individual strength, eccentric weakness, liability to wrath, capacity for being cajoled or fooled. But they rarely trust them, rarely tell them what Africans think and hope for.

Even so, a few guides to African thought seem to emerge as clearly as the white-painted steering boards on trees that line the Congo, and mark the navigable channel.

Tribalism is dying fast. Together with its essential basis, its primarily subsistence economy, the habits and disciplines of primitive collectivism are passing out of reach, out of existence. Men lost in the individualist anarchy of the towns may cast regretful glances over their shoulders, deploring the loss of the

183

group-security of their village childhood, praising nostalgically the dignity and balanced justice of chiefly society: however strongly phrased their lament they do not really want, even if they could, to go back again.

Stronger ties hold them where they are, draw them on, drive them in search of new explanations, new loyalties. Voluntary return to the village would spell defeat, would be reckoned a token of surrender: a man would lose his self-respect. 'Many hopes, no doubt, may be deceived; but, once in town, the emigrant can no longer go back to his village. For the townsman is considered an important person by those who have stayed behind; he will not want to fall from this pedestal. He stays in town: even to the point of accepting more and more poverty, of living on the charity of others who are happier than he is, and perhaps braver. . . .'(124)

In Bechuanaland, Professor Schapera finds that labour migration has 'almost entirely replaced the *bogwera* [traditional circumcision rites] as a mark of maturity', and girls admire those who have 'gone abroad' as men who have proved their manhood.(125) The case is general. Wage-labour in the towns initiates a man into the modern world. At this late stage there is no voluntary return.

Only economic crisis has availed to reverse the rural exodus. In 1954 this was beginning to occur at Brazzaville in the French Congo; but its form was typical enough — the men returned to their villages because they could not live in town, but with a determination to seek the town, once again, as soon as Europeans could employ them. For most of those who have come to town in the last ten years — and they are many millions — the 'return to the village' is present in their thoughts only as the ultimate goal of old age, or as an occasional holiday, or as a temporary escape from European injustice — or justice. They retain a kind of tribal custom when in town, and they often fête their chiefs; but their eyes are bent on other destinations and other guides.

'In the beginning,' an African writes of village opinion,

184

'tribal and other prohibitions, and equally the fear one has of the life in European towns — fear of hunger and of the forced labour one imagines must exist there — operate against the rural exodus. But the inhabitants of these towns — coming back on holiday or passing through their villages, mostly ex-soldiers, "boys", and the subjects of foreign colonies — transform this village mentality. These people of the towns make a good impression. They are well-dressed. They jabber in French, the language of the Europeans . . . They reveal the secret of their condition: money, the White man's god. In the towns, they say, there is no barter — and with money one may get everything: clothes, frying-pans, bicycles, gramophones. . . .'

And why should this attraction overcome the habit of a life-time? 'In contact with European civilization', replies this same African, 'these people find that their material development is possible only in the towns . . . And then again, in the villages most of the chiefs and elders are often loathed by the inhabitants: bad wages, hatreds, senseless *corvées*, arbitrary arrests . . . You need only spend your holiday in a village to see it all.'(126)

Village life disintegrates. 'It is a fact', writes another African, 'that the evolution of the towns penetrates even to the tribal areas. Tribal organization goes against the wishes of people who want to participate in this evolution. Villagers are getting hold of ideas about civilization. They are looking for ways of applying them to their daily life, just as the people of the towns apply them.'(127)

Even in the rural areas, the home of tribal custom, life cannot continue as it is. More food is needed for the towns, but only a radical change in African agriculture can supply it. This change means transforming haphazard tribal cultivators into a settled peasantry capable of practising a sound rotation of crops. This in turn means breaking with tribal custom, introducing an effective permanence of individual tenure. The idea of property rears its head in a revolutionary form: Africans have never owned land, but the Congo Government is now making an intelligent and progressive attempt to persuade them to behave

185

as though they owned it. With varying success, efforts are being usefully devoted to the creation of a peasantry.

There are even those who look forward to the 'settlement of agricultural communities consisting of trained and educated Africans'. These communities, argues Professor Marzorati, would be 'organized in extra-customary centres; they would certainly offer better opportunities for the introduction of new crops and scientific agriculture, than the traditional Native society where individual initiative is often handicapped by conservatism and superstition'.(128) Very true; but they would also bring the urban revolution into the surviving heart of tribal life. Not only 'urban detribalization', but 'rural detribalization' too.

Whatever beliefs may now guide an African ship's captain steering up and down the Congo, he *knows* that he is different from the villagers along the bank. He is different in the measure that he has more power to face this challenging outside world which alternately threatens and beckons, gives and takes away, preaches one thing and practises another. He knows much more than King Affonso knew, five hundred years ago, when the Europeans first appeared. King Affonso thought that the missionaries' god was the secret of the Europeans' power. A ship's captain on the endless waters of the Congo is likely to know better. The secret is elsewhere. The god is another; and it jingles in his pocket.

He knows, too, that he might be a deal worse off. Belgian paternalism is not all negative: compared with neighbouring territories, British, French or Portuguese, it has advantages for African people. It accepts the urban revolution in many of its important elementary aspects, admitting no work-bench colour-bar, encouraging security of long-term tenure in the towns (compared with the miserable absence of urban security in most British territories, and above all in Kenya and Southern Rhodesia). Its wages are higher than elsewhere: for this reason, thousands of Africans from French Brazzaville cross Stanley Pool to work in Belgian Léopoldville. It claims to provide a comparatively high level of primary education. Nearly a million children are officially said to be in one or other kind of school in the Congo, or about 9 per cent of the whole population, compared with a proportion of less than 2 per cent in French Equatorial Africa, less than a half per cent in Angola, less than 9 per cent in Northern Rhodesia, and less than 6 per cent in Kenya.(129) Even if the Belgian figures err on the side of official optimism, as seems likely, they are still comparatively high.

If a number of African peoples in rural areas appear to be dying out — the Azandi, for instance, along the fringe of the Sahara and some of those who inhabit the central basin — others, like the peoples of the Lower Congo, have recovered themselves. Even the Batwa, the pygmies, are said to be growing more numerous: they are beginning, here and there, to emerge from the forest and make long-period villages. As we have seen, urban populations are strongly established, and show at the moment a relatively high birth-rate.

And if Congo Africans may enjoy no political rights, nor may Congo Europeans: and this political vacuum, as the examples of settler government in Kenya and Rhodesia prove, can be of great temporary advantage to African welfare — even though, in Africa's contradictory way, it may also have the disadvantage of slowing up African political development by depriving Africans of useful political lessons.

Yet the 'money god' is not a comfortable master. He exacts a stiff price, whether in terms of human decency or of fellow-feeling, for admission to the modern world. The end of tribalism and the transition to urban life was in any case bound to disrupt social and collective values: under the sign of the White man's god, the process goes to an extreme in reducing community interdependence to old-fashioned nonsense, in skinning a man of the whole of his system of group-security while giving him nothing in its place, and in overturning the ancient and venerated 'good of the community' with a sheer and inescapable egotism which frightens as much as it compels attraction. It is no small irony of fate that this Most Christian paternalism in the Congo should have promoted an African society so frankly and frantically given to the pursuit of a most earthly and individualist material gain.

Africans themselves are well aware of this social disarray. Some consider the cost of this 'civilization' to be much too high, and turn away into dreams of their past. Others look more boldly for an answer. These are they who stand for the active building of a new African future. The corollary of an industrial revolution, they say, must be a social and hence a political revolution. It must be the end of colonialism.

In a highly relevant if cautious form, this argument was lately put by a distinguished intellectual of the Gold Coast. He was writing in 1949 of the townward flood into the ocean port of Sekondi-Takoradi; but his words, as will be seen, have a general application.

'We have seen the conflict of cultural values in monogamy versus polygamy; Christianity versus Tigare; matrilineal versus patrilineal inheritance; individualism versus traditional family obligations; elective municipal government versus tribal loyalties; in the discourtesy governing social relations in the new economic and governmental institutions; in the absence of a sense of social responsibility . . . in the ineffectiveness of moral and legal sanctions; and most prominently and obviously of all in increased crime, prostitution, juvenile delinquency, unbridled acquisitiveness, bribery and corruption, which are symptoms of a maladjusted society.'

All this, too, we have seen in the Congo. 'These facts make it plain that the provision of material equipment and administrative machinery alone will not solve all the problems . . . Development and welfare plans aiming at material prosperity must go hand in hand with advances in morality and social responsibility; with the strengthening and indoctrination of common cultural values through education, in its broadest sense, in and for citizenship . . . (because) it is the common cultural values that (people) accept, and the degrees of social responsibility they assume, that will determine the condition of their society.'(130)

Since those words were written we have seen in the Gold Coast some progress towards that end: Africans are taking an increasing social responsibility there, and, in spite of set-backs (for they are as open to corruption as anyone else), they are proving the truth that humanity is good in the measure that it is challenged to be good.

In the Congo there is little or no progress towards that end. 'Common cultural values', 'education in and for citizenship' — these are not compatible with colonial subjection. All that is shown to be possible under colonial subjection is the destruction of the old society. Colonialism has been the terrible though necessary hurricane which has swept away the old in preparation for the new. It shows itself incapable of building the new.

Meanwhile, the only civilization which Africans have generally acquired in this process of destruction and of clearing away is the 'civilization' that is built in the image of 'money, the White man's god', in the image of capitalism. One cannot fairly ask of anything more than it can give. The acquisitive society has done its best. The further and the fuller liberation of Africa and Africans awaits a new example, a finer challenge.

Even so, the acquisitive society has done a good deal. Anyone prone to underestimate its liberating services should take a look at Angola, slumbering next door in near-feudal servitude. Even old King Affonso, should he return from the shades, could not feel much out-moded here.

EIGHTEEN

INTO ANGOLA

To the voyager southward-sailing from the Gulf of Guinea this country of Angola shows a long lifting coast of grey and silver hills beyond the line of Atlantic surf. Here and there old slaving forts squat in primrose shadows above the blue sea. Beneath them, rare towns lie half-asleep along avenues of fronded palms. There is everywhere an air of practised poverty, dust, small change. Leaning over the steamer's rail, staring landward, one has the sense of far countries stretching into an empty interior, utterly unknown to the world at large.

This is the way Nevinson approached Angola in 1904. Months later, returning from Lobito, he travelled with a shipload of slaves. 'After we had stopped at Luanda and taken on forty-two more slaves,' he recalls in his memoirs, 'making our full complement 272 men and women, not counting the numerous babies, we called at Ambriz, and there a singular abomination occurred. For in the early morning one of the slaves, seeing the district of which he was a native not far away, slid off the fo'c'sle, where the slaves were crowded together, and tried to swim for freedom. The sea was full of sharks, and I could only hope that they would devour him; for a boat was dropped at once from the ship, and in ten minutes it had overtaken the swimmer.

'Leaning over the side, the two black men and the white officer battered his head with their oars and sticks till he was quiet, and then dragged him into the boat, laying a piece of sailcloth over his nakedness that the feelings of the ladies on board might not be shocked. Dripping and trembling, he was taken below by the doctor and the Government agent, who accompanied every consignment of slaves, and there he was chained fast to a post. "Boa chicote!" shouted the first-class passengers: "Flog him! Flog him!" . . .'(131)

In London, four years later, Sir Edward Carson and Mr. Rufus Isaacs (later Lord Reading) appeared in Cadbury *v. Standard*, a case that was closely linked to conditions in Angola and the cocoa islands of São Thomé and Principe. They agreed that no issue lay between them on the count of admitting slavery in those territories. 'We agree with them,' Mr. Isaacs said, 'that the slavery is as much to be condemned as it could be. We do not suggest there is no slavery.' To which Carson replied: 'My learned friend . . . said in the course of his opening that the question of slavery in the islands of São Thomé and Principe was not in issue in one sense — it is not in issue in the sense that it is denied — it is admitted.'

Five years later, in 1913, Sir John Harris assembled the evidence of missionaries and others after a visit to Angola: he showed that conditions were unchanged. Slavery continued.(132) In Angola itself a local storm blew up in 1924 over a factual description written by an American professor of sociology, Robert Ellsworth Ross, who obtained evidence on Angolan slavery from Protestant missionaries, and caused the Portuguese authorities to persecute these missionaries so obviously and deliberately that the memory of the 'Ross Report' is among them to this day. Ross sent his report to the League of Nations, where it was filed and forgotten of the world. From then until now, through thirty years, no detailed summary of Angolan slavery has gone through the public press, so far as I know. In 1904 *Harper's Magazine* had commissioned Nevinson to travel through Angola; and in 1954, half a century later, *Harper's* asked me to do the same.

Though limited to much briefer travel through the interior and along the coast than Nevinson's, my own inquiries reaped overwhelming evidence of slavery in the same 'contract labour' form which Nevinson, Sir John Harris and Ross described.

I came in by the back door, apprehensive of not coming in at all, and crossed from the Congo frontier by railway to the coast. I frankly told the Portuguese what I wanted to know; and they as frankly assumed that no visitor who crossed their frontier could possibly have come to criticize their master-and-slave mentality. At the same time, I ought to add that there are many Portuguese who hate slavery, and would like to see it ended: they are opponents of the Salazar régime who have sought — but scarcely found — a less constricted home in Africa.

'The political police are here, of course,' one of these said to me, 'but we are so far away from Portugal. They are not efficient. They do not bother us much.' These liberal Portuguese gave me information which enlarged my own findings: but I shall not repeat it here because I cannot give their names. Nor is it necessary: supporters of the Salazar régime, the beneficiaries of Angolan slavery, told me everything I needed to know; and publishing their names will not hurt them.

I came in from the far interior on a Belgian 'boat train' carrying homeward-bound colonials from the Katanga down the Benguela railway to Lobito, where they would take ship for Europe.

This Katanga railway runs through the sandy scrub of the southern plateau for a day and a half before it reaches the Angolan frontier at Dilolo. Apart from mining settlements there is little population in this bleak Katanga; and villages along the railway are few. But towards Dilolo there are many villages: crowds of children gather whenever the train halts, and stare and shout and beg with smiling faces and wheedling hands. These are not 'Congo natives', for the most part, but people from Angola who have settled on the Belgian side of the frontier in order to avoid forced labour recruitment in their homes on the Angolan side. Continuous emigration bleeds the frontier peoples of Angola. Families pass over into Northern Rhodesia and the Belgian Congo. (Land troubles in Nyasaland, in 1953, were partly caused by the growing emigration of Africans from neighbouring Portuguese East Africa, where conditions are possibly not much better than in Portuguese West Africa.) In Elisabethville and Jadotville I have talked to

African industrial workers whose homes are in Angola, and who, had they remained at home, would as likely as not be slaves.

Once one is through Dilolo and over the frontier beyond the Portuguese post at Texeira de Sousa, the villages disappear. Here one will pass for hours, and even for days, through country which seems without habitation. Long since, to escape labour conscription, the people have withdrawn their villages — as a railway engineer explained, throwing wide his arms with a wry excusing smile — 'far from the railway on either side'.

At Texeira, a town about as long as its station platform, we are stopped for an hour or so while everyone relaxes from the heat of the day and the annoyance of our train's arrival. This being a boat train, and everyone in transit, the affable Alfândega is far too polite to open anybody's bags: he sits in his office, signing papers, and scratches a three days' growth of beard with meditative pen. In the policeman's office there are questions: where am I going, what am I doing . . . never mind, no one seems to care. Everywhere there is a hint of down-at-heel gentility and prideful poverty, of leaving-until-tomorrow-what-ought-to-be-done-today, which is agreeable after the money-frenzied bustle of Belgian occupation. Only the police chief, stamping along the platform with suggestive cane, looks as though he remembered Diogo Cão and the grandeur that was Portugal. Only the police chief, that is, and the currency notes: for they are all history, and carry wistful lithographs of Diogo Cão presenting his Congo hostages to John II in 1485, of conquistadores founding Benguela in 1617, of Catholic dignitaries evangelizing the grateful savage. . . .

The Congo African driver gets out at Texeira and is replaced by a White driver, Angola being a country of cheap White labour as well as of very cheap African labour. For everything is relative; and a junior Portuguese police officer in Angola, I find out later, is paid rather less than a skilled African craftsman in the Belgian Congo.

At Texeira the engine summons all the steam it can, belches

N   193

flames into the evening sky, and hauls due westward into a crimson sunset. It has another seven hundred miles or so before it reaches the coast, and it will take two nights and two days to devour them.

Crossed from the far interior, Angola seems a wide wilderness of empty plains and tormented tufous hills apparently without population. Half of these seven hundred miles consists of plateau country — a continuation of the great southern upland which runs down into Rhodesia, where the soil is often bad and irrigation as yet impossible: much of it is the ill-famed 'Hungry Country' which depleted sorely the marching ranks of slaves in days gone by.

Further westward, towards Nova Lisboa, the mountains begin. They are tall and tooth-edged, etched finely along the southern skyline, climbing near by to isolated peaks above green plantation valleys where rivers run and waterfalls are many. This is good country; southward again, among other mountains, there is fly-free grazing for cattle. Into these southern mountains, long ago, there came Boer trekkers from the 'British enslavement' of the Transvaal and the Orange Free State; and some of these are still in Angola, where they form little lost communities entirely shut within themselves, half-savage, half-forgotten. Here, too, is a prospering colony of Germans who were subsidized by the Nazi Government which had thought that it would annex Angola when the war was won — and, so the Portuguese say, had designated *Gauleiters* and the rest from appropriately masterful German settlers.

The rolling stock of the Benguela Railway, carrying copper and other minerals to the coast and industrial equipment for the Congo back from the coast, proceeds across it at a leisurely pace. More properly, this rolling stock in 1954 was better named reeling stock, for much of the permanent way was still laid on sand and loose earth. Yet it would be miserly to grudge a word of celebration to the Benguela Railway, which has two reasons for fame. The first is that its engineering achievement is amazing, for it crosses not only the empty inland plateau but also the cliff-sided mountains which make a belt of desert along the coast. The second is that it is the only British-owned railway in this day and age, so far as I know, which is worked by forced labour.

It is not entirely or even mainly worked by forced labour. Exactly how many slaves it has I discovered only when I could reach Senhor Escudero, at railway's end in Lobito where the long Atlantic waves reach over to Brazil. Senhor Escudero is the general manager of the Benguela Railway, whose stock is held as to 90 per cent by a well-known British holding company, Tanganyika Concessions, registered in London until 1952 and in Southern Rhodesia since then.

A gentle Portuguese upon whom a call for courtesy is happily irresistible, Senhor Escudero occupies a modest little wooden bungalow, set among tall flowers, where the seaward-reaching spit of Lobito's harbour narrows to a strand between the sheltered water and the open sea. He is strongly of the opinion that there is no such thing as labour trouble in Angola, nor any sort of trouble; and he is happy to tell me anything I would like to know.

I would like to know how many forced workers he has. These are known in Angola as *contradados*, contract workers, just as they were in the days of Nevinson's visit and the Cadbury *v. Standard* case, when they were also known as *serviçaes*. Needless to say, nobody in Angola admits the word 'slave': nevertheless, as we shall see, *contradados* are really slaves.

Senhor Escudero calls for the files. Altogether, we find — examining the files with the curiosity of visitors to a collection of rare stamps — that Senhor Escudero has 13,453 *voluntários* and 2018 *contradados*. Not a bad proportion, he thinks: most companies have a much higher proportion. I find later that this division of Africans into 'voluntary workers' and 'contract workers' is routine practice in Angola: a practice which speaks for itself.

There is much less cruelty than in Nevinson's day. Otherwise the system is unchanged; and it is probable, on the evidence I

195

collected, that there are now many more slaves in Angola than there were fifty years ago. In those old-fashioned days they brought down the *contradados* by foot, marching them crazily across the Hungry Country beyond Silva Porto and down through the mountains along the still older trails of the pirate days before full-blown slavery was abolished. 'The whole length of the path [into the interior]', Nevinson recorded of his journey from the coast, 'was strewn with white bones — the bones of slaves.' The end of these trails still draw white scars on the grey and violet hills behind Benguela and Catumbela, where the Middle Passage once began. But the British holders of Benguela Railway stock in 1954 will be relieved to hear that nowadays their slaves are brought down in trucks and railway wagons, and almost always survive the experience. Furthermore, they are even paid a small wage, because it is in fashion nowadays to cosset Africans; and medical services sometimes exist in bricks and mortar and medical staffs as well as on paper.

Senhor Escudero and his friends consider that all is well with Angola, that Angola is a splendid colony. They see nothing strange or wrong in the mass employment of forced workers: far from concealing the system, they talk to me freely of it and think it a splendid thing.

Among the gardens of Lobito Senhor Escudero turns to me with quietly meditative eye. 'Angola,' he says dreamily, 'it's a little corner of Paradise in Africa, I always say.'

A special kind of Paradise. As I was to see later, the files of the Native Affairs Department at Luanda, its capital, show 379,000 *contradados*, or forced workers who are really slaves. A corner of Paradise that is rather nearer the other place, perhaps, than most.

NINETEEN

A MODERN SLAVERY

FORCED labour in one form or another has existed in all African colonies. It continues to exist, although only occasionally and in rural areas, in a number of British colonies. For the evidence of that one need only consult the records of the International Labour Office. What is remarkable about the present industrial revolution in parts of Africa is precisely that the need for forced labour in manufacturing and mining passes away: the people flood to the towns in search of work and wages. A relatively small amount of forced labour was still being exacted in the Belgian Congo in 1954, but only in the rural areas and mainly for the building and maintenance of roads.

Angola is peculiar because forced labour remains the flywheel of the country's whole economy. With one or two exceptions along the coast, as we shall see, Angola belongs to imperialism's pre-industrial past.

How could this general use of forced labour survive so long? Outright slavery persisted in Angola until less than a century ago, although the export of slaves had come to an end a little earlier. It was difficult to continue the export of slaves, because British and other men-of-war could and did stop the slavers sailing from the coast. Yet slavery inside Angola continued for long after it was abolished elsewhere.

The end of the oversea slave trade was indeed warmly welcomed by European settlers in Angola, for it meant a better supply of slave labour in the country itself. But the abolition of internal slavery encountered what the *Grande Enciclopedia Portuguesa* calls *grandes e nefastas resistências* among men who would otherwise face 'ruin'.(133) A decree of 1858 had declared, during a liberal turn in Portuguese government at home, that

197

internal slavery in the Portuguese oversea territories should end in 1878, twenty years later; and in 1869 there intervened another few years of 'liberalism' when, as a Portuguese writer, Senhor da Silva Cunha, indignantly says, 'the courts protected the sacred right of idleness'. But in 1875, three years before internal slavery was supposed to end, another decree announced that the ex-slaves were to labour for two years in the service of their ex-owners. Outright slavery was transformed into periodical slavery; and it is this periodical slavery, or 'contract labour', which has continued ever since.

After all, what was the use of a colony if the Natives could not be made to work? Clearly enough, a genuine end to slavery would have witnessed the massive return of slaves to their villages, where they would have resumed their tribal life with its simple code of labour linked to subsistence, and perhaps a little trade in rubber, ivory and bees-wax. The Portuguese were willing to allow this no more than any other colonizing Power: because they were poorer, less up to date, and came themselves from a country still largely pre-industrial in its attitude to work and thought, they devised means of coercion which were more primitive, more generally adopted, and perhaps more cruel than elsewhere.

The decree of 1875, which transformed outright slavery into periodical slavery, said that only 'declared vagrants' could be compelled to enter into 'labour contracts'. This failed to answer; and in 1899 another decree affirmed that *all natives* were subject to the obligation, 'moral and legal', to acquire by labour the means of subsisting or 'bettering their social condition'. This law 'consecrated the principle of forced labour'.(134) The system for which it stands is in full force today. Every African male in Angola, or in practice those above the 'apparent age' of about ten years old, is obliged to show that he has worked for six months in the year previous to inquiry, or is working at the time of the inquiry. Otherwise (up-country one should generally write 'in any case'), any African male who falls into the hands of any investigating inquiry, from the cashier's mistress up to the Governor-General himself, is practically certain to be sent for forced labour.

This is not what the constitution of Portugal says. Dr. Salazar's *Carta Organica* incorporates the rules of the Labour Code of 1928 and another labour decree of 1930; and it reads splendidly. Nothing could be more liberal and tolerant: nothing, equally, could be more unreal. Thus Article 19 of the decree of 1930, incorporated *en bloc* into the *Carta Organica*, states that 'all regulations whereby the State may undertake to furnish Native labourers to any enterprises working for their own economic development' are forbidden; and that 'all regulations whereby Natives in any part of Angola may be compelled to furnish labour for such enterprises under any pretext whatsoever' are equally forbidden. But these prohibitions are not worth the paper they are written on. They are for outside consumption, just as were King Leopold's magnificently humanitarian decrees in the days of the Congo Free State: they in no way reflect what actually happens.

Before going on to see what actually happens, it may be well to see why Britain, more than any other Power apart from Portugal, is responsible for this state of affairs. British protection has usually afforded Portugal an ample shield against criticism. The old Anglo-Portuguese alliance had assured Portugal not only of England's aid and protection for Portugal itself, but also for Portugal's oversea possessions. After its removal from Brazil's overlordship in the nineteenth century, Angola became in fact, if not in theory, a protected satellite of the British Empire. So much was this the case, indeed, that British Governments more than once felt able to offer Portuguese colonies to Germany, so as to assuage (as it was hoped) imperial Germany's desire for colonial expansion, for *Lebensraum*.

This dusty little corner of imperial history deserves recalling. In 1898 a secret Anglo-German treaty divided the Portuguese African colonies into economic spheres of interest between Britain and Germany: Germany's share was the southern part of Angola, adjoining what used to be German South-West Africa, as well as the northern part of Portuguese East Africa (Moçambique) adjoining Tanganyika, then a German possession. The remainder fell to Britain. 'At that time it was anticipated that financial difficulties might compel Portugal to sell her colonies, in which case Germany would be able to purchase her share.'(135) Portugal became alarmed at this, and managed in 1899 to conclude another Treaty of Windsor which recalled and reinforced the British protective role assumed in an earlier treaty of 1661. And in that same year of 1899, as we have seen, the Portuguese decreed periodical slavery in Angola for all African men.

Even so, the British Government remained of a mind that Portuguese territory could properly be used to appease the Kaiser's imperial ambitions. Prince Lichnowsky, German ambassador in London just before the First World War, says in his memoir that a member of the Cabinet had told him, on this point, that: 'We don't want to grudge Germany her colonial development.' Sir Edward Grey, then British Foreign Secretary, 'intended to demonstrate his goodwill towards us', continues Lichnowsky, 'but he also wished to assist our colonial development as a whole, as England hoped to divert the German development of strength from the North Sea and Western Europe to the Ocean and to Africa'. Just as a later generation of British statesmen would feel able to sacrifice Czechoslovakia to German imperialism, Sir Edward Grey and his colleagues (or some of them) felt able to be generous over Moçambique and Angola.

Pursuing this idea in 1913, Sir Edward Grey drew up with Lichnowsky, acting for the German Government, a new secret treaty when, Lichnowsky says: 'I succeeded in making the new agreement [superseding that of 1898] fully accord with our wishes and interests. The whole of Angola up to the twentieth degree of longitude [i.e. the coast and practically the whole of the interior] was assigned to us; we also acquired the valuable islands of San Thomé and Principe, which are north of the equator and therefore really in the French sphere of influence, a fact which caused my French colleague to enter strong but unavailing protests.' The Germans further obtained a treaty right to the northern part of Moçambique, as in 1898, and were even offered an option on the Belgian Congo: but this last they refused, nominally in view of 'Belgian susceptibilities'.(136)

A vain act of appeasement, as events would quickly show: but interesting as a clinical example of the imperial attitude towards Africa and Africans. In this new treaty draft of 1913 — for it was never actually signed, the Germans insisting on keeping it secret, and Grey being willing to keep it secret for no longer than a year — the two interested Powers, Britain and Germany, were not to await Portugal's willingness to sell her colonies, as in 1898: on the contrary, they might step in when they would, ostensibly because of Portuguese misrule: and as soon as one of them had 'stepped in' and taken its share, the other was automatically supposed to grab the rest. It was a nice piece of hypocrisy to suppose that Germany or Britain really cared about the fate of Africans in Angola: if Britain's day of outright massacre of Africans had lately ended with the Matabele war, Germany had smashed the Herero and other peoples of South-West Africa with a brutality which made gentlemen of Portuguese slavers.

Awaiting this happy outcome of 'Portuguese misrule', Britain in the role of Portugal's protecting Power did little more than 'note with interest' the disclosures and the protests of inconvenient travellers like Nevinson and Harris. Through all these years the quantity of forced labour used in Angola varied only with the ups and downs of colonial export prices. When times were brisk, there was need of many slaves: when times were bad, as they were in the early 'thirties, the slaves might be left in their villages where they need fear nothing worse than starvation and disease.

Since the depression of the 'thirties, as I have suggested, the quantity of forced labour has gradually increased, although it is hard to say by exactly how much. In its 1929 edition the

Encyclopædia Britannica quotes an evidently official estimate of 'labour required' in Angola at a total of 378,800, of whom some 150,000 were in 'Native industries and Native agriculture'. In 1954, by contrast, official figures in Angola showed 379,000 forced workers (none being in Native industry or agriculture) and another 400,000 voluntary workers. Against none of these proceedings in slavery has any British Government ever made effective protest.

How does the system work? One has to distinguish between theory and practice to the extent of remembering that the practice, thanks to the corruption and traditional indifference of Portuguese administration, is always much worse than the theory.

The theory is simple enough. It was explained to me by one or two large employers of forced labour, like Senhor Monteiro of the Cassequel sugar plantations and Senhor Escudero of the Benguela Railway Company, by highly placed administrators like Senhor Pereira who was head of the Native Affairs Department in 1954, and by other keen observers whose names I shall not repeat.

Employers who want forced labour indent for it from the Government-General. The Government-General allocates *contradados* according to a theoretical calculation of the number available for conscription at any one time. Approved demands for forced labour — sometimes amended, sometimes (for bigger and wealthier private employers) imposing certain medical and housing amenities — are sent to local administrators up and down the country: and the *chefe de posto*, through his local chiefs and headmen, is then obliged to conscript the number of men required by the indent or indents which he receives. I was able to inspect a number of these indent forms in the offices of the Government-General at Luanda; and also to secure copies of 'contracts' under which these forced workers are conscripted. Most of these contracts, as Senhor Escudero said, are collective contracts. They bear no relation to an agreement reached by two sides to a bargain. They are generally signed by the *chefe de posto* and the Native chief or headman who brings in the conscripted men; and are always mere window-dressing for a world which disapproves of forced labour.

Chiefs or headmen who might fail to bring in the required number of conscripted men were mercilessly flogged until a couple of years ago, according to reliable opinions I received: lately, I am told, there is less flogging than there used to be. There is no less acute a demand for forced workers, however; and chiefs or headmen are often obliged to seize men who have only just returned from a previous period of forced labour.

A correspondent of *The New York Herald-Tribune* described exactly the same system on February 15th, 1948: 'When an Angola plantation owner requires labour, he notifies the government of his needs. The demand is passed down to the village chiefs, who are ordered to supply fixed quotas of labourers from their communities. If the required number is not forthcoming, police are sent to round them up.'

According to the Labour Code, of course, the licensed recruiting agents, or *angariadores*, have to find 'voluntary contract workers' whom they must then take to the local *chefe de posto* for verification of 'contracts' and assurance that the interests of the workers are respected. But that is all just talk, like so much else in Angola where 'Native interests' are in question.

In theory, too, payment for the delivery of forced workers is forbidden. But this is seldom the case in practice. I believe it is still common form for employers to bribe Portuguese officials, and even African headmen, in order to secure priority on the delivery of slaves. Often enough, apparently, forced workers are 're-sold' by a private money transaction before they have even returned from their current term of labour service.

Advances made under the Portuguese Republic, and associated especially with the governorship of Norton de Matos, seem lost to sight. Such, at least, is the considered opinion of a Portuguese investigator, Henrique Galvão, in a report to his Government dated January 22nd, 1947. Although Senhor Galvão was at that time an ardent supporter of the Salazar dictatorship, and a member of the Portuguese National Assembly, his terrible report was never made public; and it is not difficult to see why. Two years later, however, it was published by the underground opposition; and two years after that its author, together with members of the 'legal opposition', was seized upon charges of plotting a *coup d'état* (they had supported the candidature of Admiral Meireles in 1951) and thrown into prison, where, it is said, he remains at the time of writing.

Senhor Galvão found that conditions in Portuguese Guinea and in Moçambique were somewhat better than in Angola. They evidently had need to be. He laments — and the position today is almost certainly worse than in 1946, the date of which Galvão was writing — the massive way in which, as we have seen, the people flee these colonies. 'It is clandestine emigration,' he writes, 'which, ever more rapidly, drains away the peoples of Guinea, Moçambique, and Angola; and which, in Angola, is largely responsible for the extremely grave state of depopulation (*anemia demográfica*) one notes in this colony. There stay at home only the old and infirm, the women and children and incapable. . . .' He estimates a permanent loss by emigration from these three sparsely populated colonies over the years 1937-46 of no fewer than one million people. 'Even in the Belgian Congo, where things are far less good than in Rhodesia and Nyasaland, the system is less damaging to Native interests than in Angola.'

He speaks of sickness and death. 'I maintain', he says, 'that health services for the Natives of Angola, Moçambique, and Guinea — whether paid for by Government or imposed by Government on private employers — are, with rare exceptions, non-existent.' It is 'not surprising that infant mortality reaches a figure of 60 per cent, and that a death-rate as high as 40 per cent is not rare among workers themselves'. Angola, he concludes, 'rapidly nears catastrophe'.

It is well to remember that Galvão wrote all this after travelling, as he says, many thousands of miles in Government service and with access to persons and authorities of all kinds and every degree. The clearest evidence of what is really happening to the peoples of Angola, he finds, 'rests in the steep fall of the birth-rate, in the growing number of sick and infirm, and in the general death-rate, depending as this largely does on conditions of labour recruitment and of labour itself'.

At any rate in Angola, he could find little difference between forced and 'voluntary' labour — except that the first was generally conscripted by Government, and the second by private employers or their paid agents.

He thought the worst aspect of the labour position lay 'in the attitude of the State to the recruitment of labour for private employers. Here the position is worse in Angola than in Moçambique; because in Angola, openly and deliberately, the State acts as recruiting and distributing agent for labour on behalf of settlers who, as though it were quite natural, write to the Department of Native Affairs for "a supply of workers". This word "supply" (*fornecer*) is used indifferently of goods or of men'.

After describing the methods of forced recruitment used by Government for its own purposes and for private employers, Galvão concludes that: 'In some ways the situation is worse than simple slavery. Under slavery, after all, the Native is bought as an animal: his owner prefers him to remain as fit as a horse or an ox. Yet here the Native is not bought — he is hired from the State, although he is called a free man. And his employer cares little if he sickens or dies, once he is working, because when he sickens or dies his employer will simply ask for another.' High death-rates among forced workers, he says, have never in his experience debarred an employer from being supplied with more men.

He found the same noxious system of 'forced cultivation of selected crops' — usually for the benefit of big European companies — which long existed, and still partially exists, in the Belgian Congo. Yet in Angola even this attempt at higher production is frustrated by the general abuse of labour. 'Action of the authorities against Native farmers and stock-breeders, or those who collect bees-wax and rubber, is often violent in order to make them produce more. Yet these same authorities, driven by orders, circulars, and instructions from the central administration, do not hesitate to take these Native workers away from their work and send them to "contract" labour. It was in this way that there evaporated all hope of producing rice in the Pombo and Cuango: first a forceful campaign to produce rice, and then, when the land was ready, an order for the rice workers to go away on "contract".'

The underlying violence of this system is obvious even to a brief visitor. The everyday 'hand-to-hand' violence can be obvious only to those who travel the country back and forth, or live there. It was certainly obvious to Senhor Galvão. Summing up at the end of his report, he lists eight reasons why 'employers make the labour problem difficult':

'1. Resistance by all means to a wages policy that would be fair, economic, and socially just;

'2. Bad treatment of workers; the duty to provide clothing, food and medical aid is generally forgotten; the Native is considered as a beast of burden; there is indifference to the worker's physical and moral health, to his sickness or his death;

'3. Waste of labour, which is used as though it were abundant;

'4. Quality and character of recruiting agents;

'5. Movement of workers from one place to another without regard to abrupt changes of climate — especially severe on those who must go from the interior to the coast;

'6. Extortions practised on the Natives by traders;

'7. Indifference to Native housing conditions;

'8. Vestiges of the attitude of extermination (*espirito de exterminio*) remaining from the end of the last century and the opening years of this one.'

Those who would doubt the veracity of this report might consider the cry of alarm sent up by the all-powerful Angola Diamond Company in its report for 1953 (and repeated and reiterated in its report for 1954 — see *Diario do Governo*, No. 163

of July 13th, 1954). In 1953 this company pointed out that the condition of the people of the diamond-mining district of Lunda 'was grave and well known, as are also its consequences in the physical impoverishment and social circumstances of the people. To this we have repeatedly called the attention of the Government-General. Much more than a company problem, it is indeed a national problem calling for urgent remedy'. And in 1954 — after bitterly lamenting the Government's decision to reduce the diamond-mining 'contract period' from eighteen to twelve months, and pointing out that this obliges them to 'contract' the same worker over and over again — the company's report says quite baldly that 'the battle for labour recruitment in the Lunda, so as to meet our needs, reacts directly — given the scarcity of fit workers in the District — on the critical state of the population, and increases its physical debilitation (*enfraquecimento físico*)'. To provide America and Europe with diamonds, that is, these Angolan people must pay with their lives.

Lately the Portuguese appear to have made an effort to improve the quality of their administration, although the system itself remains as it was. As the 1954 report of the diamond company explicitly says, the number of forced workers supplied by Government to private employers is actually going up, not down. Every now and then, it is true, there is legal action against officials who have too obviously taken bribes, or who, to employers' annoyance, have 'sold' forced workers twice over at the same time. In 1951 the *Boletim Oficial de Angola* notes that: 'David Nunes Lelinho was dismissed from the office of *Chefe de posto* of the administrative personnel of Angola for its having been proven in an administrative investigation that in exchange for facilities conceded in the recruitment of Native labourers in the area of the post of Cuma, where he had served from 1939 to 1941, he had received the sum of 10,000 angolars from the *Sindicato de Industria e Comercio de Peixe do Distrito de Benguela* (Industrial and Commercial Fishing Syndicate of Benguela District), 6000 angolars from the *Empreza Piscatoria de Angola*,

Angola. Perhaps the one exception — an aspect of American military investment — concerns the new highway which now runs from a point on the Benguela Railway, about seventy miles from the Congo frontier, to Chingola in the Northern Rhodesian Copperbelt, and represents both an alternative exit for Congo and Rhodesian ore and a ready-made railway bed in case of need. No doubt this highway is linked in some strategic concept with the 6000-foot asphalt runway which American money completed early in 1954 at the lost little interior town of Vila Luso, which is also on the railway. This runway was completed in the winter of 1953-54 at high speed, and with no evident regard for cost: all the asphalt was brought from the coast, six or seven hundred miles away.

Forced labour is also in general use on sugar, coffee, sisal and other European-owned plantations. Dr. Pereira, of the Native Affairs Department, told me that the Government allows 'a theoretical average' of thirty-three 'contract workers' for every hundred hectares (220 acres) of plantation; and the men are conscripted in the way I have described. Conditions are said to be bad on most of these plantations, and wages vary from about four escudos a day (about one shilling) for forced workers to rather less for 'free workers'. A British admirer of Angola wrote in 1928 that rural wages came out 'at about $2\frac{1}{2}$ to 3 escudos a day'.(138) Yet prices will at least have trebled in the interval. Not only are there more plantation workers in Angola now than there were in 1928; in real terms they are also paid less.

There is no point in trying to assess the degree of poverty of these people, for their poverty is absolute. They live in the desert lands between starvation and bare survival. Poll taxes varying between 100 and 280 escudos a year (between 25s. and 70s.) may consume most of the cash which an Angolan 'contract worker' will actually receive at the end of his 'contract'. That this is no exaggeration is suggested by a case I came across of a lad who had returned from two years' 'contract labour' in the maritime fisheries of Porto Alexandre: after paying his taxes from the 'balance of wages' which he received at the end of these two years, he had just enough money to buy a second-hand pair of trousers and a second-hand jacket. Another lad from these fisheries, returning in the same batch but after completing a *four years*' 'contract', found that after paying his taxes (for four years) he had exactly 250 escudos, or £3 2s. 6d. Conditions on the plantations up-country (though not along the coast) appear to be even worse than this.

Thirdly, there are the diamond mines of the Lunda province, an offshoot of De Beers, the Forminière and American diamond interests, with a small Portuguese participation. This Angola Diamond Company is popularly said to be a state within a state. It possesses a prospecting monopoly over five-sixths of the entire colony, and a labour conscription monopoly over most of the Lunda province, a country half the size of England. This labour monopoly makes hay, of course, of the *Carta Organica's* assurance that African workers are free to choose their employer; but nobody minds a little thing like that. Africans have to pay money-taxes. With the steady destruction of their subsistence economy, they often need money for themselves. Over most of the Lunda province they can generally obtain money only by working for *Diamang*, as the company is called; so that in this important case there is little but a name to distinguish 'free' from forced labour.

Far from their railway line, these mines are hard to visit; and a special permit from Lisbon is required. I did not visit them; but I was able to talk to experienced residents in the area of recruitment, as well as to two or three officials of the company. According to Captain Mario Costa, its agent in Luanda, the company had in 1954 about 11,000 'free workers' and about 4000 forced workers, although other reports give a higher figure for the second. Other reports also allege that forced workers are often prevented from returning home after their year's 'contract period' is over, and are made to serve a second year.

Wages are not exactly generous. Captain Costa was unable

to detach himself from more important matters for more than a few moments, but volunteered the information that 'free workers' at the mines were generally paid *less* than forced workers. Why? 'Because,' said Captain Costa, looking up with some surprise from his desk in the company's graceful eighteenth-century offices at São Paolo de Luanda, 'they are *un petit peu forcés, n'est-ce pas?*' The 'free workers', that is, are paid less because they need not be conscripted — because, that is, they are local men who have to earn money and cannot earn it elsewhere. A generous company, *Diamang*.

To this small piece of sordid information I was able to add something a little more definite by consulting a number of coloured wooden graphs erected (however strangely) for publicity purposes outside Captain Costa's door. On these boards the company has evidently intended to advertise the splendours of its 'social policy', although the effect on the visitor is not exactly warming. I quote from them. In 1947 the company had 17,500 African workers, of whom 5500 were provided 'by intervention of the authorities' — that is, were forced workers. All these African employees, 'free' and forced, received 10,050,000 angolars in wages and rations, and a further 4,450,000 angolars in 'various goods'. This gives an average money-kind wage of 830 angolars for each worker in 1947, or about £10 10s. a year. In 1947, the company paid about 32 per cent a share.

In 1953, as the company's annual report says, the number of contract workers recruited directly by the company itself 'was sensibly less than the highest figure previously registered under this heading, in 1949, but the number of contract workers supplied by the authorities — already 6235 men in 1952, or many more than ever before that — again increased to 7055'. This, be it noted, in spite of *Carta Organica* and of laws which specifically forbid, 'under any pretext whatsoever', the provision of forced labour to private employers.

Between 1947 and 1954, according to the same source, forced workers in the diamond mines were paid exactly 67

A MODERN SLAVERY

escudos a month, or about 16s. In April of this year the Government ordered that diamond wages should be raised to 120 escudos a month, or, as the company indignantly says, nearly double the previous wage. Incredible though it may seem, the company then goes on to praise itself for its generosity in continuing to pay forced workers this wage of 16s. a month for a 12-month contract instead of an 18-month contract, 'notwithstanding our right, in face of the law, to reduce it'. What the relationship between Government and company is really like, moreover, is clear from the annual report's reassurance to stockholders, on this matter of wages, that 'discussions are now proceeding with the Government-General in an effort to reach agreement on an increase in wages which might be thought reasonable. . . .'

Hard pressed by such wage demands, the company fortunately benefits from a special dispensation. In the limpid words of *Skinner's Mining Yearbook*, the Angola Diamond Company 'is exempt from taxation both as to import duties on plant and materials and export duties on diamonds'. It may be noted in passing that medical missionaries in Angola — mainly Americans and Canadians — are not only not exempt from import duties on such things as steel window-frames for hospitals, but have to pay duty even on imported bandages and drugs.

Here in all its pristine truth is a prime example of the great imperial myth that 'Africa is poor'. Nothing could seem poorer than the Lunda province: verily, it is a kind of desert. There is money for nothing, scarcely even to pay a poor wage to Portuguese district officers. There are next to no schools, next to no social services of any kind. And yet . . . the labour of Africans in this Lunda province is nonetheless sufficient to assure the profits of foreign diamond shareholders year after year, decade after decade. Of shareholders who do not even pay the import duties which over-worked and impoverished missionaries have to pay. Some people call this 'developing Africa': others, more simply, call it plunder.

It is true that the diamond company makes a contribution

213

to the public treasury of Angola: for 1953 this contribution was of the order of 87 million escudos (about £1,100,000), but the net profit for the same year, paid to oversea shareholders, was 121 million escudos (about £1,500,000), while net profit accumulated from the previous year's accounts, and paid out in 1954, amounted to another 146 million escudos (about £1,750,000). This gives some idea of the scale of tribute which diamond shareholders exact from this ruined land.

'Improvement in the general condition of rural Africans?' I listened to the opinion of a European doctor long resident in the country. 'I see none. Nutritionally, they are worse off on the whole than they were when there was more forest and wild life. The mosquitoes, ticks, flies are the same as ever. Tuberculosis must have increased ten-fold in the last twenty years.' Senhor Galvão was of the same mind: and the same opinion may be read between the lines of the diamond company's reports.

Only along the coast, west of the mountains which lift their silver ridge above the ocean, can one detect signs of gradual change towards something better.

TWENTY

COAST OF SORROW

THE Portuguese are polite to visitors, which makes the business of collecting facts more pleasant than could otherwise be possible. I met no one more polite than Senhor Escudero, whose devotion to the British shareholders of the Benguela Railway Company deserves their warm thanks. His 2000 'contract workers' — and it would be discourteous to call them anything else in Senhor Escudero's gentle presence — are treated better than most forced workers in Angola today. They receive a fairly satisfactory ration scale, and comparatively good housing is provided for them in the places where they are forced to work. Indeed, forced workers in Senhor Escudero's employment are with one or two other exceptions the only Africans in Angola, so far as I could see, in connection with whom it is permissible to use the word 'housing'. All the rest live in huts and hovels which only Portuguese courtesy could manage to describe as houses.

Their morals, at any rate, are well cared for. Second highest on the list of Portugal's civilizing exports to Angola is wine; and drunkenness is now a social scourge in all African urban quarters. But Senhor Escudero's forced workers receive only one-quarter of their wages during their time of work. 'Ils ne touchent', said Senhor Escudero with an exquisite choice of language, 'qu'un quart de leurs appointements.' Since their 'salaries' are four or five angolars (or escudos — a synonymous term) a day, this means that forced workers in British employment in Angola receive during their period of labour conscription exactly threepence or fourpence a day. 'In case', he added, 'they spend too much.' Also, no doubt, to dissuade them from running away before their 'contract period' is over.

The other three-quarters of their 'appointments' are paid,

at least in theory, at the end of their 'contract period': in practice, the balance of these earnings is filtered through the hands of a generally impoverished administrator and an always impoverished African headman, with results which are painful for the recipient. This practice of paying forced workers only a small part of their earnings during their 'contract period' is universally enforced, and is widely alleged to be one of the ways in which administrators are 'expected' to make good their pitifully low salaries.

Another polite employer who is so convinced of the virtues of the system that he speaks of it with enthusiasm is Senhor Monteiro, general manager of the Cassequel sugar plantations which reach in apple-green plenitude along the coastal plain between Lobito and Catumbela. Senhor Monteiro has about 2500 *voluntários* and about 2500 *contradados*, as well as some 500 women who also work for wages on a voluntary basis. He also has about 200 Europeans, so that Cassequel's plantation ratio is about one European to twenty-five Africans. He and Senhor Escudero, be it noted, are certainly among the best employers in all Angola.

Senhor Monteiro pays his *voluntários* a good deal more than his forced workers, thus marking a clear distinction from conditions of service in the interior. The general rate of pay for *voluntários* is 230 angolars a month (nearly £3) with which, however, no rations or housing or clothing are provided. To this there is an important exception in that *voluntários* from the Cape Verde Islands (brought into Angola in growing numbers over the past few years) are paid 100 angolars a month on a three-year 'contract period'. One imagines that these Cape Verdians are really forced workers, but I cannot be sure of this. It is the fact that they are brought over for three years for a total wage-payment — three-quarters of it being made at the end of their service — of 3600 angolars (about £45). They are brought alone, without their families, are treated as forced workers, and, one suspects, are obstructed from going home again at the end of their three years. One would need to visit the Cape Verde Islands to discover the truth of this.

The likelihood that forced labour is now being imported from the Cape Verde Islands becomes larger when one considers the fact that Senhor Monteiro is actually paying Cape Verdians less than his general rate of payment for Angolan forced workers, which is 120 angolars a month (about 30s.).

'We pay them less', he told me, 'because we have to support the cost of their travel here and back again.'

His women workers are receiving the lowest wages of all, about 80 angolars a month (20s.). All forced workers, including the Cape Verdians, are provided with a reasonably good ration scale and housed in little dormitory huts in which eight men are normally expected to occupy one small room. Senhor Monteiro said that such conditions were good: compared with the lot of most forced workers, they undoubtedly are. At Catumbela, moreover, I was shown a new plantation hospital: it seemed to be in working order, had two or three white medical attendants, and a number of African patients.

I asked him what happened when a forced worker refused to work. He looked at me in some surprise.

'Oh, but they will work. They do.'

'Still, supposing they won't?'

'Then we send them to the police station.'

'And what do the police do with them?'

'To men who won't work? Put them in prison, of course.'

Put them in prison: yes, and flog them. Witness after witness (although not Senhor Monteiro) told me this — some nonchalantly, taking the thing for obvious and natural, some with bitter loathing, some with painful memories.

This flogging is usually by a hide whip, a *chicote*. But there is also the *palmatória*. A European in whom I have every confidence, but who is no longer in Angola, has described for me a *palmatória* which he saw in use not long ago. 'It was a sort of mallet carved from one piece of hard wood, with a handle some ten or twelve inches long, the head being a disk some three inches across and an inch and a half thick. On each side of this disk five tapering holes were bored. These were in the pattern of the dots on the five of dice. The way this implement of torture was employed is this. The victim holds one hand out palm up. The operator brings the *palmatória* with a sharp forceful blow on the outstretched palm. Under the force of the blow the flesh is sucked up into these tapering holes. The lessening diameter of the holes pinches the enclosed flesh and produces intense pain. The victim then presents the palm of the other hand and the operator hits it. So the hands are struck alternately with a regular beat for the ordered number of blows.

'The Africans give *palmatória* a name of their own which might be translated "the Pain". A tough individual may take four or five blows in silence, but after that one cannot restrain his cry of anguish. At that very administration and in the time of the same administrator [a man notorious for his cruelty] I have heard him entertaining himself in his office while I waited in the outer office to have documents legalized. A most unforgettable unpleasantness. A heavy blow like hitting a log with an axe, an agonized cry with blow after blow repeating like the ticking of some Poe's infernal clock. The poor secretary nearly perished with embarrassment because an *estrangeiro* was listening in on a national pastime.' This informant thought death would follow 150 blows; others tell me not.

Do forced workers run away?

No, Senhor Monteiro said, forced workers did not often run away. Other inquiries I made enlarged upon the difficulty of running away. Along the coast, divided from the interior by its belt of mountainous desert, there is literally nowhere to run to. Men who take refuge in town, in one or other of the African suburbs or *senzalas* (traditionally: 'slave quarters') which crowd around Lobito and Luanda and the other coastal towns, are liable to be seized for forced labour unless they can show that they are in employment. They cannot become 'voluntary workers' unless their papers are in order; and they cannot get their papers in order unless they can show good reason for their being present in town . . . Running away must generally mean jumping from the frying pan into the fire, with a painful interlude at the police station to separate the one from the other. Obstinate 'deserters' are treated in a more vigorous fashion which I shall describe later.

In this way, although often less humanely, the whole economy of the coast is carried on. European-owned fisheries make extensive use of forced labour. The port of Lobito, vital American and British terminal for the export of Congo ores, is worked by about 600 forced workers conscripted on yearly 'contract period'. The commandant, Senhor Noura, was absent on the day I called at the office of the port authority, but the deputy commandant, whose name I did not catch, told me that they may shortly have to employ many more forced workers, and are building block dormitories for forced workers outside the town. This, apparently, is because American money may now expand the port facilities. One can watch these forced workers on the quayside almost any day of the week. Outside, in the blinding white light of the Avenida de Portugal, one can also watch the lorry-loads of privately-owned forced workers who are brought down by employers wanting to load or unload their goods.

Nobody pretends the system is otherwise. Senhor Monteiro's office gave a grateful shadow, on the day of my visit, to a little group of forced workers who were preparing to depart for the interior, having completed their 'contract period': they lay about in the sun while the little banner they had fashioned from a piece of cotton cloth, tied to a long pole, stood above them against a spreading tree. Senhor Monteiro thought they were probably very happy at the prospect of going home.

Yet the first glimmerings of industrialism begin to work a slow change for the better. I ran into a young American who is operating, together with Portuguese partners, a brand-new saw-mill on the outskirts of Lobito. He 'won't have a contract worker on the site', employs only free workers, pays them more than most people do, and is even breaking new ground by insisting on the payment of overtime. He has an African worker running his concrete-block making plant whose wage is no less than 50 angolars a day (about £18 a month), or twelve times the wage of Senhor Monteiro's forced workers and about seven times the wage of Senhor Monteiro's free workers. There are very few Africans, unless they are clerks, who earn as much as this. A works-locomotive driver at Senhor Monteiro's plant was making 300 angolars a month (£3 15s.), and a bulldozer team-chief (after eight years' service) was making 400 angolars (£5) a month.

At infrequent factories along the coast one may see the beneficial results of this new industrialism. *Textang*, a textile mill outside Luanda, is also employing only free workers, about 700 of them, whose basic wage is 15 angolars a day (compare Senhor Monteiro's average of 8 a day, which is also about the same as the Benguela Railway's average for free workers). A few semi-skilled workers in this mill are making as much as 30 angolars a day, which, as we have seen, is a good wage for these parts. Some of these have become responsible machine-minders and craftsmen; but I am unable to say what their working conditions may be like, because I was allowed no further than a little room inside the gate.

Senhor Pessoa, the ardent young Portuguese patriot who is general manager of *Textang*, explained to me that he has to be careful not to lose his men in police raids searching for forced labour. Every evening the personal books of all his African workers are signed by one or other of the European staff, so that, coming to work next morning, these workers may show the police that they are genuinely in employment. 'And if the police don't see that signature,' commented Senhor Pessoa, 'they'll arrest the man and take him off to the *chefe de posto*.' And the *chefe de posto*, as in duty bound, will send him to forced labour.

These few examples indicate that the shift from forced to free labour, even when employers want it, meets with great difficulties here. This ancient system of coercion is so deeply embedded that change is very slow. One has to look carefully in order to find it at all. Another telling illustration is provided by the monopoly practices of the Banco de Angola, whose attitude might have seemed oddly out of date even to the medieval Fuggers. The Banco de Angola pays no interest on deposits, makes no loans in the ordinary way of business, and extracts as much as $2\frac{1}{2}$ per cent for cashing even the humble traveller's cheque. It is too poor, it argues, to act otherwise: and proceeds to demonstrate its poverty by erecting magnificent offices in Luanda where arcades and balconies ensure that clients may sleep away their irritation, and talk away their zeal for change.

Commerce slumbers. Industry is scarcely born. A foreign businessman wanted lately to start a small factory along the coast, and deposited a considerable sum of money at the Banco de Angola's branch in Benguela. Soon afterwards he decided that he would move his residence to Lobito, about twenty-five miles up the coast. When he applied to the Benguela branch for a transfer of his deposit to the Lobito branch he found that he would have to pay a fee of $1\frac{1}{2}$ per cent: rather than do that, he preferred to draw out the whole sum in notes, pack them in cardboard boxes, and carry them by car to Lobito, where the bank clerks spent a cheerless afternoon counting them in again. Accurately enough, the Banco de Angola reflects the economic condition of the colony. In a slave economy, there is no need for financial efficiency. All may proceed along the weary lines of tradition.

There begins, nonetheless, to be a perceptible difference along the coast between forced and free labour. Up-country, as we have seen, there is practically none. Even if the number of forced workers in the interior is said to be diminishing — which I do not believe — they are replaced by 'voluntary workers' who are recruited by European recruiting agents (employing African sub-agents to whom they may pay 200 or 300 angolars a month); and this voluntary recruitment differs seldom from conscription.

Senhor Pereira — head of the Native Affairs Department and,

of course, an ardent admirer of Dr. Salazar — is typical of an improvement in the calibre of the higher ranks of the administration, as distinct from the lower ranks, which seems to have taken place within the past few years. He would probably like to see a change for the better; and he is not alone in this. The District Commissioner of Luanda showed me where he was about to start building some 2000 new huts for African workers: their average rent, he said, would be 50 angolars a month, a sum which may be compared with the 200 or 300 angolars which 'free workers' are normally able to earn, and most of which must go in the purchase of food.

Even here the system pokes its ugly face through plans for improvement. Among the earliest buildings already completed by the Luanda municipality is a splendid new prison which the District Commissioner insisted on showing me in great detail. It is certainly an improvement on the crowded little lock-up which at present serves that quarter: the day we passed this lock-up some twenty faces were peering through the bars of a big window at the 'free world' outside. Anywhere else it might seem odd to begin building a new African urban quarter by putting up a prison the size of a small town hall; but not, apparently, in Angola.

Here, too, they have built a clinic which was specially unlocked, on the day of my visit, so that we might watch an African nurse washing an African child. I am afraid it was not typical. Medical evidence suggests that the health of Africans is unusually bad, although statistics are almost completely lacking. Yet the whole population of over four millions, according to official figures in April 1954, had no more than 151 doctors. Medical services practically never reach the villages; and preventive medicine seems to be limited to erratic efforts to inoculate for small-pox and sleeping-sickness. Malnutrition is general, and its main effect is in spreading tuberculosis. Various kinds of worm, venereal disease, and other ailments common to Africa add to the physical debilitation of the people; the expectation of life must be among the lowest in the continent.

'Have you seen the maternity wing of the African hospital in Luanda?' a doctor asked me. 'No,' he went on, 'well, I wouldn't put a pig into it.'

If there are only 151 doctors in the colony there are also (see *Boletim Mensal de Estatística*, No. 4 of 1954) only 317 male and female nurses. Many of the fifty State 'hospitals' scarcely deserve the name: even in Novo Redondo, centre of a comparatively rich coffee-growing region, the principal hospital in 1954 lacked all apparatus for radiography and radioscopy. And this at a time when people were flocking to the towns.

At Lobito the African quarter, or *senzala*, lies in simmering confusion at the base of Lobito's seaward-reaching spit. It had about 20,000 inhabitants in 1954, and more were coming every month. Most of its huts and hovels are made of straw and mud, and none of its inhabitants can be said to enjoy anything in the nature of 'security of tenure'. All these people must take their fresh water from five water-points with three taps each; and a Protestant mission has lately, out of its own funds, added a sixteenth tap. This gives a rough average of 1200 people for each water tap, which is rather many in a hot and sticky climate.

In this *senzala* — to round off the picture — there are altogether two schools, one Roman Catholic and one Protestant, with about 250 children between them. Thousands of children have no hope of going to school; and bend their daily efforts, once they are over the 'apparent age' of about ten years old, in escaping the watchful arm of the police, who are likely otherwise to arrest them for 'vagrancy' and send them to forced labour.

The educational system reflects the widespread use of forced labour. In 1951-52 there was less than a half of one per cent of the African population in primary school: and this on the basis of official and therefore optimistic figures. In that year, moreover, no more than 67 Africans were at secondary school; and not one of these could present himself for the *terceiro ciclo* which gives entry to higher education.

Such was Angola in 1954. Even the slums of Africa could nowhere else show anything the like of this.

TWENTY-ONE

SÃO THOMÉ

WHEN people are treated like this, sooner or later they revolt. Yet Senhor Escudero tells me with quiet assurance that: 'We have no troubles in Angola', and he goes on to explain why Portuguese colonial policy is so much more enlightened than British or Belgian colonial policy.

It is true that no great revolt has stirred Angola since 1902, when the Bailundu people gave the Portuguese a good deal more than they bargained for. Portuguese occupation has intensified over the last few decades; a smaller Bailundu rising in 1939 was soon put down. I caught news of a small rising that was said to have occurred in the hills beyond Sá da Bandeira in 1948 or 1949, but was unable to confirm it. There was certainly a rising in the island of São Thomé early in 1953, but this, as we shall see, was something different.

Even so, there are one or two points which seem to have slipped Senhor Escudero's notice; or perhaps he was too polite to mention them.

Both among free workers and among *assimilados* (the Portuguese equivalent of the Belgian Congo *évolués*) there grows an intense awareness of the meaning and savagery of White domination. Religious sects play a part here as they do in the Belgian Congo, although it is a lesser part. Some thirty 'Simonites' were lately arrested and jailed for anti-White agitation, real or imagined, and placed in different jails up and down the country: these 'Simonites' were apparently disciples of a Lower Congo 'prophet'.

Perhaps more significantly, there is a widening belief that the outside world can help to alter life in Angola, once the facts become known. Quite a number of Africans, I think, are now willing to risk their liberty or their lives in order to make these facts known. As someone in Angola said to me, there is here 'a growing nationalist movement among Africans who are trying to get outside intervention, even if it brings down the whole house on their heads'. Even here, dimly and under shadow, one may observe the African awakening.

Growth of industrialism along the coast, slow though it is, helps this trend of protest. New United States investment will certainly strengthen the Portuguese grip on this country, but it may also, in partial remedy of this, promote more industry and break the dead hand of the Bank of Angola. Up to 1954 United States investment had scarcely made itself felt outside quasi-strategic objectives like the port of Lobito, the big air-runway at Vila Luso, and the new road into Northern Rhodesia. But a visit of American officials and private bankers to Portugal in May was accompanied by an announcement that new invest-ment opportunities would be sought both in Portugal and in Portuguese oversea possessions.(139) There is likely to be an increased demand, at any rate along the coast, for genuinely free workers.

All this, though, will be painfully slow. And meanwhile the misery goes on.

'Why don't your *assimilados* form a political grouping here, just like educated Africans in some British and French terri-tories?'

Senhor Pereira shook his head in tender forgiveness of such a silly question. 'There is no sign of that among them here. You know, it's one of the things you simply can't explain . . .' His eyes wandered to the ceiling, he grew ecstatic: 'How can one say — perhaps it is something to do with the Portuguese soul.'

It is also something to do with the Portuguese prison system. At another and more earthy part of our talk that day I had asked Senhor Pereira how many Angolan Africans were now sent to the old slave-and-cocoa islands of São Thomé and Principe, a day's sailing to the northward.

'None from Angola,' he said. The only Africans who were still sent to São Thomé, he went on, were political prisoners —

those with 'strong opinions'. For some time past, since he himself had taken office at Luanda (having come from Moçambique), he had sent an average of perhaps five political prisoners a month to São Thomé. 'Otherwise we send people we do not like to isolated settlements on the coast, south of Moçamedes.' Mainly, indeed, to the half-desert villages on the Bay of Tigers, near the empty frontier of South-West Africa. This steady flow of 'political prisoners' — the term is too narrow, for it includes all who protest against enslavement — bears witness to strong feelings about Portuguese misrule.

Now, São Thomé and Principe were Angola's familiar shadow all through the last fifty years of the nineteenth century, and for most of the present century. It was to São Thomé and Principe that the 'contract workers' of Nevinson's day were taken in bondage, there to work for the rest of their brief lives with seldom or never a hope of return. Even after the international campaign of half a century ago — which Sir John Harris was still conducting with admirable tenacity in 1913 — the islands remained the scene of mass slavery. I believe they still are.

In spite of Senhor Pereira's affirmation to the contrary, there is strong evidence that a trickle of forced workers still goes from Angola to São Thomé and its sister island. Senhor Pereira, no doubt, is the most honest of men; but he tends, in the intervals of working at his files, to become wrapped in contemplation of the Portuguese soul; and the Portuguese soul is not the best point of vantage for seeing what really happens in Angola. Both Senhor Monteiro and Senhor Escudero, who are less concerned with the Portuguese soul and more with the Portuguese pocket, told me that numbers of forced workers go regularly to São Thomé from the mainland; and three Europeans with offices on the Avenida de Portugal, alongside the port of Lobito, also said they often saw convoys of forced workers being taken into the port for transfer to the islands. Yet a growing labour shortage inside Angola does seem to be checking the export of many slaves. There is also some evidence, though it is sketchy,

SÃO THOMÉ

of forced workers being allowed to return from the islands at the end of 'contract period'.

It is difficult to be certain. I could hear of no recruitment in the traditional conscription areas to the east of Nova Lisboa; but shipment from the coast was asserted, as we have seen, by five well-informed Europeans. Furthermore, the law permits of recruitment in Angola. A decree of May 8th, 1946, fixes at 5000 the maximum annual export of Angolese workers to São Thomé.(140) Senhor Escudero thought that the total number of workers on São Thomé might be 10,000 in 1954, and this may be about right. In 1900 the official returns, quoted by Nevinson, showed 19,211 'contract workers' on São Thomé; but the growth of Gold Coast cocoa production since then has certainly lessened the economic importance of the islands. As for the maximum of 5000 forced workers who may now be sent every year, it is worth noting that the average export of slaves in the first few years of this century was in fact little more than 4000 a year. In other words, the 1946 decree changed nothing so far as permitted numbers were concerned.

Nor did it change anything so far as conditions were concerned. Its article 7 states that any contract workers not repatriated owing to the world situation 'are considered as being re-engaged by the same employers as from the date of termination of the first contract, though remaining in the position of awaiting transport for repatriation'.

The whisper of a protest can be heard even in Portugal. There appeared in Lisbon in 1953, printed in Kimbundu and Portuguese on the reverse side of a postcard (but not, as I discovered, passed by the censor) the verses of a song entitled 'The Song of Sabalu'. Here are the first two and the last two verses:

Mon'etu ua kasule   Our son, our younger son
A mu tumisa ku S. Tomé   They have sent him to S. Tomé:
Kexirié ni madukumentu   Because he had no papers.
Aiué!   Aiué!

227

Mon'etu uaririle	Our son he cried, our son
Mama usalukile	And Mamma went mad with
Aiué!	Aiué! [sorrow
A mu tumisa ku S. Tomé.	They have sent him to S. Tomé. [son
—Mam, muene uondo vutuka	— Mamma, he will return, our
Ah! Ngongo ietu iondo biluka	And then our sorrow will depart
Aiué!	Aiué!
A mu tumisa ku S. Tomé.	They have sent him to S. Tomé. [son
Mon'etu k'avutuké	Our son did not come back, our
Kalunga ua mu rié	Death carried him away
Aiué!	Aiué!
A mu tumisa ku S. Tomé.	They have sent him to S. Tomé.

There is indeed a good deal to suggest that these poor devils on São Thomé await 'transport for repatriation' until gathered to their fathers by a yet sterner hand. Labour shortage in Angola has evidently caused an acute shortage of labour on the islands, so that there is a strong temptation for employers and administration — and who shall tell them no? — to keep their slaves for years beyond the legally permitted 'contract period' of four years — and perhaps, like Sabalu, until they die.

Is the word 'slaves' too strong? But consider the plight of these men. They are seized on the mainland: they do not volunteer to go to São Thomé. Once they reach São Thomé they have no remote possibility of leaving without the help of the administration. While there they must work for the employer to whom they are sent. They have no choice of employer: the decree of 1946 reasserts an earlier prohibition on their changing from one employer to another. Should 'difficulties' arise in sending them home at the end of their two years or four years or longer, then they automatically stay in São Thomé. In none of this do they have a choice, nor any freedom to decide their own fate. Then in what manner do they differ from slaves?

Light on all this was shed by the rising on São Thomé of February 1953. News of this bloody event failed to reach the outside world, although a Portuguese officer killed at the time ('decapitated' according to the account I have, when he 'rushed into the jungle after heaving a few grenades') was given a big funeral in Lisbon. In Angola a year later the revolt was still common talk; and rumours of many killed were rife.

I first had wind of it myself when as far distant in the interior as Silva Porto on the edge of the Hungry Country. This was in more or less garbled form and asserted that 'half castes on the island' had plotted to kill all the Portuguese in the local cinema one day. Later and detailed accounts, collected mainly from eye-witnesses, show with reasonable certainty that an attempt at new enslavement lay at the base of the rising. Those responsible for the rising were not the Angolan slaves imported from the mainland, moreover, but the São Thomistas themselves, by tradition a slave-raiding and slave-possessing people (of heavily mixed racial origins) established here since the sixteenth century. São Thomistas have never done forced labour although their skins are seldom white. But in the first weeks of 1953 the governor of the province of São Thomé and Principe, one Gorgulho, issued a decree announcing that all São Thomista adult males should register for 'contract labour'. Evidently the European planters and administration were desperately short of labour, could get none or not enough from the mainland, and were willing to enslave the half-caste population.

'This decree' — of Gorgulho's — 'was posted up on public buildings and was torn down,' writes an informant who happened to be passing through São Thomé on his way to Europe a few days after the rising had occurred. He continues: 'Since the curfew was imposed, no Native dares to be out after nightfall . . . All were agreed that there had been a very considerable loss of life and that a very large number of arrests had been made. One officer and one Angolan soldier were killed during the course of the repressive measures. The number of deaths among the Natives is not known, but some persons placed the figure at "about 200". The number of arrests, likewise, is not known. One of the medical officers of the island ventured a guess that "half the population" had been arrested. It is evident that practically every Native goes about all the time in fear of being denounced and arrested.'

'With regard to possible causes,' says this informant, 'the Whites seem to credit the story that the murder of all White officials and plantation owners (or their agents) was planned, with the subsequent proclamation of independence. The alleged master-mind, a plantation owner with a degree in agriculture from Lisbon, married to a White school-teacher [i.e. the plantation owner in question was a São Thomista mulatto] was arrested with his whole family, but, instead of being sent to Lisbon for trial, is being kept in Principe. The fighting took place at or near Trinidade. . . .'

The man Gorgulho was sacked from his governorship, it is true, and in 1954 the Portuguese Government made a loan of nearly a million pounds to the province of São Thomé and Principe.(141) But the exception proves the rule. So long as an official causes no 'scandal or civil disturbance' which may break through to the outside world, his misdeeds are over-looked, even rewarded. Those few officials who mark a genuine improvement in quality — such as Dr. Pereira, for all his con-templation of the Portuguese soul — are too rare to make much real difference. To mass enslavement of Africans, engrained connivance at brutality, wastefulness, misery, the government of Salazar appears utterly indifferent. Not belonging to the United Nations, making no reports to the U.N. committee for non-self-governing territories, refusing steadfastly to honour any of the conventions on forced labour drawn up by the Inter-national Labour Office to which Portugal does belong, the government of Salazar presents a smiling face to the world and applies the whip in private. (Later, moreover, it promoted Gorgulho.)

It argues, indeed, that there is racial tolerance in Angola; and yet that is not true either. There is tolerance of intermarriage by Portuguese men with African women; there is allowance for literate Africans to call themselves 'civilized', *assimilado*: but even *assimilados* are more and more debarred from the beginnings of equality.

For the levelling effect of industrialism is nullified here by another phenomenon. Salazar's policy is to export to Africa — or at any rate to Angola — thousands of Portuguese peasants who arrive with little more than they stand up in. Between 1940 and 1950 the official census revealed a growth in the European population of 78 per cent — from about 44,000 to over 78,000. In theory these 'poor Whites' are supposed to take up holdings and become settled farmers: 'contract labour' is made available to them. In practice they accumulate along the coast and the railways as a mass of cheap White labour. This means what it always means elsewhere: competition for jobs. Inevitably, the Africans suffer; and, before anyone else, the *assimilados*. Economic discrimination rapidly becomes social discrimination. Restaurants and bars in Angola now carry a sign that is familiar from British territories of White settlement: *Right of Admission Reserved.*

Senhor Monteiro has built a cinema for his African employees and another for his European employees.

'And which do the *assimilados* go to?'

'They don't come in with us,' says Senhor Monteiro, 'I tell you, it's a problem.'

This racial discrimination seems bound to grow worse. Along most of this littoral the wages gap between the top African wage and the bottom European wage is now almost closed. With growing supplies of White labour this means that the African level is bound to be depressed; and it is of this, indeed, that *assimilados* now complain.

The traditional 'liberality' of Portuguese Native policy is in any case a lie when applied to the mass of the population. 'If my wife', said a decent European resident of many years' standing, 'likes to accuse one of our servants of being rude to her, and I take him up to the police station, they'll slash him mercilessly

— hands, arms, face, everywhere. They kick 'em around without mercy.' Flogging is generally admitted. 'If any Native gets political ideas', the same European observed, 'they'll beat them out of him right away.' And they will send him, as Senhor Pereira explained, to São Thomé or the Bay of Tigers. So that he may contemplate the Portuguese soul, no doubt, and properly admire it.

Only the twisting of language can make this system differ from slavery. The last fifty years may have brought improvements here and there; the essentials are the same. In 1904 Nevinson found that slaves were habitually sold along the coast. If that has ceased, there is still plenty of selling of 'contract labour'. Even the expansion of trade has brought little or no relief to Africans, for practically all trading facilities are in the hands of Portuguese or other Europeans. And lately, with what are probably record numbers of forced workers employed in the country's economy, there is laid upon Africans the aggravation of 'poor White' settlement, and a consequent enforcement of racial barriers against even the handful of *assimilados* of whom Salazarist propaganda boasts so much.

Writing of southern Italy, Norman Douglas has recalled a judgment on the Spanish administration of Naples. 'It was a curse of the Spanish administration,' declared a contemporary writer, 'to make the present unendurable and to sow no seed for the future . . . a pattern of what a government should not be.'(142) The judgment may serve for the Portuguese in Angola.

TWENTY-TWO

AFTER THE DELUGE

WITH the urban revolution and some of its consequences, Africans begin to make fruitful comparisons they were practically debarred from making only a few years ago. These new African cities up and down the continent are alive with rumours of what Europeans are doing or not doing, of what Africans have succeeded in achieving or failed to achieve. Even in Angola, apparently shuttered from the outside world, Africans have questioned me on the racialism of South Africa's government, have asked of the Gold Coast and Nigeria whether it was true what they had heard — that Africans there had won nothing less than a measure of self-government. One everywhere finds, faintly or strongly, a sense that the African future cannot be the same, will not be the same, as the African past and most of the African present. For all its bewildering diversity, this continent seems united by a common surge of hope — just as, in the past, it must so often have seemed united by a common acceptance of despair.

Awakening stirs in many forms. It is easy for Europeans to under-estimate its speed. Yet I doubt if any European who shares the confidence of Africans even in small degree, listens even to a few of their intimate thoughts and conversations, is treated even rarely as a trusted equal, can miss the underlifting wave of new ideas.

In part, at least, this is the sharply educational consequence of comparing what happens to Africans under different colonial governments. African advancement appears more and more as a powerful tide which flows strongly forward at one point only to be artificially checked at another, which builds up in seeming standstill only to press forward in its own time, encircles barriers and slowly overwhelms them, advances unequally but nonetheless advances.

Forced workers in Angola apparently know that their lot is peculiar to Portuguese rule. Such discrepancies now become flagrant in almost every field of everyday life. In the Katanga province of the Belgian Congo, Lamba and other African peoples are encouraged to acquire industrial skills: across the border in Northern Rhodesia these same peoples are prevented from doing so by an industrial colour bar. Until lately, Europeans in Northern Rhodesia could be heard declaring — in default of all the evidence of the neighbouring Congo — that 'their Africans' would never be 'any good with machines'. Even today, few Europeans in Northern Rhodesia would take kindly to the idea of travelling in a railway train whose engine crew was African. And yet, in the Congo across the border, all engine crews are African.

Reversing the advantage of the comparison, Africans in Northern Rhodesia have won the right to organize in genuine trade unions, and do it with efficiency and notable effect on wages. Yet Africans in the Congo — often, be it noted, of the very same tribes — are not considered 'ready for trade unions yet'. Nor are Africans in Kenya or a number of other places. But you will scarcely find an intelligent African worker who for a moment accepts this myth: with a growing clarity, he knows that his co-called 'immaturity' is nothing more in fact than employers' fear of workers' organization.

Africans in the Belgian Congo have put nearly four million pounds into savings banks since 1951: Africans in Angola, it is said by their masters, must be driven to work, forced to work — so idle and so feckless are their habits. In Southern Rhodesia a white settlers' government was cautiously moving, in 1954, towards a recognition of the need of their African factory workers (without whom the Southern Rhodesian economy would at once fold up) for security of tenure in the towns where these men must work and live. For years this government refused to face the problem: now that the problem is overwhelming, and the towns are packed with workers who cannot be allowed (and do not want) to return to their villages,

Southern Rhodesian administrators feel 'bold and progressive' in admitting that the problem actually exists. Even now they hesitate to allow Africans to own houses. And yet many thousands of town-dwelling Africans in the Congo own houses. It would seem that it is not the backwardness of Southern Rhodesian Africans which has made them unfit to own houses, but the backwardness of Southern Rhodesian Whites.

Settler after settler can be heard to say that 'we are going too fast with the African'. And yet the very same men are often those whose economic welfare depends on factories manned by African industrial workers whose demands are no more unreasonable, no more subversive of the common good, than the demands of industrial workers all over the world.

One could enlarge the field of comparison. Africans certainly do. They see that their kind of people in the Gold Coast and Nigeria, and in French Africa, have shown themselves capable of voting at political elections, municipal or territorial, and that with no more muddle and confusion than occurs in several European countries. (Indeed, the bribery and corruption and hooligan riot of English electoral history have had no counterpart here.) Yet most Belgians consider one is preaching the millennium if one tentatively suggests that men who can work so well and so intelligently as Africans in the Congo would also vote as effectively as Africans in the Gold Coast. The very word 'politics' in the Congo is matter for general European dismay; and many Belgians have apparently convinced themselves that their opinion genuinely derives from a fear of 'African immaturity' and not from a fear of losing colonial control. But can one seriously argue that a majority of these astonishingly adaptable Congo peoples are more 'primitive' than a majority of people in British West Africa and French Africa? If Africans on one side of Stanley Pool are 'fit to vote', then why not Africans on the other side of Stanley Pool?

If Native Reserves are rejected in the Congo as a policy of ruin, why do they become 'sound government' in Kenya? If passes and movement orders are 'necessary to law and order' for all Africans in the Congo, why can the government of the Gold Coast dispense with them? If Africans in their rural areas are really incapable of helping themselves, as Europeans generally assert they are, how comes it that Africans in the Eastern Region of Nigeria (having a population nearly half that of the Congo) have proved themselves capable of building their own rural roads, village clinics, village schools, village reservoirs, even village shower-baths?

The answer in all these cases, of course, rests in the difference between better government for Africans and worse government for Africans. The contrasts are not contrasts in African capacity for change, or not primarily so: primarily, they are contrasts in European opposition to change. This is a lesson which millions of Africans are now avidly learning.

From a distance, at any rate, there is no more glaring proof of this than the condition of higher and technical education in the Belgian Congo. Here, in the very cradle of an industrial revolution, where government fully accepts the need for building 'an internal market' so efficient and extensive that the Congo may be shielded from slumps in raw material prices, there is practically no technical or higher education worth the name — outside the schools of the Union Minière which I have already described. No more than half a dozen Congo Africans have ever been allowed to go to European universities, or (before the handful which started at the university college in Léopoldville in 1954) to any other university. One understands why. As the Belgian Colonial Minister said in April 1954: 'We have seen that those Natives who have been shown Europe, and given a very advanced education, do not always return to their homelands in a spirit favourable to civilization and to the Mother Country in particular.' In other words, experience in Europe is 'dangerous' for Africans because it tells them the truth about the colonial system.

For all that, Belgians in the Congo are commonly convinced that their reason for withholding university education from Africans (or secondary education but for a few) stems from

236

'African immaturity' and nothing else: I met with polite disbelief when I pointed out that the Gold Coast government had lately opened a higher technical college in Ashanti.

The argument could be pressed from other angles. The reason why municipal elections may be 'dangerous' in the Congo is not because they would lead to bribery, corruption and other social evils. They might lead to these things: Africans are no better than the bulk of humanity, even if they are also no worse. But the reason for refusing municipal elections is that these must infallibly lead to territorial elections, to radical ideas, parties, nationalism — to self-government, independence, the milking or the stopping of profits flowing oversea. Europeans may not understand this: Africans, increasingly, do.

All this says no more than that the effective limit of African development — like everyone else's — depends on circumstances; and that the circumstances of our day and age, thanks to technical and other changes, have greatly extended this effective limit. European administrations are not moving too fast for the *actual pace* of African adjustment, as Europeans often assert, but far too slowly. Flagrantly, colonialism becomes a brake not only on the movement towards greater human freedom, but also — what is after all the same thing — on the movement towards greater human wealth. More and more obviously, the system is perpetuated only at the expense of limiting the possibilities of producing wealth, quite apart, of course, from the possibilities of producing happiness.

Within the terms of what *could* happen, and not of what might have been desirable, this was not always so. Africans who imagine that all would have gone well for them without European intervention are probably in error, though excusably so: they underestimate their historical need for the revolutionary stimulus of other and more advanced cultures. Lacking civilization — in the sense of a literate urban culture such as Europe derived from the Sumerians of the third millennium — African isolation south of the Sahara could have continued to mean something very near stagnation. The supplying of this revolutionary stimulus may be the only moral and material justification for colonial conquest: but it is a real one.

We now reach a turning-point. The justification disappears. Increasingly the usefully destructive period of European contact is seen to be ended. White penetration and conquest have destroyed tribal society over most of Africa, bloodily, blindly, but irrevocably. Nothing remains of the 'noble savage' except the wistful memory of his past and a muddle of beliefs and rituals which have lost their usefulness. Nothing survives of tribalism except the enforced cluttering of 'Native Reserves' with the fragments of impoverished peoples who face despair. Having completed this unlovely but necessary mission, European contact in the form of colonialism exhausts its last conceivable value in terms of human progress. More and more consciously and clearly, these subjected peoples are now able to realize their potentiality only through their own strength and initiative, through the dynamics of their own organization — and no longer through an organization imposed on them by outside dominion.

Already, too, there are signs here and there of this destructive period of European contact being followed by a constructive period. Even when these signs are masked in their revolutionary meaning by old formulas and old ambitions, they emerge in situations which are obviously *different* from all situations in the past.

One need only reflect on the consequence for Africans of the measure of self-government which they have won in the Gold Coast, Nigeria and French Africa, where millions have acceded to modern forms of political organization. Or of the value to Africans, in preparing to build their future, of organizing in effective trade unions in Northern Rhodesia, of working at skilled trades in the Congo, of uniting in defiance of racial oppression in South Africa. Anyone familiar with Africa could extend the list: genuine contrasts with the past begin to multiply.

And already one may see what governing conditions are required if a constructive period of European contact — of outside contact — is to follow the colonial period of contact. There is needed a systematic change in the essential relationship which now links these peoples with the outside world. It is no longer, as it once was, a question of *improvement* within the same system, of a little more here and a little more there — but of a change which will place Europeans and Africans in a new relationship capable of building, on the ruins of African tribalism, a society in Africa that is fitted for the modern world. The master-servant relationship must give way to a relationship of human equality.

Many well-meaing Europeans still like to think that African civilization can best emerge under 'trusteeship', under a modified colonialism. They delude themselves. These great towns of Africa clearly show how limited a reflection of 'civilized values' the acquisitive society of colonialism is capable of achieving among detribalized Africans. No doubt a realist judgment would say that colonialism does not willingly liquidate itself, and that the African civilization of tomorrow will *in fact* emerge under a modified colonialism. But then it will be modified not by illusory notions of 'trusteeship', but by the growing struggle of African peoples who step by step assert their right to equality and independence. And in that case the cost may be high not only to Africans but also to Europeans. Appallingly wasteful in its day of growth, colonialism can be as wasteful in its day of decline. Even today, early in the African awakening, can anyone seriously believe that the cost of holding down the British empire is less than the *general* material good which the British people draw from it? What shareholders receive is one thing: what taxpayers pay is another. For there are few shareholders and many taxpayers.

It was reasonable for Mrs. Jellyby and her Victorian contemporaries to think that European intervention was good for Africa. It was right that Livingstone a hundred years ago, tramping across an Africa ravaged by the slave trade and its consequences, should see in European commerce a powerful agent of change. It was justifiable that another disinterested

239

traveller, Mary Kingsley, should fifty years ago praise in the same sense 'our great solid understuff, the Merchant Adventurers'.(143) The search for profit was not only good for some Europeans: even in face of its immediate consequences, it was also good for most Africans. But no longer. What was once a way of opening up an isolated continent — of joining this lost island of the African tribes to the mainland of humanity — is now an obstruction of that process.

And this, indeed, is widely accepted in Europe by all whose lack of stocks and shares befits them for an unprejudiced judgment. Colonial wars are increasingly unpopular among those who have to fight them. The proposition that 'Africa must advance' is accepted almost universally — and verbally even by those who are doing their best to prevent it. For the most part, the shareholders and direct beneficiaries of colonialism nowadays prefer to eschew imperial enthusiasm, at least in public, and to suggest rather that Britain's only object is to act as a disinterested and friendly trustee or guardian — at high cost to herself, moreover — while the former colonial peoples forge happily ahead to independence. There is quite a revival of the old notion of the 'white man's burden', though in an engagingly new form: the backward colonial areas of the world are pictured as places filled with bold itinerant teams of doctors and welfare workers, scientists and technicians, sweating in the jungle for 'the fluttered folk and wild' who cannot help themselves, and cannot even pay the wages of those who have come to help them.

Such teams certainly exist in Africa, here and there, and do good work. The helicopter which flies regularly over Léopoldville, sprinkling drugs to kill mosquitoes and thus malaria, is an excellent innovation for Africans as well as Europeans. A couple of years ago a Provincial Commissioner in the arid regions of north-western Nigeria was showing me how he had enabled the people of ancient Sokoto to secure piped drinking water. These efforts, and many like them, deserve praise.

Yet they remain exceptions, and small exceptions. They

represent only a tiny fraction of the knowledge and power over nature which the outside world could now give Africa, and Africa could now receive, if only . . . if only it were not for the system which prevents this transfer of knowledge. Why may not Congo Africans become engineers, soil scientists, quantity surveyors, doctors, dentists, and a hundred other desirable things? Not, any longer, because they belong to the tribal world nor because they are unfitted for entry to the modern world, but because the system will not let them. Colonial politics apart, there is no money under this system for the necessary schools.

And money, of course, is the sticking point for Europeans. No longer, perhaps, for a great number of Europeans; but still for a minority with power and influence. If the colonial system is now an obstruction for all Africans and a costly burden for most Europeans, it is still extremely profitable for the few who participate directly in its benefits. Sufficient evidence of this may be had from a few figures. A writer in *The Journal of Business of the University of Chicago* has lately offered in statistical form a splendidly clear illustration of the truth that 'poor colonial countries' have generally produced the capital they require for their own primary development.(144) He finds that the thirteen most profitable rubber plantations in Malaya and Ceylon (established from forty to forty-five years ago) have paid average annual dividends during their lifetimes that range between 23 per cent and 64 per cent. For the five best years in any single case the average annual dividend has ranged from 61 per cent to 265 per cent. Twenty profitable British investments in the tin mines of Malaya, Nigeria and Siam show annual average dividends (over periods of two or three decades) ranging between 12 per cent and 43 per cent; while the annual average of the best five years of these tin mines has ranged between 20 per cent and 280 per cent. Most of these companies, that is, have repeatedly doubled and redoubled their original capital — and have sent it oversea.

Such profits pale before the astronomical takings in Africa.

Through fifteen years, the Ferriera Estate (South Africa) has yielded an annual average dividend of 278 per cent, while the Premier Diamond Company has yielded an annual average of 367 per cent for 23 years — has in effect multiplied its originally small capital by about eighty times. In the Gold Coast the Ashanti Goldfields Corporation has yielded an annual average of 58 per cent for 51 years (its present capital is about £1,250,000); the Consolidated African Selection Trust (an American diamond investment mainly in Sierra Leone) has paid 45 per cent for 25 years (its present capital being just over one and a half million pounds); and the Rhokana Corporation (Northern Rhodesian copper) 51 per cent for 16 years (present issued capital being about £5.3 millions). These figures refer, of course, to dividends paid *after* meeting local taxes. They are again outshone by some of the major investors such as De Beers which, since 1946, has never paid less than 80 per cent on its ordinary shares, and in 1951 actually paid 200 per cent on those shares.(145)

Such examples could be multiplied. During the years of mining boom, after the Second World War, profits rose to heights never reached before. Even the original plundering of India clinks like small change in comparison with this. Not only are company profits higher: they are also more concentrated in control and probably in ownership. Thus the four big copper mines in Northern Rhodesia (a country so 'poor' as not to have been able to send more than 1179 African children to secondary school in 1953) paid dividends for 1951 respectively of 55 per cent (plus a 100 per cent share bonus), 200 per cent, $41\frac{2}{3}$ per cent (plus a bonus of four fully-paid shares for every five stock units), and $37\frac{1}{2}$ per cent; while the lead mine at Broken Hill in the same territory paid 90 per cent.

Some of the new American investors have done even better. Thus the American copper interests now working the O'Okiep mine in South-West Africa — a country of quite abysmal 'poverty' — have managed to raise their dividend from a mere 10 per cent in 1945-46 to 460 per cent in 1951-52.

No doubt it is fruitless to expect Europeans and Americans who are making money at a rate so high as this to relax their grip. Others may object that they are making it at the expense of continued African misery: others do not hold these highly profitable shares. The only African country which has so far made any consistent effort to milk these mining profits is the Union of South Africa — and that, of course, because South Africa is a country where Whites are numerous enough to demand a share in this otherwise exported wealth. In Northern Rhodesia in 1954 mining companies were still paying the same rate of company tax (before dividend, of course) as all other companies, or 25 per cent. But in South Africa the gold-mining companies are obliged to pay up to 50 per cent, and their tax is calculated not on a flat rate but on their varying capacity to pay. In good years they pay much more than in bad years.

Here and there, and notably now in British West Africa, other governments lately have striven to lessen the drain of locally produced wealth, mainly by raising mineral duties, but they are still taking only a small and sometimes insignificant proportion of wealth which continues to flow out of their grasp. Now and then, where Africans are quite unable to defend their interests, one comes across astonishing anomalies. In Swaziland, for instance, which is a small territory chronically short of funds for any sort of primary development, it was surprising to learn that a big asbestos mine pays a mineral duty of 2 per cent, while smaller and less profitable ventures must pay $2\frac{1}{2}$ per cent. And yet this mine belongs to a British company, Turner and Newall Limited, which paid in 1951-52 a dividend of 25 per cent on a capital of £20 millions.

While colonialism is evidently bad for most people, it is obviously good for some. And, as one may see in almost every African colony, a new factor now enters on the scene — massive American investment. European colonialism, weakened in its capacity for investing capital, divided in its opinions, is increasingly supplanted by American colonialism. Already we have seen a sharply growing investment of American capital in the extraction of African minerals. Soon, no doubt, we shall begin to see American consumer goods flowing into a continent whose salvation can only lie in building up its own industry, in producing its own goods. 'In twenty-five years,' according to one American businessman's forecast, 'American business will take the Western Hemisphere, the Middle East, Africa, and Australia as its prime market.'(146)

Americans who think they can 'develop' the colonial world by coming in with know-how and with dollars seem quite content to ignore the fact that they are playing the same destructive game as all the other investors who drain wealth out of 'poor' countries. The only difference seems to be that American investors are able to escape the obloquy of having to 'keep law and order'; they have the European imperial Powers to keep it for them. In some cases, no doubt, American investment will break down the stagnation of European backwardness: in Angola, for example, it will probably break the economically restrictive monopoly of the Bank of Angola, and will generally help the shift from forced to free labour. American investment tends in Africa today to put an end to outmoded ways of government and exploitation, just as European commerce once made an end of outright slavery: but, for this, American investment demands its price. 'The under-developed countries', we read, 'must help themselves to attract American capital — first by providing a stable economic and political climate and, second, by ploughing their own capital back into productive use, not into extravagances.'(147)

Extravagances? What extravagances would the peoples of South-West Africa like to indulge in if the American owners of the O'Okiep copper mine could bring themselves to accept a little less than an astronomical dividend? Perhaps a few schools, a few clinics, a few hospitals . . . How much money could be devoted to building schools and universities and training teachers in Rhodesia if American and European investors would extract no more than the rate of profit they could make in their own countries? In one year alone there would be enough money left in Rhodesia to build two or three university colleges. How many African doctors could be trained in the Congo if the American and European owners of the Union Minière would disgorge no more than half their profits? How many more drugs and bandages and window-frames for rural hospitals could Protestant missionaries import into Angola if only the duties they must pay could be paid by the Angola Diamond Company, which pays no duties? How much electric power could be produced along the Congo waterways if only its production were not necessarily limited to the production of European profit?

A factual examination of the African scene today shows that the destructive period of European contact, the colonial period, has indeed exhausted its usefulness. Most Africans are ready to enter the modern world, or have already entered it. Their past is in ruins. Their future lies ready for them.

It also shows, on the other hand, that the conditions governing this destructive period are still exceedingly advantageous to all who participate in the profits of mineral and other raw material extraction in Africa.

These two contrary goods — measured by their numerical effect, the first very great and the second very small — are in sharp and growing conflict. Out of this conflict there comes a fresh and eager spur to the African awakening. 'Troubles' are already many. And 'troubles' are bound to increase. As they increase, so, too, will the cost of paying for them. Already, by 1954, the British taxpayer was paying sorely for the mess which European settlers had made of Kenya.

Even if one imagines the African peoples as politically inert, which they are not, one can see that a constructive period of contact will nonetheless gradually supplant the destructive period. Industrial revolution is willed by Europeans, and it carries its own new set of values and relationships. But the process of change must then be very slow and very painful: the chaotic disintegration of tribal life transforming itself into urban life — such as we have watched in these Congo towns — must be extended for long into the future, and with results which must tell heavily on social peace and welfare. For evidence of this one need only look at the degradation of Johannesburg today, where industrialism has had some thirty years of life under circumstances of continued African repression.

To imagine the future in these terms is in any case an academic exercise. If the arm of the imperial Powers is now immeasurably strengthened by American participation, so, too, is the arm of African resistance strengthened by new understanding, new means of organization, new recourse to political and other forms of action.

The 'Asian problem' was once discussed in terms of what Europeans and Americans might want or do. That time is past: revolutionary changes in Central Asia, in China and in Indo-China, in India and elsewhere, have buried or are burying it fast. And already it is impossible to discuss the 'African problem' in terms only of what Europeans and Americans may want or do. Africans may still lack schools and hospitals and clinics, books and libraries and leisure, votes and representatives and parliaments, respect and dignity and equality of rights: the difference now is that they know they lack these things, they believe they ought to have them, they are determined to get them.

TWENTY-THREE

THE AFRICAN AWAKENING

EUROPEANS who govern Africa have generally seemed to imply that the whole matter — conservation, change, initiative — rests uniquely in their hands. Africans emerge as the mere objects of European policy, much as the rare and curious animals which Europeans preserve for posterity in mammoth 'national parks' up and down the continent, except that the animals look better fed.

Yet the African scene, whether in the Congo and its neighbouring territories or further afield, belies increasingly this indifferent paternalism. Many Europeans in Africa still do behave as though they need refer their 'Native policy' to nothing and nobody but themselves and their own interests: for all that, the influence of Africans begins to take a hand, begins to emerge as a paramount influence.

If one wanted the obvious and most convincing evidence of this, one might turn at once to British and French West Africa. There it is patent for all to see. Nobody who cares to spend a few days in the African parliaments at Accra and Lagos — to take only one example — will continue to affirm that Africans are not 'ripe for self-government': their management of parliamentary business compares favourably, for dignity of speech and intensiveness of effort, with most European assemblies. No African parliamentarian in the Gold Coast or Nigeria, or in the National Assembly at Paris (where some twenty African deputies sit alongside their French colleagues), has yet added to the record one tithe of the vulgar nonsense we hear repeatedly from United States congressmen. Nothing in the way of administrative or parliamentary corruption has come near the scandals connected with the late Monsieur Stavisky, or the 'piastre racket' over Indo-China in 1952.

Nothing is easier than to prove the African awakening in West Africa. It speaks from every street corner. Almost as easily, one can prove it in South Africa, if only by turning to the campaign in 1952 of non-violent resistance to racial discrimination. Over a few months of that year no fewer than 8000 African, Indian and Coloured men and women were found as volunteers to court imprisonment and violence at the hands of a notably violent police force. Most of these volunteers had never before taken part in any form of organized campaign: most of them, perhaps, had never before so much as believed that an organized campaign was possible.

Or one could find the evidence of awakening in the massive but equally non-violent opposition to the political joining of the protectorates of Northern Rhodesia and Nyasaland to the settler-governed colony of Southern Rhodesia, in 1952 and 1953, when every vocal African but for two or three unrepresentative exceptions went on record against it. One could point to the successful campaigns against petty social discrimination carried through in Northern Rhodesia by rank-and-file members of the Northern Rhodesian African Congress, illiterate, obscure, anonymous and yet powerfully on the move. One could recall the big strike of African coal-miners at Wankie in Southern Rhodesia during 1954 — in spite of all that country's laws and regulations against anything of the kind. In Uganda the leaders and chiefs of the Baganda people, who enjoyed an organized state long before the Europeans arrived, needed in 1953 no second warning in order to declare themselves against any form of federation with neighbouring Kenya. And in neighbouring Kenya the peasant war of Mau Mau, however terrible, remains inexplicable except in terms of growing African resistance to colonial rule.

This book has attempted, by contrast, to show the African awakening against a background of Congo countries which the White man's imagination has usually painted in the darkest, most mysterious terms. Awakening does not speak from every street corner in the Belgian Congo and Angola. Here there are no parties, no trade unions, no national movements, no groups of organized intellectuals, who may stand up clearly in the light of day and declare their thoughts. Here, as we have seen, there is prison for the protesting nationalist. Yet, for all that, the awakening is here. That laconic item in the Belgian Congo's official returns, '3818 political prisoners', attests its presence, not to speak in neighbouring Angola of Senhor Pereira's 'average of five a month sent to São Thomé'. And in the Belgian Congo, on the brighter side, there is the powerful emergence of an industrial working class, setting a standard of technical achievement equalled in no other part of Black Africa.

In Léopoldville not long ago an African writer — rare bird indeed — departed for the other side of Stanley Pool, to Brazzaville, where he declared that he would settle down and live, because civil liberties were greater there. And in Léopoldville, in 1953, the best local art prize was won by Benjamin Mensah, aged twenty-six, with a monumental group called *Slavery*. Mensah has had his art training in the Ecole de Saint Luc, which is directed by Roman Catholic missionaries whose achievements do them credit. His *Slavery* is one more reflection of the African awakening. In these two slaves who struggle under the weight of their chains, there is more than the passion of suffering and accusation. Mensah has managed to convey not only the carrying of chains but also, subtly, obscurely, the breaking of chains: not only slavery, but also freedom. 'The city ought to purchase it,' said the director of the school; and surely he is right.

There can be few events more stirringly hopeful than this long African search for the knowledge of life, of power over human destiny and over nature, which geography and greed have repeatedly denied them. One thing at least becomes steadily clear. Whether or not the European masters of Africa bring themselves to a surrender of their mastery, serving no longer the interests of any people anywhere, except a privileged minority, Africans will not now abandon their search. If it proves true in Africa that vested interest never reforms itself, that changes in property-relations must always be enforced, that empires crumble and are overthrown, but are never given up with intelligent foresight, then the search will be difficult and often painful, wasteful, prolonged in bitterness. Its fruitful culmination can be delayed, made more painful, infinitely more difficult: everything in Africa today suggests that nothing can avail to stop it in the end. To stop it, even now, Europeans would have to destroy their own machines, close down their own factories, barricade themselves within a framework of increasing poverty, increasing anger, increasing revolt. They cannot any longer turn back the clock for Africans without turning it back for themselves, nor bolster European privilege in Africa without impoverishing the bulk of Europeans as well as the bulk of Africans.

There is no neat ending to this story, for it is tomorrow's as well as today's. In this kaleidoscope of change, one can only hope to catch occasional glimpses of the wider truth which presses always on the heels of human liberation from its past. Thirty-five years ago an early African nationalist, 'morning star' of this African awakening, addressed a handful of like-minded Africans at the second session of the National Congress of British West Africa, an obscure body of which the world at large was almost completely unaware.

'We say,' declared Casely Hayford on that occasion, 'that we have passed the childhood stage, and that, much as we appreciate the concern of our guardians, the time has come for us to take an intelligent, active part in the guiding of our own national destiny.'(148)

Thirty years later this handful of eccentrics, had they all been alive, could have attended the opening of an African parliament in the Gold Coast; and, a year later, of an African parliament in Nigeria. Obscure no longer, their memories are celebrated as of wise men who foresaw the future and helped to shape it.

And today it is to this call, this foresight and this understanding, that the whole of Africa vibrates in deep and many-voiced reply.

AFRICAN POPULATIONS

These figures are approximate totals drawn from official reports over the past few years. They are meant only to show the comparative sizes of some of these populations, mainly in Central Africa. Altogether, there may be nearly 150 million Africans in all the lands which lie to the south of the Sahara.

ANGOLA (Portuguese West Africa)

Africans	4,000,600
Mixed	30,000
Europeans	79,000

BELGIAN CONGO

Africans	11,788,000
Non-Africans	82,000

FRENCH EQUATORIAL AFRICA (Gaboon, Ubangui, Middle Congo, Chad)

Africans	4,400,000
Non-Africans	20,000

GOLD COAST

Africans	4,000,000
Europeans	a few thousands

KENYA

Africans	5,250,000
Arabs and Goans	32,000
Indians	91,000
Europeans	30,000

MOÇAMBIQUE (Portuguese East Africa)

Africans	5,600,000
Mixed and others	40,000
Europeans	50,000

251

THE AFRICAN AWAKENING

NIGERIA
| Africans | 30,000,000 |
| Non-Africans | a few thousands |

NORTHERN RHODESIA
| Africans | 1,950,000 |
| Europeans | 50,000 |

NYASALAND
| Africans | 2,400,000 |
| Europeans and Indians | a few thousands |

SOUTHERN RHODESIA
| Africans | 2,100,000 |
| Europeans | 158,000 |

TANGANYIKA
Africans	7,400,000
Arabs and Goans	13,000
Indians	45,000
Europeans	16,000

UGANDA
Africans	5,000,000
Asians	40,000
Europeans	a few thousands

252

REFERENCES

Note: I wish to make grateful acknowledgment to the Editor of *The New Statesman and Nation* for allowing me in Chapters I and XIV, and at one or two other points, to draw on material first published in his columns.

1. M. GLUCKMAN: 'The Magic of Despair', *The Listener*, 29.4.54.
2. G. B. SHAW: *St. Joan*. I am grateful to Mr. Thomas Hodgkin for pointing out this comparison.
3. MONSIGNOR J. CUVELIER: *L'Ancien Royaume de Congo*, Paris, 1946, p. 36.
4. J. H. LAWSON: *The Hidden Heritage*, New York, 1950, p. 52.
5. *The Lusiads*: Trans. W. C. Atkinson, London, 1952, p. 212.
6. E. GUERNIER: *L'Apport de l'Afrique à la Pensée Humaine*, Paris, 1952, p. 24.
7. Quoted in M. DOBB: *Studies in the Development of Capitalism*, London, 1946, p. 114.
8. F. LE GROS CLARK: *The New West Africa*, London, 1953, p. 141.
9. H. J. SIMONS: *Handbook on Race Relations in South Africa*, Cape Town, 1949, p. 47.
10. V. G. CHILDE: *What Happened in History*, London, 1942, p. 86.
11. See A. IHLE: *Das Alte Königreich Kongo*, Leipzig, 1929, which I have largely followed. See also historical notes by E. G. Ravenstein in *The Strange Adventures of Andrew Battell*, London Hakluyt Socy., 1901, Series 2, number 6. Ravenstein was well acquainted with the important documents published in Lisbon in 1877 by the Visconde de Paiva-Manso, *História do Congo*. For Monomotapa see G. A. Wainwright in *Man*, 80 of 1949.
12. IHLE, op. cit., p. 23.
13. CUVELIER, op. cit., p. 275.
14. G. M. CHILDS: *Umbundu Kinship and Character*, London, 1949, p. 187.
15. G. THOMSON: *Aeschylus and Athens*, London, 1941, p. 35.
16. CUVELIER, op. cit., p. 31.
17. op. cit., p. 131.
18. op. cit., p. 158.
19. IHLE, op. cit., p. 150.

20. op. cit., p. 119.
21. J. T. TUCKER: *The Land of the Blacksmith Prince*, 1933, p. 16.
22. IHLE, op. cit., p. 118.
23. L. JADIN: *Bulletin* of Institut Royal Colonial Belge, No. 1 of 1953, p. 164.
24. R. DELGADO: *História de Angola*, Lobito, 1953, vol. III, p. 445.
25. JADIN, loc. cit.
25a. G. FREYRE: *The Masters and the Slaves*, New York, 1946, pp. 279, 311.
26. E. D. MOREL: *The Black Man's Burden*, London, 1919, p. 19.
27. H. PIRENNE: *Histoire de Belgique*, Brussels, 1931, p. 224.
28. op. cit., p. 226.
29. *The Times*, 16.2.1885.
30. P. T. MOON: *Imperialism and World Politics*, New York, 1927, p. 87.
31. E. D. MOREL: *Red Rubber*, London, 1906, p. 29.
32. op. cit., p. 42.
33. L. FROBENIUS: *Im Schatten des Kongostaats*, Berlin, 1907, p. 280.
34. P. MILLE: *Au Congo Belge*, Paris, 1899, p. 114.
35. MOREL, op. cit., p. 224.
36. V. VERMEULEN: *Déficiencies et Dangers de Notre Politique Indigène*, Brussels, 1952, p. 64.
37. D. WESTERMANN: *Geschichte Afrikas*, Cologne, 1952, p. 385.
38. MOREL, op. cit., p. 159.
39. Naval Intelligence Division, British Admiralty: *A Manual of the Belgian Congo*, 1920, p. 298.
40. *See Bulletins* of Centre d'Etude des Problèmes Sociaux Indigènes (Cepsi), Elisabethville, Belgian Congo: numbers 20-23 of 1953, which reproduce the proceedings of this Commission (Commission Permanente pour la Protection des Indigènes). All who are interested in African history must be grateful to Cepsi for these valuable reprints.
41. *Bull.*, Cepsi, 20 of 1953, p. 177.
42. *Bull.*, Cepsi, 21 of 1953, p. 244.
43. *Bull.*, Cepsi, 21 of 1953, p. 347.
44. *Bull.*, Cepsi, 21 of 1953, p. 378.
45. *Bull.*, Cepsi, 23 of 1953, p. 640.
46. *Bull.*, Cepsi, 21 of 1953, p. 269.
47. *Bull.*, Cepsi, 21 of 1953, p. 279.

REFERENCES

48. *Bull.*, Cepsi, 20 of 1953, p. 191.
49. *Bull.*, Cepsi, 20 of 1953, p. 192.
50. *Bull.*, Cepsi, 22 of 1953, p. 555.
51. MOREL, *The Black Man's Burden*, p. 131.
52. F. CHALLAYE: *Le Congo Français*, Paris, 1906. This was the 12th *Cahier* in the 7th Series.
53. MOREL, op. cit., p. 147.
54. H. ZIEGLÉ: *Afrique Equatoriale Française*, Paris, 1952, p. ix.
55. A. GIDE: *Voyage au Congo*, Paris, 1927, p. 17fn.
56. Admiralty, *Manual*, p. 44.
57. A. F. G. MARZORATI: 'The Belgian Congo' in *African Affairs*, Journal of Royal Afr. Socy., April 1945, p. 104.
58. Quoted by VERMEULEN, op. cit., p. 30.
59. LORD HAILEY: *Native Administration in the British African Territories*, London, 1952, vol. IV, p. 2.
60. M.WIGHT: *The Gold Coast Legislative Council*, London, 1947, p. 33.
61. CHILDS, op. cit., p. 23.
62. Quoted by VERMEULEN, op. cit., p. 24.
63. L. MARQUET: *Bull.*, Cepsi, No. 2 of 1946, p. 15.
64. loc. cit., p. 16.
65. J. VAN WING, S. J.: *Bulletin* Inst. Roy. Col. Belge, No. 2 of 1951.
66. J. COMHAIRE: *Zaire*, Jan. 1953, p. 60.
67. *The Times*, 4.5.54.
68. SIR G. RENNIE: *East Africa and Rhodesia*, 22.5.54, p. 1057. For impact on Uganda, *see* C. Legum: *Must We Lose Africa?* London, 1954.
69. E. DHANIS: *Zaire*, May 1953, p. 489.
70. Quoted by DHANIS, loc. cit.
71. VAN WING, loc. cit.
72. N. DE CLEENE: *Le Clan Matrilinéal dans la Société Indigène*, Inst. Roy. Col. Belge., 1946, p. 70.
73. Quoted by A. VERBEKEN: *La Crise de l'Evolution Indigène, Bull.*, Cepsi, No. 5 of 1947, p. 34.
74. A. W. HOERNLÉ in *The Bantu-Speaking Tribes of South Africa*, ed. I. Schapera, London, 1937.
75. M. WILSON: *Good Company: a Study of Nyakyusa Age-Villages*, London, 1951, p. 60.
76. *See* my *Report on Southern Africa*, London, 1952, p. 102, for a fuller description.

255

77. United Nations *Review of Economic Conditions in Africa*, 1952, p. 11.
78. R. VANDERLINDEN: *Bull.*, Inst. Roy. Col. Belge., No. 1 of 1951, p. 506.
79. Admiralty, *Manual*, p. 130.
80. *The Times*, 24.2.54.
81. *See The Posthumous Papers of Senator Vandenberg*: ed. A. H. VANDENBERG, Junr., New York, 1952, p. 360.
82. For these and other statistics relating to the Union Minière du Haut Katanga, I am greatly indebted to the company's general management at Elisabethville.
83. F. ENGELS: *The Condition of the Working Class in England in 1844*, p. 47 of 1953 Edn. of Foreign Languages Publishing House, Moscow.
84. op. cit., preface to English edition, 1892, p. 19 of same edn.
85. F. GRÉVISSE: *Le Centre Extra-Coutumier d'Elisabethville*, *Bull.*, Cepsi, No. 15 of 1951, p. 382.
86. op. cit., p. 385.
87. LIBOTTE: *L'Evolution du Problème du Logement au Centre Extra-Coutumier d'Elisabethville*, *Bull.*, Cepsi, No. 21 of 1953, p. 64 of supplement.
88. GRÉVISSE, op. cit., p. 370.
89. K. MARX: 'Future Results of the British Rule in India', in *New York Daily Tribune*, 8.8.1853. In Foreign Languages Publishing House edn. (Moscow, 1953), p. 392.
90. F. VAN DER LINDEN in *Revue Coloniale Belge*, 15.1.53.
91. GRÉVISSE, op. cit., p. 426.
92. *See* G. DUTILLEUX: *L'Opinion des Femmes du Centre Extra-Coutumier d'Elisabethville sur le mariage etc....*, in *Bull.*, Cepsi, No. 17 of 1951, p. 219.
93. H. BONGOLO: *A Propos des Coutumes Indigènes qui se pratiquent à la Cité Indigène de Léopoldville*, *Bull.*, Cepsi, No. 5 of 1947, p. 45.
94. B. MAKONGA in *Bull.*, Cepsi, No. 17 of 1951, p. 59.
95. G. B. SHAW: *Mrs. Warren's Profession*, Act 2.
96. G. BALANDIER: 'Approche Sociologique des "Brazzavilles Noires"': Etude Préliminaire', in *Africa*, Jnl. of Internat. Afr. Inst., No. 22 of 1952, p. 31.
97. BONGOLO, loc. cit., p. 40.
98. B. MWEPU: *La Vie des Femmes Legères, dites 'Libres', au Centre Extra-Coutumier d'Elisabethville*, *Bull.*, Cepsi, No. 17 of 1951, p. 180.

REFERENCES

99. K. A. BUSIA: *Report on a Social Survey of Sekondi-Takoradi*, London, 1950, p. 108.

100. MAKONGA, loc. cit., p. 70.

101. loc. cit., p. 77.

102. J. VAN WING, S.J.: *La Formation d'une Elite Noire au Congo Belge*, *Bull.*, Cepsi, No. 5 of 1947, p. 18.

103. GRÉVISSE, op. cit., p. 142.

104. J. VAN WING, S.J.: *Le Congo Déraille*, *Bull.*, Inst. Roy. Col. Belge, No. 1 of 1951.

105. *The Financial Times*, 3.2.54.

106. GRÉVISSE, op. cit., p. 144.

107. R. VANDERLINDEN, loc. cit., p. 512.

108. GRÉVISSE, op. cit., p. 106.

109. I am grateful to M. Marcel Soret, of the Institut d'Etudes Centrafricaines, at Brazzaville, for permission to consult and quote from his study, *Etudes de Démographie Africaine*, which contains much valuable material on urbanization in the African townships at and near Brazzaville.

110. P. CHARLES, S.J.: *Bull.*, Inst. Roy. Col. Belge., No. 1 of 1952.

111. BALANDIER, loc. cit., p. 34.

112. M. GLUCKMAN, loc. cit.

113. P. TEMPELS: *La Philosophie Bantoue*, Paris, 1949, p. 15.

114. L. MOTTOULLE: *Politique Sociale de L'Union Minière du Haut Katanga pour sa Main d'Œuvre Indigène, et ses resultats au cours de vingt années d'application*, Inst. Roy. Col. Belge, 1946, p. 5.

115. A. J. A. CARDOSO: *Angola: Your Neighbour*, 1950, p. 71.

116. VAN WING, loc. cit.

117. N. LAUDE, *Bull.*, Inst. Roy. Col. Belge., No. 2 of 1951, p. 638.

118. VAN WING, *Bull.*, Cepsi, No. 5 of 1947, p. 9.

119. Quoted by VERBEKEN, loc. cit., p. 26.

120. VAN WING, loc. cit., p. 10.

121. VERBEKEN, loc. cit., p. 31.

122. *See* Decree of 16.3.22, Section 9, *Des Sanctions Répressives* (articles 46-57); Ordonnance of 8.12.40 No. 476 bis/AIMO, modified by Ordonnance No. 155/AIMO of 8.5.42, ch. 15, *Des Sanctions* (articles 27-29).

123. N. LAUDE in *Bull.*, Inst. Roy. Col. Belge., No. 12 of 1952.

124. SORET, loc. cit.

125. I. SCHAPERA: *Migrant Labour and Tribal Life*, London, 1947, p. 116.
126. S. MOKEMO: *La Voix du Congolais*, Jan. 1954, p. 36.
127. S. LUYEYE: *La Voix du Congolais*, Jan. 1954, p. 35.
128. MARZORATI, loc. cit., p. 107.
129. Belgian Congo — official reports 1952/53: Angola — *Statesman's Yearbook 1953*, referring to 1951; British territories — Colonial Office estimates, 1954.
130. BUSIA, op. cit., p. 118.
131. H. W. NEVINSON: *More Changes, More Chances*, p. 75.
132. J. H. HARRIS: *Portuguese Slavery: Britain's Dilemma*, London, 1913.
133. *Grande Enciclopédia Portuguesa e Brasiliera*, Vol. 2, p. 611.
134. See E. W. SMITH, in *Africa*, No. 21 of 1951, reviewing J. M. da Silva Cunha, *O Trabalho Indigena*, Lisbon, 1949.
135. MOON, op. cit., p. 119. He is quoting *Die Grosse Politik*, Vol. 14, p. 347, and other German official sources.
136. LICHNOWSKY: *My Mission to London 1912-14*, London, 1918. With preface by Professor Gilbert Murray, p. 14.
137. *Boletim Oficial de Angola*, Series 2, No. 35, of August 29th, 1951, p. 757. For judgment on Sampaio Nunes, which I am not quoting for lack of space — he was dismissed for taking bribes against supplying 'contract workers' — see *Boletim Oficial*, Series 2, No. 29, of July 19th, 1951, p. 624.
138. T. A. BARNS: *Angolan Sketches*, London, 1928, p. 176.
139. *The Times*, 17.5.54.
140. *Report* of the *Ad Hoc* Committee on Forced Labour of United Nations and International Labour Office, Geneva, 1953, p. 64.
141. *The Times*, 18.5.54.
142. N. DOUGLAS: *Siren Land*, p. 170fn. of London 1948 edn.
143. M. H. KINGSLEY: *The Story of West Africa*, London, 1899, p. 154.
144. J. F. RIPPY: *The Journal of Business of the Univ. of Chicago*, April 1953, p. 110.
145. For these and other dividend figures, see *Skinner's Mining Yearbook*, London, annually.
146. *Business Week*, 31.10.53, p. 97.
147. loc. cit., p. 102.
148. *West African Leadership: The Speeches of Caseley Hayford*, ed. M. S. SAMPSON, London, 1949, p. 67.

INDEX

INDEX

260

INDEX

INDEX